London

GERMANY

AUSTRIA

FRANCE

Tripoli

Lagos

WESTE

RENEWALS 458-4574
DATE DUE

GAYLORD			PRINTED IN U.S.A.

PLUMES

Ostrich Feathers, Jews,
and a Lost World of
Global Commerce

Sarah Abrevaya Stein

Yale University Press

New Haven and London

Endpapers: Map of global ostrich feather commerce, 1883 and 1912.
Illustration, page vi: "Birds Mustering," *London Illustrated News,*
March 30, 1878.

Published with assistance from the Mary Cady Tew Memorial Fund.

Designed by Nancy Ovedovitz and set in Monotype Centaur and
Tagliente types by Duke & Company, Devon, Pennsylvania.
Printed in the United States of America.

Library of Congress Cataloging-in-Publication Data
Stein, Sarah Abrevaya
Plumes : ostrich feathers, Jews, and a lost world of global commerce /
Sarah Abrevaya Stein.
p.   cm.
Includes bibliographical references and index.
ISBN 978-0-300-12736-2 (alk. paper)
1. Ostrich feather industry—History. 2. Jewish merchants—History.
I. Title.
HD9429.F4S84 2008
382′.438524—dc22   2008031753

A catalogue record for this book is available from the British Library.

This paper meets the requirements of ANSI/NISO Z39.48-1992
(Permanence of Paper).

10 9 8 7 6 5 4 3 2 1

To my parents, Richard and Carole Stein, who gave me
an appreciation of challenging questions

To Ira and Julius Zimmerman, with whom I delight in seeking answers
And to Fred Zimmerman, the finest partner in conversation and so much else

The ostrich feather trade bewitched the Jews. . . . With
ease, they "fell into feathers." Gentiles used to say that
. . . Jews "served a new God, the ostrich."
LEYBL FELDMAN, *Oudtshoorn, Yerushalayim d'Afrike*
[Oudtshoorn, Jerusalem of Africa]

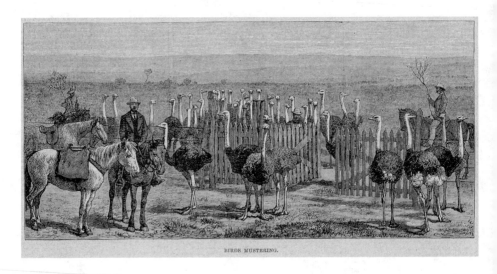

BIRDS MUSTERING.

CONTENTS

The story I have to tell here—one spanning three continents, the boom and bust of a single global market, and the Jewish cultural world—began with a single Yiddish book. For nearly twenty years, I have collected illustrated books in Yiddish. Most were published in the United States or Eastern Europe in the 1920s and 1930s, the golden decades of popular Yiddish culture. There are volumes printed on inexpensive paper with pale ink, others with gold-edged leaves and dazzling art deco prints, the delirious scenes of Russian Jewish life imagined by Marc Chagall, or Todros Geller's colorful portraits of Native Americans. Amid this visual luxuriance, Leybl Feldman's *Oudtshoorn, Yerushalayim d'Afrike*, published in Johannesburg in 1940, stands out. Devoted to the history of Jews in a small town in the South African province of the Western Cape, once the world's center of ostrich farming, the volume's cover depicts a line of ostriches poised between the setting sun and a gravestone—on which the book's title is inscribed (fig. 1).

Scholars of Yiddish culture are well acquainted with *Yizker-bikher*, memorial books to the hundreds of Jewish communities annihilated by the Nazis and their collaborators during World War II. Leybl Feldman's book about the town of Oudtshoorn is a different sort of memorial—a commemoration not so much of lives lost to methodical violence but of livelihoods lost to the caprice of global markets. In this context, the cover of *Oudtshoorn, Yerushalayim d'Afrike* appears jarring, audacious, even unseemly. How could anyone think of mourning the loss of an ostrich farming center in South Africa in Yiddish when, at that very moment, the Jews of Europe were falling prey to genocide? Did Jews have a place in the history of ostrich farming, or ostriches a place in modern Jewish history?

Figure 1. The cover illustration from Leybl Feldman's Yiddish-language *Oudtshoorn,
Yerushalayim d'Afrike*, published in 1940. "Jerusalem of Africa" is inscribed on a tombstone,
as if to signal the lost eminence of the town and its Jewish merchants in the global feather
trade. (Courtesy the National Yiddish Book Center, Amherst, Massachusetts)

These questions intrigued me, but they were unsettling, for they carried
me to a geographic and conceptual landscape that appeared marginal—even
frivolous—to a scholar of modern Jewish history. My interest piqued, I added
Feldman's book to that mental list that all scholars maintain of tantalizing
leads that invite pursuit. Fifteen years passed before I broached the riddle of
Feldman's study. Even then, I did not think I would write a book about Jews
and plumes.

My engagement with Feldman's book deepened during a research trip to
South Africa in 2004, when the story of Jews and ostriches—still not the focus
of my attention—exerted an unyielding and ever more fascinating pull. And
I quickly recognized the serendipitous nature of my research. In South Africa

(as, subsequently, in Europe and the United States) I encountered rich archival material and generous contacts in the feather world.

As I buried myself in the history of the global exchange of ostrich plumes, I came to appreciate the complex rationale of Feldman's elegiac study of Oudtshoorn. Oudtshoorn was the "Jerusalem of Africa," not only because its Jewish immigrants from Russian-controlled Lithuania obtained, for a time, unimagined wealth and privilege on its soil, but because for Jews in the feather trade, as for consumers and sellers of feathers the world over, it was a global fulcrum. Although few, if any, turn-of-the-century women who adorned themselves with ostrich feathers thought about their plumes' provenance, the bulk of the feathers they wore came from this small town in southern Africa. No less surprisingly, most of their plumes—like most of those from the world's secondary site of supply, the southern Sahara—had been conveyed, manufactured, and sold by Jews situated in a complex web of trans-hemispheric supply. Jews thus represented an unappreciated and even hidden link between African sites of supply, European and American female consumers, and disparate parts of the globe.

More compelling still, Feldman's book did not speak only of Jewish success. Although for a time some Jews experienced Oudtshoorn as Edenic, in the wake of a cataclysmic bust in the global feather market that began in 1914 they came to see it as cursed. Following the crash of the feather trade, Feldman wrote:

> The [ostrich feather] dealers, speculators and exporters were reduced to poverty, feeling as hard done by as the ostriches had formerly felt after being plucked. Their poverty grew so great that they found themselves literally without a crust of bread. The majority of Jews in Oudtshoorn were reduced to starvation. The Oudtshoorn shopkeepers formed relief organizations. They obtained wagonloads of fish from Mossel Bay and collected donations for other food. Jews no longer went out to buy feathers. Instead they wandered the streets of Oudtshoorn in dire straits like victims of fire, dejected and desperate. The prosperous town of Oudtshoorn lost the glitter of its former wealth and the winds of poverty began to blow from all sides.[1]

This shattered town was not, perhaps, altogether different from Jewish Eastern Europe in 1940. Like Oudtshoorn, that other world—Feldman's erstwhile home—also was poised on the brink of destruction, not yet imaginable in scope. Did Feldman sense any of this? Does that tombstone stand for more than one endangered community? To elegize Oudtshoorn in Yiddish was perhaps to mourn (if only half consciously) for a traumatized Jewish world—and for the unfolding obliteration of lives, culture, and possibilities in the Ashkenazi heartland of Eastern Europe and across its diasporic breadth.

For all of these reasons, Feldman's account of Oudtshoorn Jewry is nuanced, even masterful. Even so, I suspect that Feldman was unaware of just how multilayered and geographically wide-reaching a history of Jews and ostrich feathers could be. As my inquiries into this topic deepened, I was stunned to learn that Jews played a crucial and visible role not only in the South African branch of the feather trade but in its North African, Ottoman, French, British, and American wings as well. Furthermore, Jews in the industry were immensely diverse: Ashkenazi, Sephardi, Judeo-Arab, and Anglo; citizens of nation-states, colonial subjects, and protégés of royal courts; white-collar and blue-collar workers; immigrants and native born, men and women, adults and children. The story of Jews and the feather trade is not, as Feldman intimates, a single tale of transplanted Eastern European Jews realizing the aspirations and traumas of their homeland on southern African soil. The truth is far more textured—and, I think, far more interesting as well.

To write a history of Jews and the feather trade, I realized, was to tell a story of unimagined global connections: a history of disparate people and places linked by ephemeral and material threads. Shifting my geographic and conceptual focus away from terrains and subjects more "obviously" Jewish or familiar could thus allow me to meditate on the constitution of the modern Jewish world—and the wider world as well. Those ostriches in haunting parade on the cover of an illustrated book, it turns out, were dancing to a complex and richly Jewish rhythm. To pursue their story—to read that image as a summation of complex histories, variegated routes, multiple geographies, numerous forms of production and consumption—is to relinquish the distinction between the fundamental and the frivolous, between things historically weighty and those light as a feather.

The Pursuit of Plumes

The plume was of medium length, fairly broad, with a remarkably dense, strong quill. In 1910 it was shipped to a representative of the Cape Colony government by the British consul in Tripoli, who was able to say of its origins only "that it had been brought by a party of Arabs who had crossed the Sahara Desert from the Southern Soudan."[1] Cape officials immediately recognized it as the feather they had been waiting for. For months these bureaucrats had been collecting feathers from wild ostriches "wherever they were found in the world" with the goal of procuring a special one: the elusive Barbary plume, a feather coveted the world over for its dazzling fullness, width at the crown, and so-called double fluff—that is, density or compactness along the flue.[2] Month after month feather samples had arrived, each as unpromising as the one before. Particularly disappointing were the long, narrow, drooping feathers of the wild Moroccan bird, which Cape agriculturalists had mistakenly anticipated would be of the Barbary variety.

The Sudanese feather was different. Where South African ostrich plumes were weak and spare in the flue, with drooping, thinly tipped barbs set far apart, this feather was robust, taut, and glossy. It was precisely the sort of feather most desired by consumers in Europe and the United States. Were the bird that produced this specimen to be found and brought to South Africa, theorized the Cape officials who held it in hand, it could be crossbred with the hearty Cape ostrich, resulting in a bird of "physiological vigour" whose plumes would dominate the international feather market.[3] Quickly, plans for a secret, state-sponsored Trans-Saharan Ostrich Expedition were hatched. None involved could anticipate how very close to their goal they would come or how completely it would elude them.

Ostrich feathers were valuable commodities at the beginning of the twen-tieth century, their value per pound almost equal to that of diamonds. Great Britain, the world's principal feather conduit and the single largest national importer of ostrich plumes, bought between £1 million and £2 million worth annually from 1903 to 1914. France imported an average of 76 million francs' worth from 1907 to 1911, and the United States, which like France acquired most of its ostrich feathers through London, during the same period purchased between $1.08 million and $5 million worth a year.[4] Most of these feathers came from the ostrich farming region of the Little Karoo, a section of semi-arid plateau located in the Western Cape region of southern Africa. (Technically the ostrich farming centers studied here are located in the southern Cape, just south of the Swartberg mountains and some thirty to seventy miles north of Mossel Bay. For purposes of comprehensibility, I use the more popular "Western Cape," a region into which the southern Cape is often considered to be subsumed.) Since the 1860s, the British imperial government had actively facilitated export-oriented ostrich raising in the Oudtshoorn District of this region. State sponsorship coupled with soaring demand ultimately resulted in feathers being ranked fourth in value among commodities exported from the Union of South Africa, following gold, diamonds, and wool, and secured the Cape's status as the world's principal ostrich feather supplier.[5]

Yet throughout the period of the ostrich feather boom, and indeed for cen-turies before, it was merchants in North Africa who supplied the plumes most admired by European and American consumers: the elusive Barbary plume. "Barbary" in this case was misleading. The vast majority of ostrich feathers exported from North Africa came not from the Barbary coast but from wild (and some domesticated) birds that were hunted by settled and nomadic farm-ers in the southern Sudan and the semi-arid Sahel—from Timbuktu to the Darfur region—whence they were ferried by camel caravan and eventually by post to ports in the north (fig. 2). Demand for these feathers was so extensive that scholars of North and West African trade credit this commodity with single-handedly revitalizing the institution of the trans-Saharan camel caravan in the last decades of the nineteenth century.[6]

So lucrative a commodity quickly garnered the attention of colonial authori-ties and foreign emissaries in North and West Africa. The turn-of-the-century Ottoman and French regimes, both of which had holdings in these regions,

Figure 2. Postcard that likely pictures domesticated "Barbary" ostriches in French Sudan, ca. 1900. (Courtesy www.struthie.com)

wished to capitalize on the trade in plumes in and across their colonies, if necessary by diverting traditional camel caravan routes to their advantage. At the same time, French and American consular agents, civil servants, and agricultural economists were debating whether, in imitation of the British, their own governments ought to facilitate intensive ostrich farming in Algeria or Senegal (in the case of the French) or, for the Americans, in California, Arizona, Florida, or Texas. While French efforts to follow through on these ambitions lagged, ostrich farms emerged in the American West, Southwest, and South in the early 1880s, and the entrepreneurs behind these farms fantasized that they might be the foundation of a fully domestic ostrich feather industry. In 1913, Representative Carl Hayden of Arizona, sponsor of a successful bill for the appropriation of funds for America's ostrich farms, assured his colleagues in the House that the "riches" had been put into "ostriches," and no country could afford to stand by.[7]

But many in the industry believed that success depended on demand, demand on quality, and quality on stock. According to this equation the bird that produced the "double fluff" was the proverbial goose who could lay the golden egg. Thus the arrival of a long sought after feather on the desk of a Cape bureaucrat produced great excitement. To these administrators, the elusive "double fluff" appeared to be the last crucial ingredient for constructing a lucrative global monopoly. So it was that, in possession of a feather and in search of a bird, the government of the Union of South Africa sponsored a secret expedition to southern Sudan. The expedition was led by Russell Thornton, the official agriculturalist for the government of the late Cape Colony (recently superseded by the Cape Province, a constituent of the Union of South Africa formed in 1910). Accompanied by Frank Smith and J. M. P. Bowker ("competent authorities on the subject"), Thornton set sail in August of 1911.[8]

Thornton and his colleagues traveled via London and Paris to West Africa and docked at Forcados, at the mouth of the Niger River. Thence they journeyed by paddleboat to Baro, where they employed 107 Hausa porters and set out—by horseback, foot, and train—for the camel caravan entrepôt of Kano. In Kano, the party checked the stock of all incoming feather caravans. The work was tedious, the sandstorms trying, the caravan leaders protective of their wares. According to expedition member Smith's unpublished memoirs, the longed-for lead at last arrived:

> After many disappointments a parcel of feathers of undoubtedly the right type was brought in one day for sale. These were immediately pounced on and the vendors eagerly questioned as to where the feathers had come from. They turned out to be a party of Tuareg Arabs who had come from a district beyond Timbuktu. They stated that their particular district was isolated by a strip of a hundred miles of desert from any other habitable part. They also said there were numerous ostriches there, both wild and in semi domestication, and that it lay in the French territory.[9]

The travelers cabled the South African government for approval to pursue the treasure. Months passed, in the course of which the men suffered from heat and bouts of fever. Finally, the expedition members got word that the South African government had granted them authority to spend £7,000 for the procurement of 150 ostriches. First, however, they were obliged to seek permission from French authorities in Zinder (in present-day Nigeria, 150 miles north of Kano) to export live ostriches from French colonial terrain. This the French commander in Zinder promptly refused. Appeals by the British government to the French government also met with resistance; like the British, who forbade the export of live ostriches and ostrich eggs from the Cape, the French saw no reason to permit the purloining of this coveted colonial resource.[10]

In spite of the lack of permission, and aware that the South African government would deny any association with them in the event they were apprehended, the explorers proceeded into French Sudan, chased, or so they believed, by French and American spies, the latter of whom ("persistent men who had

'shadowed' them across hundreds of miles of desert") were purportedly sponsored by an aspiring American feather magnate.[11] To deceive their pursuers the
expedition divided into three parties, with each one following a different route
and purchasing quantities of worthless ostriches as a subterfuge. Reconvening in
Timbuktu, the adventurers managed to obtain 156 Barbary birds with the assistance of the emir of Katsina. While a malarial Thornton was tended by a Catholic missionary, the ostriches were encased in eight-by-eight-foot pens of palm
leaves and carried by porters roughly a thousand miles overland to Lagos.[12]

The contraband was shipped to Cape Town in the summer of 1912, and men
and birds were welcomed with great fanfare. The ostriches that survived the
journey—140 of the original 156—were transferred to the Cape's Grootfontein
Agricultural College to be acclimated and inbred.[13] Among those heralding the
poachers' work was Senator Charles Southey, an experienced breeder of birds,
who declared with triumph: "We have the double fluff feather. [Our competi-
tors] do not. This new shipment will help to cultivate that double fluff, and it
will take years for any other country to catch up with us. In point of fact . . .
I do not think they will ever be able to catch us up."[14]

The exuberance of this success was to be short-lived. "Unfortunately,"
expedition member Smith reminisced in 1944, "before this fixing of the [cross-
bred ostrich] type could be completed . . . the whole ostrich feather industry
crashed. Ostrich feathers were no more in demand as articles of adornment,
and the only use that could be found for them was for the making of ostrich
feather dusters."[15] American feather merchants saw their finest white plumes
adorn cheap kewpie dolls, while the feathers of London-based manufacturers
sold only "when they are made as unlike ostrich plumes as possible."[16] Smith
himself spent two years in England trying to "revive an interest in feathers,"
but found it "a hopeless fight—the ladies simply would not have feathers at
any price."[17]

Russell Thornton's expedition encapsulates the dynamism of the global
ostrich feather trade in the early twentieth century, in particular the struggle by
modern empires, nation-states, and individual merchants to capitalize on the
flow of this luxury good from Africa and the boom-and-bust trajectory of a
single commodity. But there is one strand of this story that is less visible—the
crucial involvement of Jews in trans-hemispheric ostrich feather commerce.

The apparent absence of any Jews in the preceding tale stands in inverse relation to their actual importance in the global exchange of plumes in general, and to the Trans-Saharan Ostrich Expedition in particular. The historical occlusion of Jews from these stories has roots in the inglorious dénouement of the feather boom, when rumors of a Jewish feather mafia circulated globally, but also in the contemporary moment, when public discussion of the relationships between Jews, power, and capital is widely perceived as a reactionary tendency. In telling the history of Jews' prominence in the global ostrich feather trade at the turn of the twentieth century, this book takes shape around a confluence of significance and silence.

JEWS, PLUMES, AND GLOBAL COMMERCE

In turn-of-the-century North and South Africa, in Europe, and in the United States, Jews were the principal middlemen (and women) of plumes. In the Cape, over 90 percent of feather merchants—numbering roughly five hundred at their peak—were Yiddish-speaking immigrants from Lithuania in the Russian Empire. Some of these traders operated on an infinitesimal scale, buying individual plumes from Boer and Jewish farmers or colored farmworkers before reselling them to Jewish small-scale or large-scale feather exporters. ("Colored" in the South African context at the time means people of mixed race, primarily the descendants of black Africans and Boers, whites of Dutch ancestry who had migrated northeastward from the Cape Colony in the 1830s and 1840s to escape British rule.) Others, operating more ambitiously, contract farmed the plumage of thousands of birds at a time, essentially dealing in feather futures.

South African Jewish feather exporters shipped their plumes monthly (or even more frequently) to representatives and partners in London; there, the city's colonial produce brokers offered the feathers at auction every other month to an international collective of mainly Jewish feather merchants. Hundreds of Jewish ostrich feather dealers, wholesalers, and manufacturers operated in the British capital, and thousands of Jewish blue-collar workers—the majority immigrant girls and women from Eastern Europe—labored in London as unskilled or semi-skilled feather handlers. So hugely overrepresented were Jews in London's ostrich feather trade that it was said to be one of the city's "chief Jewish monopolies."[18]

Not all ostrich plumes handled in London were from South Africa: lesser quantities (but the highest grade) reached London across the Mediterranean after traveling along a densely Jewish chain of supply. Overseeing the Mediterranean ostrich feather trade was a handful of Jewish family firms, most of which were Sephardi and Livornese in origin. These merchants acquired their plumes in the southern Sahara and Sahel and, in tandem with other Jewish and non-Jewish feather merchants, helped to finance the trans-Saharan camel caravans that ferried feathers to port cities in North Africa. Still other plumes destined for export to Europe reached North Africa from what one nineteenth-century writer called "the celebrated ostrich feather sea port" of Aden, where Yemeni Jews were said to monopolize the trade and processing of plumes.[19] In North Africa's ports themselves, untold numbers of poor Maghrebi (sometimes called Judeo-Arab) Jews staffed the local feather processing industry; in late-nineteenth-century Tripoli alone, it is estimated that some two hundred Jewish families were supported by occupations linked to the feather trade.[20] As for the Thornton expedition, its key informant and adviser was a Sephardi Jew of Livornese descent who represented a Tripolitanian feather family's Parisian office.

After being sold at auction in London, most African ostrich feathers were exported to New York and Paris for resale: if still in a "raw" (or unfinished) state, they would be manufactured in these cities as well. Jews were visible in the Parisian feather trade, but it was in New York that their preeminence in the industry was most striking. In America, Jews occupied every tier and link of the ostrich feather commodity chain. Most of the thousands of feather merchants, manufacturers, and blue-collar workers who operated in New York were Jewish. In the American West, Southwest, and South, Jews constituted the financiers and "feather go betweens" for entrepreneurial ostrich farmers.

Notwithstanding Jews' significance to the history of this and other globally traded modern goods, the story of Jews and modern trans-hemispheric trade has never been systematically explored. This is not accidental. On the contrary, a number of historiographic trends have made the telling of this history untenable. First, a study of a single ethnic group's relationship to global supply falls in the as yet untheorized interstices of economic and cultural history. Economic historians have paid careful heed to processes of supply, of course, but in most cases have not interrogated the involvement of ethnic communities or diasporas in the shaping of individual commodity chains. Cultural historians, on the other hand, though increasingly engaged with practices of consumption, have by and large avoided the terrain of supply. Historians of modern global commerce, colonial economics, and consumer culture, for their part, have neglected Jewishness as a category of analysis.[21] And, finally, scholars of Jewish culture have been understandably wary of linking Jews to the global market in luxury goods—or to the proliferation of capitalist markets in colonial settings—for fear of reinforcing anti-Semitic stereotypes. As a result of these intersecting trends, though studies of Jews' investment in localized economies are numerous and explorations of discourse on Jews' relationship to commerce probing, there is little serious research on Jews' involvement in trans-national or trans-hemispheric commerce, particularly for the modern period.[22]

One example illustrates this point. A number of sophisticated studies have explored Jews' involvement in the turn-of-the-century textile industries of London, Paris, and New York: some of these are comparative in orientation; some thoughtfully explore the significance of Eastern Europe as a dynamic background to the development of the trade.[23] A large body of scholarship outside Jewish studies, meanwhile, pivots around the complex conditions that shaped the production and consumption of cotton in colonial and metropolitan settings.[24] But when it comes to the ways Jews in the European or American textile industries interacted with or influenced the global market, we know next to nothing. My point is less to pin an imagined set of phobias on my colleagues than to point toward a field of inquiry that may be rife with new insights. By interrogating the connections between Jews and global commerce we may develop, on one hand, a heightened appreciation for Jews' place in the modern world, and on the other a more textured sense of how trans-hemispheric trade was arbitrated by individuals and on a quotidian level. To produce precise historical insights about Jews, commerce, and the modern world, we must dispel the stigma associated with linking Jews to capital and international exchange.

Although few studies have explored the theme directly, Jews were profoundly implicated in modern global commerce: not only through their involvement in the fashion and textile industries, or because of their widely acknowledged overrepresentation in the fields of brokerage and financing, but through the trade of precious stones and metals, legal opium, liquor, and oil, among other commodities. Indeed, Jews intentionally moved into new markets in modern colonial settings, facilitating the conveyance of novel goods to the metropoles of Europe and the United States.[25] Other scholars (problematically, as we shall see in a moment) have used qualities possessed by Jews in general to explain these trends. Jews have been called quintessential "service nomads" of the modern period because they were outsiders—urban, literate, peripatetic, and in possession of contacts of kith and kin over seas, oceans, and political boundaries. Similar qualities, it has been argued, allowed Jews to rise to prominence in trans- and extra-regional trade in the ancient Mediterranean, the early modern Atlantic, or in such hubs of early modern global commerce as Antwerp, Hamburg, Amsterdam, Livorno, and Bordeaux.[26]

Indeed Jewishness was an asset to many in the modern feather trade, just as it was to merchants in other industrial contexts and periods. Jewishness served for some as a magnet to the industry and for others as a tonic that facilitated commercial relationships. More astonishingly, it influenced the pace and geographic makeup of the global feather market as a whole. Jewishness was a variable and subtle concept for those in the feather industry, and its meaning and import fluctuated across sub-ethnic diasporas, as across gender, class, and regional lines. In every instance, however, the fact of being Jewish had a bearing on individuals' movement into and experience of the feather business. A history of the modern ostrich feather trade that pivots around Jews is thus not simply another in a series of studies on single commodities such as cod, salt, sugar, coffee, or tea.[27] To borrow loosely from a scholar of feminist commodity chain analysis, this approach presents "an alternative rather than an additive" to the history of modern commerce, highlighting as it does the centrality of a particular ethnic and mercantile group to global exchanges.[28] In certain moments and industrial contexts, Jewishness functioned as the glue that bound together a global market.

And yet it would be misleading to pin Jews' success in feather commerce on general Jewish traits. Jews did not succeed in the feather market simply because they were Jews: indeed, they were still Jews when so many of them failed. Furthermore, the qualities that pushed Jews into global commerce in general, and into the pursuit of plumes in particular, were not universally Jewish. Instead, Jews involved in various echelons of the turn-of-the-century ostrich feather commodity chain embarked on the commercial adventures they did in part because of the particular skills, expertise, and contacts they possessed as Ashkenazi, Sephardi, Maghrebi, and Anglophone Jews—and as rich and poor, immigrant or native-born, South African, Mediterranean, British, or American men and women. Thus despite their historic expertise in transnational plume commerce and despite the existence of some Sephardi contacts on the ground, Sephardim broke into the Cape feather market rarely relative to their Ashkenazi peers. On the other hand, not a single Ashkenazi feather firm appears to have penetrated the North or West African feather markets, despite the higher quality of plumes in these regions and despite the peripatetic and entrepreneurial nature of so many Lithuanian Jewish feather families from the Russian Empire. By contrast, London, New York, and Paris seemed to level Jewish difference in the industry: in these cities robust numbers of Ashkenazi, Mediterranean, and Anglo-Jewish merchants, manufacturers, wholesalers, and blue-collar feather workers collaborated and competed with one another, gathering together in a single bourse—London—to vend their wares. Even here, however, Jews in the industry strategically balanced interaction and dissociation, and sub-ethnic specializations emerged. Thus feather processing in London and New York was almost entirely Ashkenazi in constitution, while Sephardim in these cities inclined toward manufacturing and wholesale; large numbers of Tripolitanian Jewish feather exporters, though competitors, settled densely near the Parisian Porte Denis after the demise of the trans-Saharan caravan route that linked Kano and Tripoli.[29] If Jewishness wove together the modern feather trade, sub-ethnicity delineated it strand by strand, place by place, and industrial niche by industrial niche.

For some of these reasons, the story of Jews' participation in the modern ostrich feather trade is not the same story one might tell about Jews' relationship to commerce generally, or in another epoch or industrial niche more specifically. The modern character of this history can be seen in three principal arenas. First, modern forms of communication and transportation intensified the boom-and-bust trajectory of the global feather market. Jewish and non-Jewish traders in earlier periods also monitored the ebb and flow of markets, but the invention of the steamship and the telegraph allowed farmers, merchants, wholesalers, and manufacturers in the ostrich feather trade to react instantaneously to subtle shifts in their volatile market. The facility with which information and goods traveled across the globe, through the ostrich feather industry, and between sites of supply and demand thus determined the success, vulnerability, and quotidian practice of individual industry participants.

The demand of consumers for more exotic fashion also weighs on this story far more conspicuously than it would in earlier periods. Fantastic numbers of plumes were bought by late-nineteenth- and early-twentieth-century consumers (about whom we will learn more shortly), and an extensive and geographically complex chain of supply emerged to accommodate their desires. Even for ostrich feather trading routes that spanned the Red Sea, the Sahara, and the Mediterranean basin and had operated continuously since the ancient period, the scale of modern feather commerce required merchants to conduct business in new cities, with new partners, and in a different fashion than they had before. The history of the ostrich feather boom and bust and the intertwined story of Jews' preeminence in this global commodity chain were shaped by the desires of a modern consumer society of unprecedented scale.

If the demands of consumers remapped feather commerce in the modern period, the actions of nation-states and empires carved new contours for this global industry. Nineteenth- and twentieth-century representatives of the American, British, French, Ottoman, Moroccan, Cape Colonial, and South African governments—policy makers, consular agents, social workers, agricultural experts, social scientists—had a profound influence over the development and, in some instances, the stagnation of feather commerce in areas under their control. Jews in the feather industry experienced state intervention (and inaction) acutely and asymmetrically. To offer but two contrasting examples: while the British state's nurturing of the feather trade proved a boon to Jewish merchants in the turn-of-the-century Cape Colony, the Moroccan court's dwindling ability to patronize privileged merchants ensured that the modern feather boom eluded local Jewish traders, including those whose families or firms had been in the business for generations. In these instances and others, the interaction of states, individual merchants, and commercial networks proved crucial to the shaping of a complexly interdependent modern global economy.

The speed with which information traveled across the globe, the voracious demands of consumers, and the commercial cultures of empires and nation-states are historical factors that delineate the modern feather trade from its early modern incarnation and modern Jewish traders of plumes from their early modern predecessors; these factors also point to the inadequacy of general historiographic explanations for Jewish commercial success. Relevant, too, are the idiosyncratic natures of single industries. One could argue that any careful history of Jews' involvement in modern global commerce must take into account the particularities of individual commodity chains. Given the intricacy of the story of Jews in the feather trade, we would expect an equally complex historical foundation to undergird Jews' (or any other ethnic mercantile group's) participation in the trade of other goods. For example, Jews were influential traders of legal opium, diamonds, gold, and wool, all commodities sold globally at the turn of the twentieth century; but the story of each of these commodity networks, like the story of the feather trade, was inflected by the histories of the colonies, empires, states, or cities in which the commodity was extracted, refined, or traded, by the race and class relations particular to these regions, by the relative stability or volatility of the commodity in question, and by the particular histories of the merchants involved. In sum, the specific human capital Jews brought to their commercial pursuits was an alchemy of ethnicity, sub-ethnicity, and regional, political, and social circumstance. A contribution of this work is to understand a particular global commodity through the lens of its most prominent ethnic traders, manufacturers, and handlers and, in so doing, to produce insights into the symbiotic relationships of discrete contexts, commodities, and cultures in the modern period.

What led Jews to occupational pursuits associated with the feather trade? As I have suggested, the reasons varied in each of the global hubs of the feather market and depended on the particular immigrant history, class, and role of the individual, family, or firm involved. Certain leitmotifs, however, persist. Jews gravitated to this commodity chain because they had a background in similar industrial and mercantile trades, because they had contacts across the Anglophone, Eastern European, and Mediterranean diasporas, and because many were immigrants poised to move into new or expanding industrial niches. Some of these factors pushed Jews into other commodity chains, including diamonds and textiles, but no other commodity chain was shaped by all of them.

The extensive Eastern European Jewish diaspora was pivotal to the expansion of the global ostrich feather trade. Just as the feather boom was gaining steam, mass numbers of Jews from Eastern Europe were settling in the major new hubs of the feather trade: roughly a million and a half in New York City, 150,000 in Britain (with the majority in London), 80,000 in Paris, and

10,000 in South Africa. For the most part, these émigrés did not move with the intention of joining the feather trade. (Exceptions may be found among Russian-Lithuanian Jews who migrated to the Cape Colony.) Instead, the bulk included young men and women experienced as skilled workers or artisans whose migration was motivated by a crisis at home and the quest for social and economic ascension elsewhere.[30] Neither of these opportunities could be found easily in the Russian Empire, where the vast majority of Eastern European Jews resided. Change was afoot for Jews in late-nineteenth-century Russia—Jewish youths were increasingly entering Russian government-sponsored schools and becoming more Russian in cultural orientation, they were joining novel political and cultural movements including socialism, Zionism, and Russophilism, they were witnessing the erosion of traditional pillars of Jewish society, and they were gravitating toward the region's new industrial centers. At the same time, Jews were, as a group, overpopulated, underemployed, and unemancipated, with no real hope of political change. Despite the rise of a Jewish middle and upper class, Jews throughout the Russian Empire faced widespread pauperization, residential and professional restrictions, and a rise in anti-Semitic sentiment by state officials and the Russian public.[31] These factors, coupled with the lure of various potential homelands, led to the mass intra- and extra-regional migration of millions of Eastern European Jews between the 1880s and the outbreak of World War I.

In London, New York, and Paris, tens of thousands of these immigrants—mostly girls and women, but boys and men as well—moved into skilled, semi-skilled, and unskilled positions in ostrich feather manufacturing. The industry appealed to Jewish immigrants from Eastern Europe and their children because of their background as artisanal and industrial workers, because they were young, working-class, and transplanted, and because they were in search of new professional opportunities. Jewish girls and women gravitated to blue-collar feather work in particularly large numbers (relative to Jewish boys and men): they represented a large percentage of the East European Jewish diaspora, had a tradition of serving as providers in Eastern Europe, and were experienced in the needle trades.[32] As further inducement (and not coincidentally), ostrich feather manufacturing was concentrated in or near the heart of dense immigrant Jewish neighborhoods: London's East End, the *Pletzl* of Paris, and the Lower East Side in New York.

Feather merchants, manufacturers, and wholesalers of Eastern European origin benefited from being a part of a modern diaspora as well. Trans-Atlantic feather commerce relied on the flow of capital, commodities, and bodies back and forth between Eastern Europe, the Cape, London, Paris, and New York; contacts across these cities and regions—and, in some cases, the existence of Yiddish as a shared language—facilitated success. These global connections are illustrated graphically in the business stationery of H. Barron Company, Ltd., a turn-of-the-century import-export firm operating in the Cape, London, and New York run by three Jewish brothers of East European origin. The company's letterhead pictured ostrich feathers undertaking a single, seamless journey from the ostrich-spotted Little Karoo to Cape Town's bustling harbor and thence to the welcoming arms of the Statue of Liberty. Overlaying this image was the imprint of a single handshake, evidence of the presumed security a family firm was meant to provide (fig. 3). Though fraternity did not always guarantee harmony for the Barron brothers, diasporic conditions undoubtedly facilitated commercial opportunities.[33]

Members of Mediterranean Jewish diasporas who worked in the feather trade also benefited from trans- and extra-regional contacts of kith and kin. Sephardi and Livornese merchants had traded in ostrich plumes since the early modern period, operating in the principal port cities of Marseilles, Livorno, Venice, Trieste, Cairo, Alexandria, Benghazi, Tripoli, and Essaouira (Mogador) and relying on Jewish and non-Jewish trading partners along the camel caravan routes that extended south across the Sahara and the Sahel.[34] As feathers rose in value in the last decades of the nineteenth century, more Jewish merchants and family firms moved into the business or shifted their European representatives from the Mediterranean to London, Paris, and New York, all centers of modern feather commerce. Some prospered as a result, especially those Livornese Jewish feather families based in Tripoli who benefited from the fiscal protection of the Ottoman state. (Jewish feather traders and financiers in Morocco, by contrast, found themselves increasingly unable to rely on the impoverished royal court for the accustomed subsidy and protection, and the modern feather boom thus by and large eluded them.)[35] Diasporic contacts, state sponsorship, expertise acquired over time: all this influenced Mediterranean Jews' ability to operate as feather exporters and financiers in some contexts.

As it did for some Jews of Eastern European origin, poverty drew other

Figure 3. Business stationery of H. Barron Company, ca. 1919. The multiple addresses and illustration narrate the path of plumes exported by this family firm from the Cape of Good Hope to New York harbor. (Courtesy C. P. Nel Museum, Oudtshoorn)

Mediterranean Jews to the industry. Like the East European Jewish feather handlers who worked in New York or London, Maghrebi Jews were drawn to feather processing because they were poor and because they had expertise in related trades—in this case the tanning and processing of skins. In contrast to their Ashkenazi peers, however, Maghrebi Jewish feather processors were not immigrants but impoverished locals largely bereft of overseas connections and the capital required to emigrate and better their lot. Thus while some Mediterranean Jews sought out feather trading as a lucrative pursuit, others were driven to the industry by a shortage of options, finding in it no real hope of ascension.

Jewishness abetted commercial alliances not only within but across sub-ethnic Jewish diasporas. There was, indeed, a certain intimacy to the global feather trade, notwithstanding its intensely competitive nature. Edward Schuman, whose father founded the first American ostrich feather duster company, has recalled that traveling Jewish feather merchants frequently slept on his family's couch, among them a representative of the Barron family and Marcel Habib, a Jew of Tripolitanian and Livornese origin who came to dominate the Parisian ostrich feather market in the mid-twentieth century.[36] The Schumans were not alone in creating alliances across sub-ethnic and political boundaries. Isaac Nurick, for example, was a Cape-based feather merchant who immigrated to South Africa from Russian-controlled Lithuania. Nurick collaborated with *landsmen* in the Cape and developed business alliances with non-Ashkenazi Jewish merchants in London, including an Anglo-Sephardi feather seller named Dan Andrade, who for years had farmed birds and bought and sold plumes in the Cape, and a Jewish feather merchant of Mediterranean origin named Isach Hassan. Nurick hired these men to spy on the competition, work as auction shills, and inform him on the state of the trade more generally. Because of the quasi-legal nature of these relationships, and because of the competitiveness and paranoia to which so many feather traders were prone, correspondence among these men was marked by discord and occasionally written in code.[37]

Other such examples abound. The Anglo-Jewish Salaman family oversaw what was said to be "the largest wholesale ostrich feather business in the world," based in London with operations in South Africa, France, and the United States. The Salamans' ostensible Northern European origins and long-standing roots in Britain were a source of pride for some in the family. At the same time, their business clearly benefited from a daughter's marriage to Alfred Aaron de Pass, a Sephardi merchant experienced in the whaling, sealing, guano, fur, and fishing industries of the Cape who assumed a position of leadership in the Salamans' commercial affairs.[38] And there is the story of Alfred Mosely. British born and educated, Mosely profited in the early years of South Africa's mineral revolution and permanently relocated to the Cape. During what appeared to be a resurgence in the feather market in 1919, Mosely collaborated with his London-based brother and with a Jewish merchant in New York by the name of J. A. Stein to finance an American ostrich feather farm in Atlanta, Georgia.

Given the preponderance of Jews in the feather trade, one might ask whether Jews such as these collaborated with one another by chance. Certainly a Tripolitanian Jewish merchant from Livorno living in London was not the obvious bedfellow of a Lithuanian Jewish émigré working in the Cape. And yet given the volatility, competitiveness, and trans-hemispheric nature of the modern ostrich feather trade, the forging of personal alliances eased by shared religion was crucial to doing business.[39] Indeed, one did not have to be Jewish to recognize the importance of developing contacts across the Jewish feather world.

European merchants and Muslim chiefs involved in North Africa's feather trade were known to employ Jewish interpreters and secretaries to conduct business correspondence in Judeo-Arabic, the lingua franca of regional Jewish feather traders.[40] Similarly, many Boer ostrich farmers in the Western Cape acquired the Yiddish required to conduct business with Jewish feather buyers.

Not surprisingly, the reasons for Jews' preponderance and success in the feather trade were neither readily recognizable to nor appreciated by non-Jews in the industry. European and American observers of the feather trade, Boer ostrich farmers, North African Muslim merchants: all complained that Jews conspired to keep non-Jews out of the business, thereby maintaining a monopoly. Hekkie Schoeman, a prominent Boer ostrich farmer, described being shocked to discover firsthand how much ostrich plumes were commanding at auction in London. He returned home determined to sell his feathers directly to brokerage firms in London, thereby eliminating the need for the services of the Jewish feather buyer on whom he normally relied. Schoeman prepared his own bundles for auction and, after first asking his regular buyer what the plumes were worth, sent them to London himself. To his great dismay, he discovered that the feathers earned him less at auction than his buyer originally offered. An infuriated Schoeman attributed his failure to the influence of "the Jewish mafia" and determined that he had little option but to patronize his regular buyer once again.[41]

What Schoeman did not realize, and what eluded so many of the non-Jewish Americans, Europeans, and North Africans who echoed his concerns, was that success at trans-hemispheric trade required expertise, background, and contacts. These skills were acquired by Jews in the feather trade not because they were predisposed to maintain cabals and not because they were Jews ipso facto—not even, as a contemporary scholar has argued in another context, because they were primordial middlemen—but because of the particularly complex intricacies of feather grading, sorting, and selling. These complexities, and the intense volatility of the market, created a large premium on industry-specific information—a premium paid in recognition of the sub-ethnic and commercial backgrounds of the parties involved, the contacts they had at their disposal, and the feather fluency they acquired over time.[42] This anecdote about Hekkie Schoeman thus translates into one of the central arguments of this book. Jews brought certain elements of human capital to the ostrich feather trade: background in like industries, contacts of kith and kin within and across sub-ethnic diasporas and political and oceanic boundaries, copacetic relations with the reigning authorities, geographic mobility, and, no less important, economic need. These factors rendered them uniquely well suited to pursue feather commerce and, in turn, they proved crucial to the expansion and profitability of the feather market as a whole.

SUPPLY, DEMAND, AND THE ARC OF A BOOM AND BUST MARKET

Thus far I have suggested that Jews were well represented as purveyors of goods—and ostrich feathers in particular—in the modern international market. I have also speculated that the occlusion of these stories stems, at least in part, from historians' failure to sufficiently analyze the symbiotic relationship between ethnicity and particular commercial networks. One might rephrase this argument by suggesting that a cultural historian's perspective may bring something new to the field of economic history. Cultural historians, too, may benefit from an emphasis on global supply.

In spite of the recent proliferation of excellent scholarship on modern practices of consumption, cultural histories of supply remain scarce.[43] This trend reflects how fully cultural history has overtaken economic and business history in recent scholarly generations; it also betrays cultural historians' unease at tackling the sources and themes traditionally considered the domain of economic historians. Whatever the cause, cultural historians' avoidance of the story of production relations is limiting, for where modern goods come from and how they reach the consumers who desire them is a crucial component of the history of modern consumer society and the modern world more generally. Like histories of consumption, histories of supply can emphasize the importance of transnational currents of capital and culture and the interconnectedness of metropoles and colonies. But an attention to supply may move these insights in new geographic and conceptual directions. Studying the full width and breadth of a given commodity chain highlights global interconnections in and across colonial contexts whose links to metropolitan consumers have not yet been developed, and their relation to particular mercantile groups. A focus on supply thus emphasizes pronounced interdependencies between seemingly disparate markets, regions, and cultures.

When it comes to the ostrich feather trade, one cannot artificially separate the history of supply from the history of demand. This point was made quite clearly in 1918 by a prominent Cape ostrich farmer addressing a government-sponsored commission inquiring into the causes of the feather crash:

> Fashion has always been cosmopolitan and international. How it will be after the [First World] war I do not know; as little as I know whether there will be a sudden extensive revival of demand. . . . But judging from what is secure to judge upon—the experience of the past—I cannot see to what other conclusion we can come than that we have to do here with an uncertain, arbitrary, whimsical love of luxury, that this is finally the conclusive base of the whole of our feather industry, and that those among us who put our capital and work in such an industry ought to realize that we have to do this from the nature of the business at our own risk, because we cannot expect it to be durable.[44]

Such an astute assessment of the ostrich feather boom and bust was rare for a member of the industry. This was in part because the personal success of all involved depended on the stability of the feather trade. But it was also because the arc—or, more specifically, the apex—of this market was impossible to anticipate with precision. When the ostrich feather market was booming, there was little indication that plumes would have a more finite appeal than, say, diamonds, another volatile luxury good of South African origin then capturing a large international market. Indeed, contemporary observers often compared the relative durability of these goods, suggesting that a fine ostrich feather "is an investment for life," and noting that the plume "has been in fashion for centuries past, and will probably be for centuries to come. It holds its place like the diamond."[45]

But the ostrich feather did not share the same fate as the diamond. Beginning in the 1930s, the De Beers diamond syndicate created a cartel to control prices, simultaneously managing an aggressive and astonishingly successful advertising campaign to convince global consumers that diamonds were enduring, classy, and a mark of fidelity.[46] Similar attempts at influencing consumers were undertaken a decade or so earlier by those in the feather industry, but these efforts were insubstantial, underfunded, and ill-timed. Partly as a result, by around 1915, ostrich feathers had come to be viewed as fragile, dated, and tawdry.[47] What made the ostrich feather so appealing to turn-of-the-century consumers? Why did it then fall so precipitously from grace?

American and European women's thirst for feathers as objects of adornment undergirded the vigorous modern global market in ostrich plumes. Fashion watchers like Lucy Hooper, a regular contributor to the American women's periodical *Peterson's Magazine*, noted that trends in ostrich feather wearing, like so much else in the fashion world, emanated from Paris. From time to time, Hooper explained, the British or American woman showed signs of "growing amazingly independent of the Paris fashions." But, for the most part, ebbs and flows in the turn-of-the-century ostrich feather market of France, Britain, and the United States (and, on a smaller scale, Germany) ran parallel and took their cues from the French capital.[48]

A variety of feathers, including those of the ostrich, had adorned the hats, fans, and clothes of elite European and American women since at least the second half of the eighteenth century. Ostrich feathers, however, were not widely employed by the fashion world until the 1880s, the first of three decades in which women's hats were worn large and elaborately trimmed. Then, feather-bedecked fans and boas prevailed. From the 1880s to roughly the outbreak of the First World War, when feathers fell out of fashion, ostrich plumes proved a highly versatile and popular commodity, a ubiquitous feature of trans-Atlantic women's fashion (fig. 4). Though the length, hue, and shape of the plumes ebbed and flowed over the duration of the feather boom, and though there were dips and peaks in the market, the overall appeal of ostrich feathers endured. "A well dressed woman nowadays is as fluffy as a downy bird fresh from the nest," wrote one fashion observer of the period. Declared another: "If you would be fashionable this winter, you will be beplumed."[49]

Women's evolving patterns of consumption partially explain the feather boom. Urban working- and middle-class women in the United States and Europe were gaining ever more opportunity and desire to consume at the turn of the century: the many fashion choices they faced were outlined in new kinds of media targeting the female shopper, fashion magazines among them, while the objects they coveted were displayed ever more alluringly in novel shopping neighborhoods.[50] If women were willing and able consumers, however, there was something particularly magnetic about ostrich feathers. In contrast to "fancy feathers" (that is, the plumage of wild birds) or artificial flowers, both popular millinery accouterments of the period, ostrich plumage was considered fashionable all year round. What's more, ostrich feathers were

Figure 4. French trade postcards featuring models with ostrich feather hats ca. 1910.
(Courtesy www.struthie.com)

deemed acceptable embellishments for women young and old, of all "sizes and complexions."[51] With at least fourteen varieties and countless grades available, ostrich feathers' appeal also crossed class lines. Women of means, the first to wear the plumes, were drawn to the highest grade, "prime white" feathers, of which the Barbary plume was preeminent, but lesser grades of ostrich plumes were widely used throughout the fashion industry.[52]

For trendsetters like Sarah Bernhardt, ostrich feathers may also have been appealing as emblems of colonial conquest and a cosmopolitan sensibility.[53] Even American ostrich breeders who were acutely sensitive to consumers' potential loyalties to the American-made good boasted of their birds' African origins. In one promotional pamphlet titled "My Life by Daddy Ostrich," distributed by a California ostrich farm, the titular bird confides: "My native country is South Africa, but I was born in Sunny California."[54] Popular journalistic accounts, too, dwelled on the feathers' exotic roots in the "Dark Continent," where they were ostensibly worn on "the head-dress of the African king."[55] Black African and colored men and women in southern Africa were indeed known to wear ostrich plumes ornamentally; ironically, this proved a source of discomfort for white residents and travelers in the region, who found feather wearing among men emasculating and among women a bastardization of white fashion norms. White women in South Africa may even have spurned feather wearing because it was done by poor non-whites; according to one source, "the lady of fashion—who is [the feather industry's] best customer—refuses to wear feathers on her hat if her servant is also wearing them."[56] (The wearing of feathers by urban and educated black and colored women in South Africa, by contrast, does not appear to have taken off until the 1930s or 1940s—after feather wearing had already fallen out of fashion in Europe and the United States.)[57] American and European narratives on feather wearing in Africa were innocent of these nuances. These sources stressed, instead, that ostrich feathers left southern and northern Africa in a disgraceful state—covered in guano and dirt, gray, matted, and straggly—only to be transformed into pristine objects of adornment by feather handlers in London, Paris, and New York.[58] The ostrich feather so admired by turn-of-the-century European and American women consumers, it would seem, was Africana refined.

Complementing its exotic African origins, there was something about the raw physicality of an ostrich plume that held appeal. Fashion critics called the feathers sinuous and sensual and noted that, when moored to the hat, fan, or boa, they lent their wearer the impression of movement and freedom. Like the modern woman, who moved and encountered space in new ways, the plume embodied emancipation and mobility.[59] Feathers fluttered, reflected light, were soft to the touch, and were said to "refine many hard lines."[60] To borrow freely from Judith Walkowitz, one could say that these physical features, coupled with the larger sociopolitical context in which the plumes were traded, imbued ostrich feathers with the enticing and transgressive qualities of cosmopolitanism. Feathers were reminiscent of the modern dance of Maud Allan, which Walkowitz has described as "a pleasurable, stylized form of imaginative expatriation, associated with privileged mobility; and, second, a debased condition of deracination, hybridity, displacement and racial degeneration—all the dangers of the unplaced."[61] So resonant were ostrich feathers as colonial booty and cosmopolitan trope, they and, indeed, entire flocks of the birds were displayed at world's fairs in Chicago, Philadelphia, Paris, and London, by the Smithsonian Museum in 1914, at the Panama-California Exposition of 1915, and in the British Empire Exhibit of 1924, where the queen herself clipped plumes from a live bird.[62] Ostrich feathers, it seemed, could be found wherever there were arbiters of style: a consignment of £20,000 worth of the plumes was lost during the sinking of the *Titanic*.[63]

Ostrich farmers and entrepreneurs in South Africa were not naive beneficiaries of the ostrich feather craze. On the contrary, they served as a largely invisible "corner" in the triangulation of trans-Atlantic fashion. Those in the feather industry in the Cape actively monitored—and, when the feather market was depressed, attempted to influence—feather fashion across the Atlantic. According to an unpublished study of Oudtshoorn from 1948:

> The farmers, many of them illiterate, became passionately interested in what women were wearing in London and New York and Paris. The late Mr. Ockert Fourie, one of the finest breeders of birds, used to take the feathers of the ostriches he intended mating down to the sea and find out whether the moisture would affect the flue. . . . Leaders of the industry in Oudtshoorn traveled to Europe to see their feathers being sold and marketed and made up by the world's courtiers and milliners.[64]

When it came to ostrich feathers, fashion currents ran not only on a north-to-south trajectory, but east to west as well.

Given the exertions of Fourie and his peers, why did those in the feather industry not succeed in micromanaging consumers' desires, as the De Beers syndicate was able to do less than two decades hence? What caused feather boom to turn to feather bust; what determined the immense volatility of this modern commodity?

The first answer has to do with social politics. The campaigns of bird preservationists, combined with the support of consumers and disorganized resistance on the part of the millinery and feather trade, represented a profound blow to the feather industry. These campaigns resulted in the adoption of a series of anti-plumage bills, including in the United States the Lacey Act of 1900, the Migratory Bird Act of 1913, and the Tariff Act of 1913, and in Britain the Plumage Act of 1921. These laws, like most bird preservation efforts, sought to halt the obliteration of wild bird species at home and tropical birds overseas. Ostriches, of course, were not a target; they, as distinguished from hummingbirds, herons, or egrets, were farmed and not killed for their feathers. Advocates of the industry—who imagined that bird protectionist legislation would actually prove a boon to the ostrich feather trade—pointed out further that farmed ostriches were "treated with the greatest kindness, and their lives are prolonged as long as possible," while the harvesting of ostrich plumes was "as painless as cutting human hair" or "trimming one's fingernails."[65] These distinctions mattered little to feather consumers. Once feathers were branded cruel and unfashionable, women buyers were inclined to make no distinction between types of plumes or birds. With American and British anti-plumage legislation on the books, international demand for ostrich feathers fell, as did the amount plumes commanded at auction.[66]

Even before the full effects of bird protection legislation were felt, the fashion world had reason to turn against feather wearing. World War I was pushing European and American women into the workforce, stimulating demand for more utilitarian clothing—including hats. Beginning in late 1914 and early 1915, fashion journals and trade bulletins on both sides of the Atlantic dispensed with the ornate, deep-brimmed hats that had been so recently celebrated, promoting instead more austere and streamlined options: a simple toque, a peaked cap adorned only with a ribbon band, or, in time, the ubiquitous cloche.[67] The popularization of the automobile had a further impact on women's headgear. Enormous hats were impossible to keep in form or place in open cars; elaborate feather accessories fared badly in such circumstances.[68]

Those in the ostrich industry were also culpable. In the early years of the twentieth century, ostrich farmers and feather buyers in South Africa were feverishly engaged in contract farming and informal speculation, and as a result they were raising ever more birds. Brokerage firms, feather wholesalers, and manufacturers in New York and London, meanwhile, were stocking great quantities of feathers in anticipation of a rise in value.[69] In hindsight, these activities may appear reckless and imprudent, but at the time they seemed shrewd.

The feather crash that began in the late winter of 1914 brought financial and personal ruin to ostrich farmers, feather merchants, manufacturers, sorters, wholesalers, and handlers across the Mediterranean Jewish diaspora and in southern Africa, Europe, and the United States. The most tenacious tried to ride out the feather bust, and some even experienced a bout of success when consumers' interest in plumes revived briefly in 1919. Many more were left bereft of business, pride, and reputation. There are stories of new slums created to house communities disenfranchised by the crash, of feather merchants committing suicide rather than face their debts, of husbands selling their wives' jewelry and even their oven door to remain solvent, of large-scale exporters reduced to itinerant vegetable hawkers, of feather ghost towns and feather orphans, of farms littered with the carcasses of ostriches no longer worth the cost of their feed.

In times of bust as in times of boom, all those engaged in the ostrich feather trade, from the large-scale manufacturer with operations in four countries to the unskilled immigrant feather handler, proved immensely sensitive to the volatility of the global market. This was no less true for Jews than for non-Jews. The forms of human capital that facilitated Jews' movement into the commerce in plumes did little to insulate them from the feather crash. Indeed, in certain respects Jews proved particularly vulnerable to it, and, more specifically, vulnerable to the ways the feather bust was interpreted and managed in the various hubs of the global feather industry.

In North Africa, the final evisceration of centuries-old feather trading networks paralleled the erosion of ancient Jewish regional economic practices and of the global importance of Mediterranean trade more generally.[70] Increasingly unable to rely on the protection of the state and in certain respects jeopardized by the encroachment of European control, many Jewish traders and family firms left the region altogether. In the wake of the feather crash in South Africa, the state ceded to the demands of an Afrikaner nationalist agricultural movement eager to edge "middlemen" and "speculators"—both thinly veiled terms for Jews—out of the feather industry. Once valued for their extra-regional contacts, Jews were now disparaged for their cosmopolitanism and recast as ruthless speculators inclined to prey on economically vulnerable farmers. The state also stepped in to monitor the British feather industry after 1914. Arguably its agenda was laudable: the creation and enforcement of a minimum wage scale for London's blue-collar feather workforce. But in this context, as well, the feather industry's vulnerabilities were pinned on Jews. Even Britain's extensive debates about anti-plumage legislation were imbued with the faintest tinge of anti-Semitism.[71] Finally, New York State, America's ostrich feather manufacturing center, began an intense scrutiny of the feather industry after the crash. Its authors proved far more discreet than their British peers on the topic of Jews' prevalence in the field, but the American popular press was not always so demure. Among the countless cartoons that parodied the collapse of the feather trade were those that hinted that this was a story not about failed business in general, but failed Jewish businesses in particular.

In each of these contexts, Jews' prominence in the feather industry was strategically remembered—vilified and legislated against here, officially noted and popularly scorned there—and, in equal measures, strategically forgotten. Such forgetting was, for example, an ingredient in the various retellings of

Thornton's Trans-Saharan Ostrich Expedition, the first of which emerged even as the expedition members were returning to South African soil. In these narratives, the feather boom was driven by state power and individual bravado. Jews are missing, but so too is any practical representation of the trans-national nature of plume commerce. Both of these qualities were essential and obvious features of the modern ostrich feather market. None with any knowledge of the turn-of-the-century ostrich feather trade could be innocent of its global makeup, or of Jews' importance to it. Nonetheless, for the historical and historiographic reasons we have seen, this story has become increasingly inaccessible with the passage of time.

HISTORIES LOCAL AND GLOBAL

To uncover the story of the elusive ostrich plume, we—like the feathers whose path we will follow—must move back and forth through local and global terrains. This book explores how Jews fostered and nurtured the supply side of the global ostrich feather industry at all levels and stages—from feather handler to financier and from bird to bonnet—and over the varied geographical and political terrains in which the plumes were grown, plucked, sorted, exported, imported, auctioned, wholesaled, and manufactured for sale. Our main chapters are organized geographically and chronologically and explore how the feather boom and bust played out in each of the four major regional and urban hubs of modern ostrich feather commerce: the Western Cape; London; the southern Sahara, North Africa, West Africa, and the Mediterranean basin; and in New York and the American West, Southwest, and South. As they move geographically, these chapters also progress sequentially along the length of the global ostrich feather commodity chain.

In a rough chronological progression, the following chapters explore Jews' involvement in the production, financing, purchase, and preparation of plumes in South Africa, the southern Sahara, West Africa, and the Mediterranean and their export to London; the auction, wholesale, and manufacture of plumes in the British capital; and the subsequent export of "raw" and manufactured feathers to Paris and New York (among other metropoles), where they were manufactured and wholesaled once again. None of these chapters stand alone. Readers will encounter the same individuals, events, and feather work in multiple chapters, with their histories unfolding gradually. These cross-references are necessitated by the economic and geographic logic of the turn-of-the-century feather trade, according to which individual plumes could be transshipped no less than four times between North Africa and London, or conveyed from the Cape to London to New York to Paris before being returned to New York for public sale. A spiraling narrative also serves to emphasize that participants in the feather industry were rooted in global—as well as in local, national, and imperial—landscapes. Accordingly, while each of the chapters of this work is densely local, readers shouldn't lose the sense that they are also integrated into something larger. In the end, this is a study that thinks globally yet examines locally, exploring rich case studies to understand a global market, trans-hemispheric networks, and the ebbs and flow of international demand.

This narrative demonstrates how deeply trans-hemispheric currents of capital, bodies, and goods affected modern Jews and, conversely, how profoundly Jews shaped the modern global economy. If it threatens to confirm stereotypes about Jews' intimacy with commerce or capital, it must be remembered that this is also a story about failure, about how elusive—and historically contingent—profit and expertise can be. Though focused on commerce, it is also an exploration of Jewish culture, identity, and communities—Jews' encounter with and place in the modern world. If these cultural themes remain in the background of my story, it is not because they are irrelevant to the Jewish historian, but, on the contrary, because we have already paid them so much heed. By displacing such themes, I intend to raise, if not to fully answer, two broad historiographic questions: What might result from the blurring, and possibly even the erasing, of the line that divides economic and cultural history? And how does the arc, or even the engine, of modern Jewish history change if we invite commercial practices to center stage?

CHAPTER I

The Cape of Southern Africa: Atlantic Crossings

On August 30, 1912, Isaac Nurick shipped seven cases packed with 1,708 ostrich feathers from Oudtshoorn to London. The cases, which would sail aboard the steamship *Saxon*, bore his trademark, which featured Nurick's initials and the first letter of his town. The feathers, and six more cases besides, were to be received by the National Bank of London and sold at public auction in December, likely by one of Nurick's favored brokerage firms, Figgis and Company or Hale and Son. Insured for a total of £11,500, the thirteen cases represented a particularly vigorous season's work for Nurick.[1]

At the close of 1912, South African ostrich feather buyers like Nurick had reason to be satisfied with the state of their business. It was true, as Nurick's London-based associate had warned in correspondence as much as a year earlier, that American and French buyers had been losing interest in plumes for some time.[2] Yet fears about waning international demand for feathers had circulated before; for the moment, the ostrich feather market was still quite strong. Reports on the state of "South African Produce Markets" published monthly in the *South African Agricultural Journal* concluded that the last major ostrich feather auction in London (in June 1912) had witnessed "a good demand for all classes of goods."[3] Overall, nearly a million pounds of ostrich feathers, valued at roughly £2.6 million, were exported from the Cape in 1912, yielding the largest gross income for ostrich feathers ever seen. Over a twenty-year period, the value of Cape ostrich feathers had trebled.[4]

In Oudtshoorn, Nurick was feverishly capitalizing on the ostrich feather boom. In November 1912, he engaged in an ambitious bout of contract farming, purchasing the entire plumage of roughly 1,355 birds that were, at the time of sale, not yet ready to be plucked.[5] Advance contracts like these, which were

endemic to the feather trade, had made many feather buyers and ostrich farmers rich. To be sure, some had lost their wealth once or twice over, particularly
between 1886 and 1896, when shifts in fashion caused the value of ostrich
feathers to plunge by 75 percent, but the ostrich farming district of Oudtshoorn, and the town of Oudtshoorn in particular, were marked by grand
"feather mansions" that bore testimony to the success of its wealthier white
inhabitants. In the autumn of 1912, as thirteen cases of his feathers wound
their way to auction on London's Mincing Lane, Isaac Nurick paid no heed
to his industry's own promotional material, which described ostrich plumes
as "fancy feathers of fickle fashion" (fig. 5). Yet the mercurial feather market
would ensure that in a few years' time ostrich feathers would be nearly worthless, and many buyers, him included, would be deeply in debt and bereft of
business, pride, and reputation.

The story of the highly lucrative, if ultimately short-lived, trans-Atlantic
ostrich feather trade of the late nineteenth and early twentieth centuries had
roots that ramified over several continents and pushed deep into previous
imperial and colonial histories. It was anchored, first, in the shtetls, or small
towns, of Chelm and Shavli in the Lithuanian province of the Russian Empire. This was the provenance of the vast majority of the feather merchants
of the Cape, the first generation of whom had surely never seen an ostrich
before arriving in southern Africa as penniless single Jewish men.[6] Once in the
Cape, Jews developed business and personal relationships with colored workers
and Boer farmers, buying feathers from these locals or entering into business
partnerships with them. Some Jewish feather buyers maintained small-scale
operations, buying and selling feathers in small quantities or plume by plume
and never developing contacts overseas. Others, like Nurick, took their supply
to the international market, plying the millinery, fashion, funeral, and costume
industries of London, Paris, Berlin, New York and beyond.

The pages that follow tell the story of Jews' preeminence as feather buyers
in the Western Cape. I am interested in several interrelated questions: How did
Jewish immigrants from the Russian Empire come to dominate the lucrative
South African ostrich feather trade? Why were Lithuanian Jewish immigrants
so well poised (in the language of Leybl Feldman) to "fall into feathers"? Were
the Russian shtetls from which these feather merchants came merely sources of
abundant, cheap mercantile labor, or did they provide a particularly apposite set

of circumstances for incubating feather merchants? Finally, in what ways was these feather merchants' work as buyers and sellers of ostrich feathers structured by their Jewishness, and, conversely, was the texture of their Jewishness influenced by their vocational pursuit?

THE RISE OF THE SOUTH AFRICAN OSTRICH FEATHER INDUSTRY

Before the 1860s, ostriches ran wild in large numbers in southern Africa, the Sahara, and the Sahel. In southern Africa, the birds were hunted and killed for their feathers by Khoisan and colored residents and by white settlers and travelers, all of whom valued the plumes as adornment or sold them for profit.[7] In 1863 the first ostrich was domesticated in the Cape; one year later, the first effective ostrich egg incubator, an apparatus called "the Eclipse" that allowed for the controlled breeding of birds, was patented.[8] Over the course of the next five decades, ostrich farming in the Western Cape took hold in the semi-desert Little Karoo region, where the number of domesticated ostriches skyrocketed from next to nothing in the early 1860s to 776,000 in 1913.[9] By that year, when the price of ostrich feathers reached its peak, the plumes were ranked fourth in value among commodities exported from the Union of South Africa.[10]

As international demand for ostrich feathers grew, Boer, British, and some Jewish farmers in the Oudtshoorn District exploited the suitability of the region for ostrich farming to continuously expand and intensify their operations. Hermanus (Armaans) Potgieter recalls being shocked by the sum Jewish feather buyers gave him for wild ostrich hides and feathers that he had acquired on a hunting expedition in the 1860s. Shortly thereafter, he leased a farm in Oudtshoorn District and began raising ostriches himself. Less than a generation later, the firm he established, Potgieter Brothers, was the largest bird holder in the Cape.[11] In the early nineteenth century, grain, viticulture, and tobacco had been the principal crops farmed by Boers in Oudtshoorn District: these crops were cultivated on a modest scale, such that farmers could deliver goods to market themselves.[12] The region's absence of grass made cattle and sheep farming difficult, and low precipitation rates (less than an inch annually, on average) further limited farmers' flexibility. Because of the expansion and intensification of ostrich farming around the turn of the twentieth century, however, Oudtshoorn evolved from a relatively isolated rural economy to an

Figure 5. The Jewish feather merchant Isaac Nurick (with cane), surrounded by family, associates, and his finest "prime white" ostrich plumes, ca. 1911. An immigrant from Russian Lithuania, Nurick prospered in Oudtshoorn during the feather boom but fled South Africa for London after losing his and his wife's fortune in the feather bust. (Courtesy C. P. Nel Museum, Oudtshoorn)

industrialized center linked to the metropoles of Europe and the United States. Thus, though class, labor, and race relations in Oudtshoorn were in many respects distinct from elsewhere in South Africa, the dramatic growth of ostrich farming in the district coincided with South Africa's agrarian and mineral revolutions and contributed to the changes that forever transformed the Cape.

What made the Oudtshoorn region so hospitable to ostrich farming? As ostrich farmer N. H. O. Gavin explained to a state-sponsored irrigation committee in 1913, the Karoo's arid climate was "essential to the production of the finest feathers." The climate in Oudtshoorn allowed ostrich farmers to pluck adult birds three times in two years, or every eight months, a frequency of harvesting not possible even in neighboring Grahamstown, where rainfall was more frequent.[13] Other environmental factors made the Oudtshoorn District well suited to ostrich farming. High levels of lime in the alluvial soil of the region's river valleys presented ideal conditions for growing lucerne (or alfalfa), which provided superb nourishment for ostriches and allowed a high density of birds to be raised per acre of farmland.[14] These conditions, combined with the escalating value of ostrich feathers on the international market, ensured that ostriches could earn a farmer five to six times more than wheat for the same amount of cultivable land. In the last decades of the nineteenth century, the quantity of wheat and grapevines grown in Oudtshoorn plummeted as the production of lucerne and ostriches soared.[15] As early as 1864, *The Times* of London declared the ostrich industry so promising that it was "likely to eclipse the gold mines of Australia, California, and Vancouver."[16] In this and other sources, young British men were advised that they were certain to find both adventure and fortune in ostrich farming.[17]

Indeed, ostrich farming brought great riches to some in Oudtshoorn District. The wealth of Oudtshoorn grew at three times the rate of other rural areas in the Cape Colony, as well as that of the colony as a whole.[18] The value of fixed property grew dramatically, leading wealthier farmers to partake of a land grab and, as a consequence, to a rise in tenant farming in the district.[19] To accommodate Oudtshoorn's growth, the number of wells in the district increased from two to forty-six from 1891 to 1911.[20] Boer and British farmers and Jewish large-scale feather buyers were the principal beneficiaries of the feather boom. As a result of their success, the "valuation per head of European population" rose faster in the Little Karoo than almost anywhere else in the Cape.[21] Farmers built extravagant "feather mansions" to display their wealth: luxurious homes adorned with, in one contemporary's description, "paneled walls, tiled bathrooms, hand-painted friezes; the finest mahogany, walnut, and oak furniture . . . imported mostly from Birmingham, but also from the Continent, . . . [and] gilt concave mirrors, silver and Sheffield plate, the best Irish linen."[22]

There were, however, many who could not benefit from—and indeed were economically disenfranchised by—the surging ostrich industry. Large numbers of Boers who once worked on local vineyards as *bywoners* (labor tenants dependent on and employed by landowners) were thrust into unemployment by the feather boom as the high price of land made such arrangements undesirable for landowners. Boer and colored wage laborers of the district also found themselves redefined as surplus labor as a result of the ostrich feather boom. This was because relative to other crops, ostriches—and the lucerne they thrived on—required scant labor. The birds needed little tending, and many farmers hired workers for a short time only every eight months, when it was time to harvest feathers from the adult birds.[23] As feathers translated into wealth for British, Boer, and Jewish farmers, and for Jewish feather buyers in the Cape and abroad, it produced underemployed populations of Boers and colored wage laborers and farmer bywoners. Once employed on vineyards and wheat farms, these families relocated from rural areas to the town of Oudtshoorn itself, which doubled in size between 1891 and 1911.[24] In the process, the feather boom served to further narrow the economic opportunities of the colored and Boer working class.[25]

While the ostrich feather boom had diverse effects on residents of the Western Cape, Jews proved a crucial link in the chain of economic changes that shook Oudtshoorn at the turn of the twentieth century. This was because Jews were responsible for readying Oudtshoorn's new agricultural product for consumption and sale on an international market. Jewish immigrants from Russian-controlled Lithuania were able to dominate the buying and selling of ostrich feathers in the Western Cape because they had the human capital this vocation required: practical skills inherited from former homes, commercial and familial ties in requisite locations, shared languages with business partners at home and overseas, and copasetic relationships with the reigning authorities. Through their role as feather buyers, Jews brought the economic realities of a global commodity chain into the heart of the South African hinterland.

JEWS AND PLUMES IN THE WESTERN CAPE

Why did Jews of Russian-Lithuanian origin come to dominate the South African branch of the trans-Atlantic feather trade? Lebanese, Greek, and Chinese merchants were, like Jews, among the most visible small-scale merchants in southern, western, and central Africa, but these other groups did not enter the ostrich feather trade.[26] On the other hand, Sephardi Jews, who were well represented as shop owners and traders in southern and central Africa, and perhaps more importantly were crucial middlemen in the ostrich feather industry in northern and western Africa, entered the South African ostrich feather trade in very small numbers.[27] These Jewish and non-Jewish merchants did not penetrate the feather trade because they lacked the precise skills that rendered Lithuanian Jews well suited to South African and trans-Atlantic plume commerce—skills the following pages will continue to explore.

We may measure Jews' influence in the trans-Atlantic trade of ostrich feathers thanks in part to government decree. According to statutes passed in 1883 and 1887, all persons carrying on "trade or business" in the Cape were required to purchase one of a series of licenses, one of which authorized the owner to "deal as a buyer of ostrich feathers" at a cost of £5.[28] Feather buyers were further required by statute and under threat of fine and hard labor to note the date on which they purchased feathers; their number, weight, and description; the name, residence, and occupation of the vendor; and the price the feathers commanded.[29] In the years that followed, the Oudtshoorn post office—the agency responsible for dispensing official feather buying permits—was so inundated with requests for them that, in October 1907, the Central Association Farmers Congress resolved that a special board should be created to vet future applications.[30] No less important, in deference to the statutes of 1883 and 1887 and their heightened enforcement in the first decade of the twentieth century, feather buying became an increasingly formal affair.

From 1909 to 1914, Isaac Nurick maintained meticulous "ostrich feather ledgers" detailing the quantity and type of feathers he bought on a daily basis, the price paid, and the name and occupation of the seller. From these quotidian records, we can learn in great detail not only about Nurick's business but about the ostrich feather trade more generally. Over the course of three years (1912–14), Nurick did business with roughly three hundred feather buyers and farmers. But more than 80 percent of those he bought feathers from were feather buyers, and almost all of these feather buyers have recognizably Jewish names (at a time when roughly 1,000–1,500 Jews were permanent residents of Oudtshoorn District).[31] Nurick's habit of buying almost exclusively from Jewish feather merchants was not idiosyncratic but reflected the ethnic economy of the ostrich feather market in Oudtshoorn and the Cape more generally. Leybl Feldman, author of the Yiddish-language study of Oudtshoorn Jewry, has suggested that during the boom years 90 percent of Oudtshoorn's ostrich feather merchants were Jews.

Even before Feldman's account circulated, Jews' dominance in ostrich feather buying was accepted by those inside and outside the industry. In 1887 and 1901, articles in London's *Jewish Chronicle* reported on Russian Jews' ascendancy in the trade in the Cape, noting that "this business is almost entirely in the hands of the Jews."[32] American accounts also dwelled on Jews' visibility in the feather industry. An 1886 article in *Forest and Stream: A Journal of Outdoor Life, Travel, Nature Study, and Shooting* emphasized the trans-Atlantic ostrich feather trade's Jewish and highly organized nature—two features, it seemed, that went hand in hand.[33] Accounts like these were little exaggerated. The vast majority of individuals who acquired feather buyer licenses were Jews: lists of their names were regularly published in the *Oudtshoorn Courant* for all the industry to survey.[34] In 1913, almost all of the 277 licensed feather buyers in Oudtshoorn were Jews, and many more no doubt operated illegally.[35]

Who were these feather buyers? The vast majority were young men who had recently immigrated to the Cape from Russian-controlled Lithuania. Their re-location, as we have seen, was part of the mass migration of Eastern European Jews that commenced in the early 1880s; the Jews who left Eastern Europe in the years that bracketed the turn of the twentieth century tended to be young men and women in search of economic and social opportunity.[36] Relatively few of these émigrés chose South Africa as their home, but the roughly forty thousand Eastern European Jews who did relocate to South Africa—drawn in part by reports of the riches of the region's gold and diamond mines—represented a highly visible population in the colony.[37] Jews were also overrepresented in certain expanding trades spawned by South Africa's mineral and agrarian revolutions—the prostitution, liquor, diamond, gold, and feather industries among them.[38]

Most future feather buyers came from two towns in Russian-controlled Lithuania, Chelm and Shavli.[39] The provenance of these immigrants was signifi-cant, for it meant they had at least a passing familiarity with certain industries that resembled the feather business: the textile, tanning, hide and leather, and fur trades, in which Jews were significantly overrepresented in Eastern Europe in general and in Lithuania particularly.[40] These industries, like the feather com-merce, obliged participants to have expertise in promoting and assessing fashion trends. Merchants in these industries—like the feather trade—were also rooted in rural and urban or small-town cultures and economies. Most famously, Eastern European Jews were experienced itinerant merchants, accustomed to transmitting goods for sale between country and town. This would constitute an essential task of the feather buyer, particularly the small-scale one, who tended to enter—or dabble in—the industry while working as a *smous*, or traveling salesman.[41]

That Lithuanian Jews in the Cape were part of a mass migratory movement also enhanced their ability to serve as feather buyers. Just as this diaspora afforded a vibrant cultural network, so too did it facilitate Jews' involvement in trans-national and trans-regional commerce, allowing feather buyers like the Barron brothers to rely on fathers, brothers, or cousins, with whom they shared a language as well as ties of kith or kin, as business partners in Cape Town, New York, London, and Paris.[42] Jews' success in the trans-Atlantic ostrich feather trade also depended on the exchange of bodies and capital between the Cape and Eastern Europe and not simply unidirectionally from Eastern Europe to South Africa. Jews in the Cape wrote letters back home, sent money to family members who had not emigrated, helped fund the passage of other Eastern European Jews to the Cape, and themselves visited and sometimes even permanently returned to Lithuania. The resulting migration of fiancées, wives, children, and future business partners created stability and business opportunities for feather buyers in South Africa and beyond.

To illustrate these points, let us return to Isaac Nurick. Nurick's entry into the feather trade was in many ways typical of his peers. He left Shavli in the late 1880s with his father and future business partner, Abraham. How they made their way to Oudtshoorn is unclear, but it seems probable that they were drawn by reports of the lucrative trade in feathers rooted in the district. Nurick's initial foray into the feather market was in 1888, when he acquired his first feather buyer's permit.[43] Odds are that he began as an itinerant feather buyer, as did many future exporters. A year later, he entered a business relationship with Max Hotz, one of the first and eventually one of the foremost feather buyers in the district. Hotz would be both partner and friend to Nurick throughout his career.[44] In January 1898 Abraham and Isaac Nurick inaugurated the feather buying business Nurick and Son. To fund the nascent company, the pair secured a loan from Oudtshoorn's Standard Bank, signing their names in the bank's signature book in the cramped and wavy hand of those unfamiliar with the English language. (In later years, Nurick's correspondence and business ledgers would become more stylish and formal.)[45]

At this time a young bachelor, Nurick attended the Queens Street shul, the rather more modern and well-to-do of the two synagogues in Oudtshoorn.[46] According to family lore, he "used to gaze upstairs at the ladies' gallery at a beautiful young girl whom he presumed was engaged."[47] This woman was Annie Sanders, Nurick's future wife. Sanders had been born of Eastern European Jewish parents in Melbourne in 1872.[48] The Sanders family had moved to the Cape already fairly wealthy, but Annie's father, Wulf, met with extraordinary success in the ostrich feather trade and quickly enriched them further. Accordingly, when the relatively poor *greener* (new immigrant) Nurick fixed his gaze on Annie Sanders in synagogue, he was falling in love out of his financial and social league. Fortunately for him, Annie had just emerged from a failed betrothal, and the circumstances surrounding this event were apparently traumatic enough that her parents were eager to see her engaged anew.[49] Nurick was offered her hand, and the pair was married on February 28, 1893.[50] It was appropriate that the match joined two feather merchant families. For Nurick, as for so many Jewish feather merchants, personal and commercial relationships developed in tandem, and both were insulated by the existence of a trans-hemispheric Eastern European Jewish diaspora.

At the turn of the twentieth century, Nurick was not among the wealthiest feather buyers in Oudtshoorn—the most prominent were Morris Aschman, Marcus Hotz, Samuel Lazarus, Herman Lewin, Jacob Nochamson, Max Rose, and Moses Sanders (fig. 6). Still, Nurick's family was well off and respectable, having even acquired one of the first motorcars in town.[51] His success at feather buying distinguished him from most in the industry. Jewish feather buyers tended to operate independently and on a very small scale. Because they were unlikely to maintain or preserve business records, and because many of them did not remain in the feather trade for long, we know the least about these smallest-scale feather buyers. Many must have been like S. Jaffe, who, for a time, paid weekly visits to Nurick. During these encounters, Jaffe sold Nurick a small collection of feathers, earning an average of £5 but frequently as little as £1 a week before disappearing from Nurick's feather ledger after a last entry on February 28, 1914.[52] There is no record of Jaffe acquiring a feather buyer's permit, no record of his keeping a permanent address in Oudtshoorn or joining a synagogue, and no record of his marrying, having children, or dying in the district. Presumably Jaffe—like so many other young Lithuanian Jewish men in South Africa—heard rumors of the lucrative trade in feathers, traveled to Oudtshoorn to seek his fortune, dabbled in the business for a spell, and settled elsewhere, participated in return migration, or died young. Jaffe's path was one favored by many; in 1889 alone, thirty-eight of forty-six Jewish men naturalized in South Africa identified themselves as feather buyers.[53]

Every Monday, itinerant buyers like Jaffe would leave town on foot or by donkey, horse, or oxcart to roam the district on feather buying journeys that lasted a few days or a week at a time.[54] There are many tales of these itinerant merchants, some romanticized, others rather more lugubrious. Lily Jacobs (née Safman), who spent her childhood on an ostrich farm in the Oudtshoorn District, recalled the stories of Jewish *smous* who were attacked and robbed while they wandered the district; according to her account, her father, a Jewish ostrich farmer, frequently aided itinerant Jewish feather buyers in distress.[55] But recollections like this are in the minority: most references to these small-scale Jewish feather buyers focus on amicable relations with Boer farmers, eased by the linguistic similarities between Yiddish and Afrikaans. Alex Miller remembered the great kindness Boer farmers extended his father, who worked as an iterant feather buyer during the boom years. Until he acquired a horse and cart, Miller's father roamed the region on foot, leaving Oudtshoorn every Monday morning and returning Thursday evening. Miller recalls:

> I must tell you the farmers in Oudtshoorn were very, very good to Jews. . . . [T]hey used to call them people of the Bible and they were very religious, the Afrikaners in those days, extraordinarily religious, they used to go out of their way when a Jew couldn't eat the meat, they used to prepare eggs in a special vessel. . . . [M]y father used to take along all his own stuff but sleeping over you've got to have something to eat. . . . They were absolutely friendly, hospitable, and they used to have special private rooms for the Jewish people to stay in.[56]

This sanguine image of the feather world was shared by Leybl Feldman, who described small-scale itinerant feather buyers operating as something of a brotherhood. "So great was the competition that the dealers came to a mutual understanding," Feldman wrote. "If one buyer met another at a farm, a *yakhtsu* [contract] was proclaimed: one of them would buy the parcel and thereafter share either the goods or the profit between them. If many buyers met at the

Figure 6. Joseph Lazarus (1886–1945), ostrich feather merchant, ca. 1911. Lazarus immigrated to Oudtshoorn as a young child from Russian Lithuania, entering the feather trade in cooperation with his father, Samuel, and brother, Isaac. (Courtesy South African Jewish Board of Deputies Archive, Johannesburg)

same farmer, they would call out, 'A *khasene* [wedding]!' which meant that one of them should buy the feathers and share the profits among all of them."[57] To others, cooperation between feather buyers was bald conspiracy. Robert Wallace, a British scholar of agricultural economics, wrote in 1896 of "the usurious practices of feather peddlers, frequently German, Polish, or Russian Jews of a low type, who swarm about the country as feather buyers." According to Wallace, these feather buyers "bewilder[ed] the ignorant and imperfectly educated farmers" by charging inflated interest and conspiring to keep prices low.[58]

The real tenor of feather buyers' cooperation no doubt fluctuated over time and in accordance with market conditions, but it is easy to imagine that the quality of these relations tended to lie between Feldman's and Wallace's accounts. There were, after all, reasons for feather buyers to collaborate—or even conspire—with one another. From peers, a buyer could learn about the quality of a particular farm's feathers, the projected date of a farmer's plucking, the state of the market abroad, and so on. Jewish feather buyers were, however, also competing with one another for business, and those in the industry were known for their competitiveness and even paranoia. Anne (Chana) Berman recalled that her grandfather Isaac Nurick insisted even that his own children remain discreet about the family business. In her words:

> My mother [Cissie Nurick] told us that one of the first lessons she learned from her father when she was a young child was never to speak to strangers about their father's business. Apparently a neighbour (a competitor in the feather business) questioned the children about their father's activities. Innocently they answered him and when Isaac arrived at the appointed business meeting found that his neighbour had arrived earlier and had received the business instead. He returned home in a terrible rage. So you see there was very intense competition.[59]

To protect their interests and expand their business, large-scale feather buyers like Nurick employed small-scale buyers to travel from farm to farm, buying feathers and brokering contract-farming relationships. From a complex lawsuit filed after the crash of the feather market, we know a great deal about one such employee of Nurick's, a man by the name of Abelkop. Over the course of 1913, Abelkop traveled the Oudtshoorn District, buying feathers and extending at least £4,000 worth of promissory notes in Nurick's name.[60] Abelkop appears to have purchased feathers not only after they were clipped, but also in advance of their harvesting, through contract-farming agreements. In July 1913, for example, Abelkop approached the brothers Petrus Erasmus Smit and Daniel P. Smit and suggested they embark on contract farming with Nurick as their sponsor. The Smits purchased twenty ostriches from Abelkop for £9 each, agreeing that in eight months' time, Abelkop would, in Nurick's name, buy the first plucking of the birds' feathers for £100. This kind of arrangement was typical of the ostrich feather industry, and it functioned quite successfully while the price of feathers was stable or increasing. When the bottom fell out of the feather market, however, contract farming in general and the Nurick-Abelkop-Smits relationship in particular proved disastrous for all involved.

Advance purchase contracts—buying feathers in advance of their harvest—were common in the trade. Many of these contracts were underwritten by the Standard Bank, which provided loans to many feather merchants and backed the promissory notes they extended.[61] Technically speaking, feather buyers were not engaged in speculation; unlike the typical speculator or financier, Cape ostrich feather buyers like Nurick both intended and had the capacity to take delivery of the feathers they contract farmed. Nonetheless, feather buyers in general and Jewish feather buyers in particular were habitually referred to as "speculators" by the farmers they dealt with, the banks that financed them, and by American and European observers of the industry who wrote about ostrich farming and the feather trade. The conflation of the categories of "feather buyer," "speculator," and "Jew"—which has been perpetuated in superficial studies of the feather trade—reiterated stereotypes about the Jewish financier who made no real contribution to the local agricultural economy.[62]

All participants in the feather trade, whether small-scale itinerant merchants like Jaffe or large-scale exporters like Nurick, participated in Oudtshoorn's Friday feather market. After spending several days, a week, or longer on the road, itinerant feather buyers tended to return to town on Friday morning to sell their feathers and to spend the sabbath in town, often with families. They were joined by Jewish merchants who lived in surrounding districts but who used Oudtshoorn's Friday feather market to ply their goods and assess the state of business, and by the larger-scale feather buyers who lived and worked in town. Alex Miller, who grew up in Oudtshoorn, recalls in an oral history how, for smaller-scale feather merchants, attending the Friday market was a necessity.

> The poor people always had to come to the rich people because they were the buyers of the feathers, they had stores, offices, and they were agents for the English market so you must come to them, pick out the feathers and they give you a quote, every morning, every weekend there were different prices according to the market.[63]

Large-scale buyers like Nurick used the weekly feather bazaar to supplement their own collections, amassed through contract farming, with the plumes that small-scale merchants had to sell. Thereafter, these large-scale buyers would ready shipments for London, where the feathers would reach an international collective of feather wholesalers, manufacturers, and buyers.

The financial effects of a bullish feather market rippled through Oudts-hoorn. Reggie Kahn described the pleasure of market days from the perspective of a child. After her father finished selling feathers, he would return to the family farm with presents for Reggie and her friend Sally, daughter of the Kahn's Jewish farm manager. She recalls of her father: "He used to come back with fashions of clothing, shoes and dresses and hats, Sally and me we used to walk out on the high street . . . [in] the most beautiful crinoline dresses and hats."[64] Leybl Feldman's description of Oudtshoorn's Friday feather market is particularly vivid, conjuring up the spirit of a shtetl marketplace before Shabbes.

> From early Friday morning up until Sunday night, Jews so to speak domi-nated the town. On Fridays the spirit of the Exchange and the market-place ruled Oudtshoorn. With the arrival of the ebullient, excitable feather dealers, Oudtshoorn began to buzz and seethe. In the centre of town, where the offices of the industry and the bank were situated, and particularly at the Ostrich Feather Merchants' Association, which was a kind of bourse, the pavements were thronged with Yiddish speaking feather merchants.[65]

Though Feldman's description of the Friday marketplace is wonderfully vibrant, his inclination to conflate Oudtshoorn and Chelm is overblown. The Friday exchange—like the feather trade itself—never functioned as a Jewish-only affair. Boer ostrich farmers, essential to the industry, also took part in Oudtshoorn's Friday market; many brought their families to town for the weekend, not only to participate in Friday sales but to attend church on Sun-day (fig. 7).[66] Even more important, a complex cauldron of racial and power dynamics undergirded feather sales in and from Oudtshoorn, and these, too, shaped Jews' place as the region's principal feather dealers.

OUDTSHOORN WAS NO SHTETL: EMPIRE, RACE, AND THE TRANS-ATLANTIC FEATHER MARKET

The success of the Oudtshoorn feather market, of course, depended on the work of Jewish merchants as well as Boer farmers. But two additional factors were instrumental to the smooth working of South Africa's trans-Atlantic feather trade: the existence of a large pool of colored wage laborers and the nurturing

Figure 7. Feather exchange behind Prince Vincent Building, Oudtshoorn, ca. 1911. This photograph features the ostrich farming brothers Hermanus Lambertus Potgieter (seated at right), Jacobus Ernst Potgieter (tableside), and, behind them, Jan Hendrik Potgieter (in a pale suit). On the day this photograph was taken, £5,000 worth of plumes were exchanged. (Courtesy C. P. Nel Museum, Oudtshoorn)

of the British imperial government. These forces had an intertwined impact on Jews in the feather industry. Together, they eased Jews' absorption into plume commerce and white society, allowing them to benefit from privileges of whiteness denied to Jews in other South African industries and contexts.

The most physically trying labor associated with South Africa's feather trade fell to colored wage laborers, who were responsible for the day-to-day tending of birds and for the plucking and sorting of feathers.[67] Reggie Kahn, whose family owned several ostrich farms in and just outside the Oudtshoorn District, remembered that her family employed no fewer than two hundred colored workers.[68] Similarly, the family of Lily Jacobs employed a Jewish manager to oversee its ostrich farm and colored workers to oversee the birds themselves.[69] In their reliance on a largely colored labor force, these farms appear to have been typical of those in the district generally, where roughly half of the agricultural workforce was categorized by the state as "non-white" or "non-European."[70]

Colored workers were also the district's principal feather pluckers and sort-ers. Before an ostrich was plucked, it was corralled into a small wooden enclo-sure and hooded: confinement and blindness soothed the cantankerous animals, allowing them to be quickly plucked or clipped.[71] Ostriches are notoriously strong animals, and especially in the early days of the industry, when feathers were plucked (rather than cut at the base), one had to be enormously careful "to prevent [the ostriches] from administering those terrible kicks to the pluckers of which they are capable, and which are delivered with a force sufficient to break a man's thigh," according to an account in *The Times* of London.[72] As one observer noted, "it is very rough to handle" an ostrich, "and bruised hands, arms, and fingers, are generally exhibited after a day's ostrich-plucking."[73]

Once plucked or cut, ostrich plumes needed to be sorted, a second task that fell to colored wage laborers. In Oudtshoorn approximately 200–250 colored sorters, many children among them, were employed to assemble feathers into lots for export.[74] Feather sorting was a dirty and dangerous profession. Ac-cording to the findings of a South African commission devoted to exploring the causes of tuberculosis, sorters worked in small and ill-ventilated spaces that were "hot, vitiated and laden with dust and feather particles." The airborne dust, "consisting of powdered earth, dirt, and small particles of broken feathers and quill scales," lodged in workers' throats and lungs, dramatically increasing their risk of tuberculosis, among other diseases (fig. 8).[75]

It is striking that in all the other hubs of the global ostrich feather trade, including those in North Africa, Britain, and the United States, the menial tasks associated with feather handling fell to Jewish workers. That this was not the case in the Cape suggests that even the poorest Jews in the feather trade—immigrants who were as economically desperate as their peers in Lon-don, New York, or Tripoli—maintained a level of racial and social privilege that distinguished them from non-whites.[76] To understand how and why this came to be, we must meditate on the ways in which the colonial system shaped the feather trade.

None in the feather business—not Boer ostrich farmers, colored wage labor-ers, or Jewish feather buyers—operated free of state intervention. Investments in infrastructure by the Cape government were critical to the viability, success, and racial composition of the ostrich feather industry. The expansion of this industry depended, first, on state-sponsored improvements in transportation.

Figure 8. Ostrich feather sorting room, Oudtshoorn. This unidentified group includes
five "colored" feather sorters, including one boy (standing), and two more formally dressed
white men, who are probably feather merchants and possibly ostrich farmers.
(Courtesy C. P. Nel Museum, Oudtshoorn)

These included the building of the mountain pass linking Oudtshoorn and
George, which, notably, relied on convict labor, and the railroad that connected
Oudtshoorn and Port Elizabeth.[77] These transportation routes facilitated the
explosion of the ostrich feather industry at the turn of the twentieth century,
for they made possible the relatively quick and safe conveyance of goods. Second, the state-sponsored postal service allowed feather buyers to communicate
with contacts overseas and intra-regionally. Regular communication with business partners abroad was particularly important for feather merchants whose
goods were destined for auction in London, because they needed to anticipate
changes in fashion and accumulate their own feather stock accordingly—buying
more or less of a given type of feather in accordance with consumers' current
or predicted desires. More directly, the Cape Colony regulated tariffs on ostrich
feathers, eggs, and birds as a way of supporting the industry. At the height of

the feather boom, for example, unmanufactured (or "raw" or "undressed") ostrich feathers were permitted to be exported free of tariff, which more or less rewarded South Africans while, beginning in 1883, heavy taxes were placed on exported birds and eggs to discourage the anticipated development of competitive ostrich farms in Algeria, Australia, Argentina, and the United States.[78]

Finally, the colonial government had a role in controlling the racial composition of the feather industry. This was achieved through the aforementioned statutes that required buyers of ostrich feathers to obtain licenses. Though these laws were theoretically intended to quash illegal feather buying, they—and the fees they stipulated—had the additional effect of limiting feather trading by less affluent Khoisan and colored people, who had previously sold feathers to white merchants. Jews in the industry, it should be noted, also perceived this legislation to be racial in inspiration, but interpreted it as directed at driving Jews out of the feather trade. When the Central Association Farmers Congress proposed in 1907 that a special board be created to vet feather buyer applications, Jewish feather buyers perceived the suggestion as bald anti-Semitism. Outraged, they created the Oudtshoorn Jewish Vigilance Committee, an organization that would defend "the poor unfortunate ones who would suffer by the proposed legislation."[79]

State investments in infrastructure that supported the feather industry, like the involvement of colored workers and Boer farmers in the feather trade, discredit the suggestion that the trade of ostrich feathers was an exclusively or predominantly Jewish affair—an argument offered, oddly enough, both by anti-Semitic observers of the industry and by the few studies that lionize Jews' prominence in the feather world.[80] The implications of enmeshing Jewish feather merchants in the context of colonial policy and race relations are, however, greater still, for they suggest that in this case, at least, Jews were not merely accidental subjects of imperialism, but were able to succeed as trans-hemispheric traders in part because of an exploitive colonial system that privileged whites. What forms of human capital Ashkenazim brought to the feather industry were thereby complemented by their relationship to the colonial state. Together, these phenomena served as the bedrock on which a predominantly Jewish trans-Atlantic feather empire could be built.

But Jewish entrepreneurship was not always matched by state or social sanction in turn-of-the-century southern Africa. While Jews who partook of the feather boom functioned as and reaped some of the benefits of being white settlers, in other instances South African Jews straddled or elided the racial and social boundaries established by the colonial order.[81] Jews who owned or oversaw the notoriously foul eating houses frequented by black workers all but imprisoned on Kimberly's diamond and gold fields (the so-called kaffir eateries), for example, were considered *vayse kaffirs* (white kaffirs) by their Yiddish-speaking peers.[82] To colonial administrators, missionaries, and other European settlers, meanwhile, Jews' whiteness and Europeanness was dubious at times: Jews were occasionally spoken of as "white niggers," who would never gain full entry into white colonial society.[83] Nor were white and black the only colors through which South African Jewry moved. Immigrant Jews, particularly those from Eastern Europe whose primary language was Yiddish, were labeled *greeners,* or new immigrants, by Jewish settlers more established than they, and "Peruvians" by non-Jews, who blamed Jewish immigrants for crime and the illicit sale of liquor, diamonds, and women, especially to black consumers.[84] One Yiddish-language study of the Jews of South Africa argued in 1937 that, over time, Jews who worked with black Africans on the diamond and gold fields or as proprietors of small or itinerant shops became "less green and more black."[85]

The idea that one's commercial interlocutors could "bleed" color—infecting one, in this case, with a tinge of blackness—generally did not threaten Jews in the feather trade. While Jews who worked as *smous,* shopkeepers, sellers of alcohol, or traders in diamond and gold regularly interacted with black Africans, Jewish sellers of feathers did not. This is not to say that racial hierarchies did not shape the feather trade—clearly the colored population of Oudtshoorn was barred from certain aspects of the feather trade by decrees both formal and informal. For Jews, however, the absence of a black African labor force in the feather trade seems to have rendered the racial politics of the ostrich industry relatively benign, at least while the feather market was strong. Put simply, Jews in the trade were immune from much of the hostile racial labeling to which their peers in other industries were vulnerable.[86] In the South African context, it would appear, Jews had the ability to change their hue by involving themselves in different commercial pursuits or commodity chains.

Still, participation in the feather industry did not render Jews permanently immune from anti-Semitic sentiment: when the feather industry flagged, many

Boer farmers blamed Jews. This accusation, which found expression in the na-
tionalizing of the region's agricultural economy in the 1920s and 1930s, resulted
in the squeezing of most Jews out of the South African feather industry.

THE GLOBAL FEATHER CRASH AND THE WESTERN CAPE

In 1911, the world's only professor of ostriches, J. Duerden, assured participants of the Ostrich Farmers' Association that "ostrich farming is a permanent
feature of South African farming life."[87] Duerden's speech was delivered two
years before the Cape feather market reached its peak, and three years before
it began its precipitous and permanent decline. At the time Duerden addressed South Africa's ostrich farmers, they were raising ever more ostriches.
The number of farmed birds in the Cape had more than doubled in less
than ten years. During the same period, the value of Cape feathers had nearly
trebled.[88] Flush with success, ostrich farmers had failed to diversify their gains.
Most poured their profits back into the industry, planting lucerne and rearing
ever more birds. As we have seen, when the value of the ostrich plume was
high, investment in other agricultural crops in Oudtshoorn District declined.
Furthermore, neither the region's ostrich farmers nor the government of the
Cape invested in the district's irrigation system, which would have permitted
crop diversification should the need arise; instead, Oudtshoorn District relied
on outdated furrow irrigation techniques that were useful for little more than
ostrich farming.[89]

The threat of rampant oversupply did not, however, rest on farmers' shoul-
ders alone. Brokerage firms and individuals in London and New York were
stocking great quantities of feathers in anticipation of a rise in their value.
This had the effect of insulating South African farmers from the feather boom,
but also rendered all the more acute the impact of a would-be feather bust.
"Even should trade in the United States recover soon," the *Agricultural Journal
of the Union of South Africa* reported in 1912, "it might be some time before we
felt the benefit of it here, as, notwithstanding the huge and steadily increasing
population of that country, the manufacturers there have such heavy stocks
on hand at the present moment, it would take a considerable time before they
would find it necessary to replenish them."[90] Finally, in their zeal to expand
their operations, ostrich farmers' ambitions were stoked by feather buyers, who,

with the aid and encouragement of banks, were feverishly engaging in contract farming and informal speculation. Among these buyers was Isaac Nurick.

As late as March 1914, Nurick was still actively buying for London's June feather auction. Indeed, it appears that he invested over £30,000 in ostrich feathers from early January to early March of that year, with the goal of auctioning them in London in June. Meanwhile, Nurick was also continuing to engage in contract farming. In partnership with several others, he paid the Potgieter Brothers £7,273 for the plumage of 2,078 birds in February or March 1914, and bought the plumage of 361 birds for £1,353 from the farming partners O'Fourie and LeRoux some weeks later.[91] Alas, June feather sales in London and on the Cape saw a dramatic decline in prices, and many of the plumes offered were not even sold. In their monthly report on the trade, the brokerage firm of Messrs. John Daverin and Company relayed the bad news: "As head-gear, ostrich feathers are not worn at all in Paris or America, and hardly at all in England or the Continent; and even the extremely low prices at which feathers are being landed in England fail to tempt manufacturers to buy.... We cannot advise our clients to look for any improvement in the present state of affairs until some change in the fashions occurs, and no one can say when this is likely to happen."[92] Two months later, Isaac Nurick's business was in liquidation.

In personal correspondence with me, Nurick's grandchildren have discussed his handling of the feather crash. More than one mentioned that Nurick was a proud man who could not bear to declare bankruptcy and insisted on honoring all of his debts.[93] According to several of their accounts, he even used the estate of his wife, Annie, to pay off his debts, despite the fact that she was suffering from breast cancer and they had eight children to support.[94] In fact, the collapse of Nurick's business was both messier and more unpleasant than his descendants recall. The correspondence of his liquidator, Arthur Bentley, reveals the financial catastrophe Nurick faced in painful detail. Much of Bentley's work entailed calling up promissory notes which Nurick had received, or announcing the liquidation of I. Nurick and Company (as Nurick and Son had been renamed) to those in receipt of a promissory note bearing Nurick's name.[95] Exchanges between Bentley and Nurick's creditors, and between Bentley and those indebted to Nurick, indicate that after the value of feathers plummeted, Nurick was caught between the farmers whose future feathers he had promised to buy and the banks that had extended him credit to engage in contract farming. Because of the speculative nature of the trade, few involved in the ostrich feather economy—ostrich farmers, feather buyers, and banks alike—could easily pay or call up their debts.

One thorny legal battle handled by Bentley, a lawsuit filed against Nurick by the farming brothers Petrus Erasmus Smit and Daniel P. Smit, demonstrates the conundrum unleashed by rampant ostrich feather speculation. In July 1913, Nurick's assistant Abelkop, acting on behalf of I. Nurick and Company, had sold the Smits twenty ostriches, promising to buy the first plucking of the birds' feathers for £100. Abelkop further agreed that if the £200 mortgage on the Smits' farm was called up as a result of this transaction, Nurick would advance the Smits the requisite money. Eight months after the Smits bought the birds from Abelkop, they were pressed to pay their mortgage. However, the ostriches they had purchased were not yet ready to be plucked, and Nurick refused to advance them enough money to pay the bond. Two months later, Abelkop "did the plucking of [the ostriches] himself in so negligent a manner that in consequence thereof eight of the said birds died from exposure, to the value of seventy two pounds."[96] Abelkop's ineptitude, Nurick insisted, was his own doing, and Nurick himself was not to be held responsible.[97] Nurick now demanded back the £100 he had paid against the birds' next crop of plumes, while the Smits demanded that their promissory note be extended, that Nurick advance them money to cover their mortgage, and that he reimburse them the cost of the ostriches' upkeep. Meanwhile, because Nurick's business was in liquidation, the Bank of Africa had possession of the Smits' promissory note to Nurick. When this came due, the bank held Nurick responsible.[98] In response to inquiries about the status of the money owed him by the Smits, a notary public in Steynsburg advised Nurick: "I do not think that you could expect to recover anything unless proceedings are instituted, and, even then it is a question what you could recover for debtors' farm is mortgaged very heavily. . . . [I]t is possible that both farm and loose assets may not realize [funds] sufficient to pay the bonds." A handwritten note on the side of this letter confided that the Smits were also in debt to another feather dealer, J. M. Joubert.[99]

Nurick's legal struggles with the Smit brothers represent only one of many difficult encounters that Bentley brokered after I. Nurick and Company entered liquidation.[100] Bentley wrote to countless farmers in a comparable position to the Smits, demanding they honor promissory notes that Nurick held in his possession. In response, he received requests for renewals and references to hard times. Presumably it was also Bentley who filed in Nurick's letter book notice of the bankruptcy of his erstwhile partner Isach Hassan, submitted to London's Board of Trade in February 1914.[101] Some ten years later, Nurick remained without income, reliant on the financial support of his sister and in "very poor financial circumstances."[102] When his wife succumbed to cancer in 1918 "after a long period of great suffering," Nurick fled Oudtshoorn for London, leaving his eight children in the care of his eldest daughter, Cissie.[103] Poverty stricken, he became an itinerant hawker of vegetables and other goods. He saw only two of his children again before he died.[104]

Nurick's business failings were by no means exceptional. The feather crash, coupled with a devastating drought that lasted from 1914 to 1916, left countless Cape ostrich farmers destitute. In Oudtshoorn, thirty-four farmers and twenty-nine merchants claimed insolvency in 1915, compared with five and seven, respectively, who had filed similar claims four years earlier.[105] There were Boer farmers who committed suicide rather than suffer the humiliation of losing their farms, while the fabulous feather mansions of Oudtshoorn were auctioned off for little more than the price of their doors and windows.[106] By 1916, the municipality was on the brink of bankruptcy, crime was rampant, especially by youths, infant mortality had risen dramatically, and poverty had become ubiquitous. With the ostrich and building industries obsolete, colored and Boer workers were unable to find jobs in any industry other than tobacco production, which in turn meant that tobacco factories, lacking competitors, had no check on wages and working conditions, both of which were abysmal.[107] New slums were created to house Oudtshoorn residents dispossessed by the feather crash, many Jews among them.[108]

In the wake of the slump of 1914, for all but a very few Jewish families, the luxury of the ostrich boom was gone forever. There were, it is true, momentary highs in ostrich feather sales—in 1919, 1925, and 1931—and this enticed some to stay in the business, among them Max Rose, the Barron brothers, and the Klaas family. Still, the industry did not permanently regain its footing until the end of the twentieth century. By then, a variety of forces had conspired to disperse and otherwise disintegrate Oudtshoorn's Jewish community, rendering a renewal of its past glories unthinkable.[109]

A ghostly description of Oudtshoorn's Jewish feather merchants in the wake of the feather crash has been offered by the Yiddish dramatist Peretz Hirshbein, who visited Oudtshoorn as part of a trip to South Africa, New Zealand, and Australia in the early 1920s and who narrated his trip in a Yiddish-language travelogue serialized in the New York daily *Der tog.* To Hirshbein, Oudtshoorn's Jews appeared lost and dazed following the collapse of their business, able to do little more than "wander the streets buying feathers from those who didn't have the strength to part with their beloved birds forever."[110]

Hirshbein's haunting picture is mirrored in other sources. In 1940, Leybl Feldman concluded his elegiac study of Oudtshoorn Jewry by suggesting that the "'Jerusalem of Africa' has nearly disappeared."[111] Sixty years later, Isidore Barron, a third-generation Jewish ostrich farmer, offered a more complete eulogy. Punning on the Yiddish appellation once tenderly given to Oudtshoorn, Little Jerusalem, Barron said: "Alts vos is gebliben is di kleynkeit" (Today, all that is left is the littleness).[112]

Part of the tragedy of ostrich feather bust, viewed from the perspective of Jewish history, occurred only later. In the years after the bottom fell out of the feather market, Jews were further displaced from the industry, or at least from whatever future prospects it had, by increasingly nationalist-minded Boer farmers who blamed "middlemen" for the implosion. Such expressions of discontent had been voiced even as the crash was unfolding. In the early months of 1914, the *Oudtshoorn Courant* published numerous articles by ostrich farmers that blamed feather buyers for starting the feather slump and accused them of benefiting from it at farmers' expense. Middlemen with contacts abroad, speculators, buyers, foreigners—all thinly veiled code words for Jews—were described in the paper as nefarious parties that should be barred from the industry in the future.[113]

It took two decades for these hostile sentiments to translate into a transformation in the ethnic composition of the feather business. During this period, the racist and xenophobic Nationalist Party gained popularity in Oudtshoorn District and in South Africa more generally, based in part on its support for Afrikaner control over industry.[114] A central tenet of the Afrikaner nationalism of this period was support for the cooperative movement. Born of socialist and volkish nationalist sentiment and influenced by the anti-Semitic and Nazi-inspired Greyshirts, the cooperative ideology sought an exclusively Afrikaner dominance of agriculture. As it gained popularity and political power, the cooperative push succeeded in squeezing most remaining Jews out of the ostrich industry. Today, the few Jews who remain in the business remember the cooperative movement with open disdain.[115]

Deeply understanding the history of South Africa's feather boom and bust, and Jews' place within it, requires situating these stories in a global context. To this end, we must follow the path of Cape plumes to and through the global feather hub of London, where the vast majority of African ostrich feathers were auctioned to an international collection of wholesalers and merchants. In the next chapter, we follow the feathers of Isaac Nurick and Cape-based Jewish feather exporters like him, considering how these plumes—and the Jewish merchants, manufacturers, and feather handlers who worked with them—fared on the trans-hemispheric market. Serving as our liaison to this world is the Jewish family-owned feather firm of I. Salaman and Company.

CHAPTER 2

London: Global Feather Hub

On June 17, 1884, Myer Salaman visited London's Billiter Street Warehouse on Mincing Lane to preview plumes being stored for public auction. In recent years, Myer had come to be the powerhouse behind I. Salaman and Company Ostrich Feather Merchants, a company created in 1816 by his father, Isaac, and based in London's Falcon Square.[1] According to Myer's son, Redcliffe Nathan Salaman, Myer built I. Salaman from a small one-man operation into "the largest wholesale ostrich feather business in the world, with depots in Cape Town, Port Elizabeth, and Durban [and] for a time possessed ostrich farms up-country, in addition to offices and warehouses in London, Paris, New York, and Buenos Aires."[2]

On this particular summer day, Myer was armed with a catalogue published by the brokerage firm Dalton and Young, which was offering the first lots at one of the two biggest ostrich feather auctions to take place in London that year. An auction catalogue was indispensable to any feather buyer of the day, and was distributed not only to buyers in London but to firms overseas who were likely to bid.[3] This catalogue contained myriad information about feathers destined for sale, including their type and size, the emblem of the seller who shipped them across the Atlantic or Mediterranean, the case in which they were packaged, and the name of the ship on which they sailed. This information allowed diligent feather buyers not only to select the kind of feathers they desired but to buy from particular sellers they had come to trust, or indeed to buy particular lots toward which a seller might direct them. Ostrich feathers' quality was knowable by the seller but difficult for all but the most experienced buyer to determine before processing. Feathers' finicky nature led to competitiveness among buyers and occasional trickery among sellers.

Figure 9. Ostrich plumes being scrutinized by prospective buyers at the Cutler Street warehouse in the City of London. Each numbered case corresponds to a particular catalogue entry identifying the provenance, seller, and importing ship. (Courtesy Museum of London)

Myer had written his name and the address of I. Salaman and Company (44/7 Monkwell Street, Falcon Square) on the cover of his catalogue, and his amble through the warehouse on Mincing Lane was not hurried.[4] The plumes he surveyed were not to be auctioned immediately. According to rules established by the London Produce Brokers' Association in 1879 and observed by participants in the ostrich feather trade, all goods destined for auction were put on display at the Billiter Street Warehouse for two days prior to sale (fig. 9).[5] During this period, according to industry member Arthur Douglass, the author of a crucial study of the feather trade in 1886, imported feather cases were

opened, and the feathers exposed on tables with wire divisions to separate each lot, one long table under the windows being reserved for intending purchasers to examine the feathers on. The warehouses are open for a few days before the sale, and intending purchasers go with their catalogues, the great dealers examine and fix their valuations on every case, the smaller buyers only valuing those cases that are likely to suit their wants. On entering the warehouse the visitor is taken in charge by one of the attendants, who remains with him as long as he is in the building, and carries any lot he wishes to examine from the feather tables to the table under the windows.[6]

As Myer toured the warehouse, he recorded his observations in the margins of his feather catalogue, as did at least one associate—perhaps his father, Isaac, or his brothers Abraham and Nathan, who were also involved in the family business. "Fair stuff," reads the notation on one page, while other pages describe feathers as "flashy," "wooly," or "poor." Lot 162 was dismissed with a terse "NO," another with the phrase "not to buy." Like all experienced feather buyers, Myer was aware that a practiced eye was critical to success in the industry. As one of his competitors wrote of the feathers displayed for European buyers: "it sometimes happens that small sticks, stones, lumps of clay or other useless but weighty materials accidentally find their way into the bundles."[7] To guard against such deception, to ensure they bid only on the finest stock, and to evaluate the ever-changing feather market, ostrich feather buyers from across Europe and the United States viewed the inspection of feathers at Billiter Street as a crucial link in the international feather commodity chain. According to the *New York Times*, all New York feather merchants sent representatives to London, where they examined plumes with the intensity of "New York commission men look[ing] over consignments of California fruit on the Erie pier."[8]

London did not become the commercial heart of the global ostrich feather trade by chance: arguably the ideal commercial setting for the ostrich feather market could not have existed anywhere else. Other cities—including Cape Town, Tripoli, Paris, and New York—were hubs of the trade, and there were regional cities in England where feather manufacturing took place.[9] By the turn of the twentieth century, however, the only logical epicenter for international feather sales was the British capital. London maintained a thriving artisanal culture in the late nineteenth century, particularly when it came to the importing and finishing of high-value consumption goods. The city was home to the world's busiest port; it was a commercial bridge between modern colonies and metropoles, between the Atlantic and Mediterranean worlds, and between Europe and the United States. More specifically, London was the

Cape Colony's principal trading partner, and by the late nineteenth century the colony, under British oversight, had been actively transformed into the world's principal ostrich feather supplier. The rise of London as global feather hub was enabled by, and indeed a manifestation of, London's own evolution into a turn-of-the-century world market, an international center of finance and industry, and, not coincidentally, a center of cosmopolitan cultural forms.[10]

Seen from the vantage of Jewish history, London, a city increasingly defined by immigrant and working-class culture, was particularly hospitable to an emergent industry overwhelmingly populated by Jews. Jews were well represented in all tiers of the supply side of Britain's feather industry. In 1883, Jews constituted, by one estimate, 57 percent of dealers in ostrich feathers and 43 percent of ostrich feather manufacturers in the British capital, a preponderance that rendered the ostrich feather trade one of London's "chief Jewish monopolies."[11] The feather industry's blue-collar workforce, too, was largely Jewish in composition, as the hundreds of small feather manufactories that dotted London's East End were staffed principally by Jewish women and girls.[12] What's more, over the course of the feather boom, the number and overall percentage of Jews in the industry seem to have grown steadily, leading the Ostrich and Fancy Feather and Artificial Flower Trade Board to conclude unambiguously that "the Ostrich Feather trade before the [First World] War was in the hands of East End Jews."[13]

In London, as in South Africa, the ostrich feather trade was undergirded by an immigrant Jewish community poised to fill an expanding industrial niche. From 1880 to 1914, between 120,000 and 150,000 Eastern European Jews found their way to Britain, with many more passing through London en route to other destinations. Between 60 and 70 percent of this population settled in London's East End. This was a young population, and most found employment in the "sweating" industries of retail and manufacturing, of which ostrich feather processing was a part.[14] London was also home to a diverse Jewish mercantile and manufacturing community, which allowed a wide swath of Jews (not just those of East European origin, but North African, Sephardi, and Anglo-Jews as well) to pursue ostrich feather manufacturing and sale. Some of these businessmen and women segued into feathers after trading in other commodities from North or South Africa: the Sephardi merchant Alfred Aaron de Pass, for example, who married into the Salaman family, came to feathers after working in the whaling, sealing, guano, and fishing industries of the Cape, while the Ashkenazi Mosenthal brothers entered the trade after dealing in South African mohair and wool. Others moved into feathers after working in other retail industries, such as textiles, which shared characteristics with the feather trade.[15]

Although diverse circumstances pushed Jews into London's feather industry, all participated in a wheel of global commerce whose hub was the City of London and whose spokes reached across Europe and the Mediterranean, into colonial and pre-colonial northern and southern Africa and the United States. To gain a feel for this world, we must first understand why London assumed the status of the world's modern feather bourse in the late nineteenth and early twentieth centuries. Thereafter, we may return to the feathers themselves, pursuing them through the London market from importer to broker, broker to wholesaler, wholesaler to manufacturer, manufacturer to feather handler, feather handler to feather exporter or merchant. By way of conclusion, we will return to the story of I. Salaman and Company to trace how a single (London-based but geographically expansive) Jewish-owned firm weathered a volatile century of feather trading.

LONDON AND THE SHAPING OF THE
MODERN GLOBAL OSTRICH FEATHER MARKET

When the Salaman family first entered the feather business in the early decades of the nineteenth century, the global and the British ostrich feather markets were pale precursors of what they would become. Demand for ostrich plumes was limited and unreliable, and few merchants or wholesalers could afford to devote themselves wholly to the feather trade.[16] Insurance documents allow us to track the net worth of London-based feather dealers from this period: in the early decades of the century the Sun Fire Office insured two ostrich feather merchants, both of whom were Jewish and had a modest valuation. Judah Imschwartz's business was assessed at £700 in June 1817 and £400 in December 1819; Jacob Davies's business, which was assessed seven times between 1820 and 1826, was deemed worth an average of £2,000. Isaac Solomon, a merchant who did not specialize in plumes, also purchased a meager insurance policy from Sun Fire in 1825. This man, who may or may not have been the founder of I. Salaman and Company, had his business assessed at £1,100, including:

> household goods wearing apparel printed books plate in Wilson dwelling house only situated as aforesaid Brick Eight hundred fifty pounds.
> Jewels therein only one hundred pounds
> China and glass therein only fifty pounds
> Wearing apparel therein only (in twill) one hundred pounds.[17]

The small and fluctuating fortunes of merchants like these suggest that one could hardly expect to become wealthy in feathers in London in the early nineteenth century. Perhaps for this reason, all of the sellers of feathers insured by Sun Fire appear to have worn more than one professional hat: Sun Fire labeled Solomon a merchant, Davies a furrier and dealer in ostrich feathers, and Imschwartz a furrier and dealer in ostrich feathers and artificial flowers.[18]

The inchoate nature of London's early-nineteenth-century feather trade reflected the modest demands of consumers, but it was also shaped in the absence of dedicated ostrich feather suppliers. The Cape Colony had not yet emerged as a center of ostrich farming: this dramatic transformation of the region was still fifty years in the making. Prior to the ascendancy of the South African feather industry, most ostrich plumes destined for European consumers came from wild birds hunted in the southern Sahara and Sahel. These plumes reached London only after being carried by camel caravan to port cities in North Africa, whence they were sent by Jewish mercantile firms across the Mediterranean to associates in Livorno, Venice, Trieste, and Marseilles (among other port cities). Seen from the vantage of the eighteenth and early nineteenth centuries, these cities, far more than London, were the world's feather hubs. Livorno, in particular, could claim the role of Europe's and America's plume gateway before the mid-nineteenth century.

As a direct result of British colonial policies in and toward the Cape, this mercantile geography began to evolve in the 1860s, just before the onset of feather mania. British investments in South African and trans-Atlantic communication and transportation networks facilitated the expansion of white-dominated export-oriented industries in the Cape, and the ostrich industry in particular. The Cape's monopoly on feather production was furthered by British regulation of tariffs on South African ostrich eggs, feathers, and birds and by laws that prevented the export of live birds and their eggs.[19] Perhaps most important, the privileged trading relations that bound metropole and colony ensured that most feathers exported from South Africa were directed to London. We have already seen how these measures facilitated the rapid growth of the Cape ostrich industry; of interest here is how they changed the landscape of the British and the international feather trade. British support for the Cape-based ostrich feather industry ensured that London imported an ever larger percentage of ostrich feathers from its colonial possession in southern Africa, thereby largely circumventing (though not altogether attenuating) the older but still vibrant Mediterranean feather trade. Thus the Cape, which had supplied a virtually negligible quantity of Europe's ostrich feathers in the first decades of the nineteenth century, was supplying Britain fifteen times the value of feathers from North Africa by 1895; thirty-eight times in 1900; and more than a hundred times in 1910.[20] The increases are impressive, especially because certain individual feathers from North Africa (including the legendary Barbary plume) continued to be more highly valued than those from South Africa.

As ostrich feathers from the Cape took hold of the European market, the geography of the global industry evolved. By the 1870s, it was clear that London was to become the principal American and European feather supplier.[21] Even feather wholesalers in Paris, who once absorbed 75 percent of Livornese imports from North Africa, now traveled to London to buy Cape ostrich feathers.[22] At the same time, as buyers of feathers from across Europe and the United States increasingly depended on London for feather purchases, North African feather exporters began to redirect their plumes there rather than to Livorno, Marseilles, and Paris. In addition to diminishing Livorno's importance as a center of the feather trade, this shift in mercantile practice diminished the global significance of the Mediterranean as a feather conduit. Ostrich plumes were shipped across the Mediterranean into the twentieth century, especially from the Ottoman-controlled port of Tripoli. However, these feathers supplied an increasingly marginal portion of the European and American market. Mediterranean feather commerce was endangered for other reasons as well, principally because of the emergence of east-to-west trading routes that redirected plumes to the West African coast.[23] Putting the story of the decline of trans-Saharan and trans-Mediterranean feather traffic aside, the following point must be stressed: as a result of Britain's dominance of the trans-Atlantic ostrich feather business, the Mediterranean trade, though still crucial to North and West African economies around the turn of the century, was increasingly assuming a secondary position of importance to the global market.

Certain turn-of-the-century observers of the industry attributed these transitions solely to the evolution of steam navigation, but this theory underrated the political complexity of global plume commerce.[24] With feathers, as with tea, the British clearly stood to gain by producing a luxury commodity "within the confines of their own empire," as historian James Walvin has described the shifting sources of tea imports in the late nineteenth century.[25] Indeed, striking financial benefits followed London's seizure of center stage in the ostrich feather world. By 1876, large-scale public auctions were being held every other month in London (monthly and twice-monthly auctions would come in time), and it was at these that buyers from Britain, the United States, France, Austria, and Germany acquired the bulk of their ostrich feathers. The subsequent expansion of the British ostrich feather market was exceedingly rapid. In 1893, Great Britain imported nearly £475,000 worth of ostrich feathers, 98 percent of which were from the Cape. In 1912, the peak year of the feather boom, 943,000 cubic pounds of ostrich feathers valued at roughly £2.2 million were imported to Great Britain. This was nearly three times the amount imported by France and nearly five times that in Germany—for both of these countries, the great majority of ostrich feathers were transshipped through London. In the same year, roughly £772,000 worth of ostrich feathers were reexported from Great Britain, with the bulk destined for the United States (fig. 10).[26]

To accommodate the explosion of the global ostrich feather market, ostrich feather brokers, merchants, wholesalers, manufacturers, and feather handlers in London began to grow in numbers and operational scale. A thorough study of the industry was begun by the Board of Trade only in 1919, after the feather market had already crashed, when even the survey in question called "the industry a dying one."[27] Yet statistics on the state of the trade in the aftermath of the crash hint at just how vibrant Britain's ostrich feather economy was but six years earlier, when the market was at its height. In 1919, 2,000–3,000 skilled female workers and 200–300 skilled male workers processed ostrich plumes in the British capital; when interviewed by representatives of the board, ostrich feather merchants and manufacturers testified that this represented as much as an 85 percent reduction of the erstwhile feather workforce.[28] This would mean

THE INCUBATING ROOM.

A BIRD SITTING.

HELPING OUT A WEAK ONE.

COOLIE WITH YOUNG BIRDS.

FINDING A NEST.

THE FEATHER ROOM.

Figure 10. Published alongside an account of South Africa's ostrich industry by Anthony Trollope, this pictorial synopsis shows the seemingly natural flow of feathers from British farmers in the Cape Colony to London's colonial produce brokers. An instrumental advocate of Britain's expanding ostrich feather industry was Arthur Douglass (middle left), owner of the three-thousand-acre ostrich farm pictured here, inventor of the first ostrich incubator (upper left), and author of an influential 1881 book on ostrich farming. (From "Ostrich Farming in South Africa," *Illustrated London News*, March 30, 1878, courtesy University of Oregon Knight Library)

that as many as 2,000 boys and men and 20,000 girls and women were working in the trade at its peak. According to a state-sponsored inquiry in 1884, these workers labored in "thousands of domestic workshops at East End," many little more than converted dwelling houses.[29]

As London's blue-collar workforce grew, so too did the number of ostrich feather manufacturers and dealers who employed them. In 1919 it was estimated that just over thirty ostrich feather manufacturers and dealers existed in London.[30] This figure represented a dramatic reduction in the number of such firms that had once operated. Over the course of the sixty or so years of the feather boom, hundreds of such businesses announced themselves annually in the London Post Office Directory.[31] The number of London's ostrich feather brokers, too, was on the rise at the turn of the century, while the auctions they oversaw became more frequent, well attended, and successful. To monitor so dense an industry and to set statutory minimum wages for its notoriously ill compensated "sweated" workforce, the British Board of Trade (a Committee of the Privy Council) created the Ostrich and Fancy Feather and Artificial Flower Trade Board in 1919. Until the late twentieth century, the twenty-five members who sat on this board met twice monthly, tracking and monitoring the industry.[32] The extensive paperwork gathered and generated by this board, held by the National Archives of the United Kingdom, represents a crucial source for this study.

But why did Jews come to monopolize Britain's feather industry? To answer this question, we must proceed along the length of Britain's ostrich feather commodity chain, tracking the passage of feathers from ship to shop—to and through auction and manufacture, from importers to brokers, auctioneers, wholesalers, and feather handlers—all before the plumes reached retailers in the millinery, fashion, or funeral industries in Britain and beyond.

OSTRICH FEATHERS FROM SHIP TO SHOP

During the modern feather boom, most ostrich feathers reached Britain from North and South Africa on steamships, bundled in wooden cases lined with tin or specially prepared paper that had been sewn into canvas; by one account, a single ship could carry as much as a million pounds sterling worth of plumes, and these left the Cape several times a week.[33] In an ironic twist, plumes from the Cape traveled on ships that had once been filled with South African–bound Russian Jewish immigrants, many of whom passed through London en route to their new homes, and including some destined to become feather merchants.[34] Upon arrival in London, the feather cases were stored on docks and dockside warehouses—what Jonathan Schneer has termed the "nexus" of the imperial metropolis that was London—where luxury items from the colonies including fruits, nuts, oils, spirits, tea, cinnamon, shells, and feathers (among countless other goods) were stockpiled.[35] In the early years of the ostrich feather trade, potential buyers came to the docks to scrutinize the newly imported plumes.[36] As the market accelerated, however, this arrangement proved cumbersome, and the presentation of feathers was relocated to the warehouses at Billiter Street visited by Myer Salaman.

Before the plumes reached the Billiter warehouses they needed to be retrieved by the import firms that had invested in them. This was accomplished in one of two ways. Some companies followed a path favored by the London and Kano Trading Company, a firm that oversaw the export of ostrich feathers, tanned skins, and horns (among other commodities) from the southern Sahara to London. This company had only a titular London base (its main British offices were in Liverpool), so company managers arranged for the brokerage firm of Lewis and Peat to hire a "Dock Company" to retrieve their plumes and "render [a] report evaluation as soon as the parcel is worked."[37] Other African Jewish feather exporters maintained offices or associates in London that were responsible for the retrieval of their goods; Sybil Honikman, descendant of a Jewish feather family based in Oudtshoorn and London, recalled visiting the docks as a student with her father.

> When . . . my father met me in London, [the] first thing he did was went [*sic*] on a trip to the docks, the warehouses, and climbing over lugs and bags of spices we got to a warehouse where a fellow in a white coat met us and he led me by the hand to a corner where there were bags of feathers. Every bag had a black diamond, and inside [the diamond were] the letters I.J.H. and he said, those are the feathers we buy, and no others. Those are my father's initials, you see, and they could depend upon the quality.[38]

As father and daughter left the dock, Honikman remembers passing an elaborate ostrich feather fan that was being either stored or displayed on the docks. It was, reminisced Honikman, "a gorgeous thing dyed brilliant colours and I can remember my father making a sweeping bow to the feather fan."[39] This gesture, deliberately stagy as it feels, points to the delicate role middlemen like Honikman played in the global feather commodity chain. Jewish feather merchants like Honikman were, on one hand, crucial to facilitating flows of capital via Britain from the colonies and independent states of Africa to consumers in an international market. On the other hand, these merchants sought to profit from global fashion trends to which they paid obeisance but over which they had little control. Both cocksure and submissive, Honikman's bow to the feather fan was canny metonymy for the feather traders' condition.

Feather importers next entrusted their plumes to brokers, who offered them in monthly auctions held in London's Commercial Sale Rooms. Of the year's auctions, those in June and December were particularly significant. Feather exporters in the Cape and North Africa saved their best and largest quantity of stock for these events, which attracted the greatest number of feather buyers from overseas. All such auctions were overseen by established brokerage firms that specialized in ostrich feather sales, including, most prominently, Lewis and Peat, Hale and Son, and S. Figgis and Company. Though Anglo-Jews have a long history as brokers, there is no evidence that the brokerage firms that handled ostrich plumes were Jewish-owned.[40]

The history of these brokerage firms remains to be written, but we may draw preliminary conclusions about their role in the feather trade. Each of the main ostrich feather brokers worked in various forms of "colonial produce" in addition to plumes. Lewis and Peat, for example, began as spice brokers. By 1909 most of their roughly £6 million turnover was in rubber.[41] Thomas Hale, co-founder of Hale and Son, began his career as a "West Indies broker." By the 1850s he was a partner in "Ellis and Hale, drug and colonial brokers," a firm that specialized in the sale of ivory.[42] One of Ellis and Hale's first accounts in feathers may have been brokered with the Jewish merchant Joseph Samuel, brother of Marcus Samuel, future founder of Shell Transport and Trading Company. The Samuel family firm was at this time importing various luxury goods to Britain, fishing about for the one that would secure its fortune. That oil rather than feathers, tea, sugar, or shells (all commodities in which the family then dealt) would allow them to reach this goal could not have been predicted at the time. In 1863, Joseph Samuel entrusted Ellis and Hale with a series of shipments of goods procured in the vicinity of the Moroccan port of Essaouira (Mogador). Among these goods were ostrich feathers, whose sale ensured that the Samuel account with Ellis and Hale rose from £603 in 1863 to £4,338 in 1864.[43] Perhaps this was just the sort of windfall that could sway a colonial broker in favor of a particular commodity; soon after, Hale entered into business with his son, Thomas Jr., and the resulting firm, Hale and Son, focused on the handling of ostrich feathers for roughly the next forty years.[44]

The story of Hale and Son reminds us that if colonial produce and ostrich feather brokers were not themselves Jewish, their day-to-day operations (and their success or failure) depended heavily on the Jewish merchants with whom they worked. In the case of the ostrich feather trade, this relationship was most intimate and crucial at auction time. Feather auctions were not open to any potential buyer, and individual consumers, in particular, were barred from these monthly events. Consumer participation was not in the interest of the London Produce Brokers' Association, the agency that established the rules observed at feather auctions, for were consumers in attendance they would circumvent the wholesale houses that were the principal clients of brokers. At the same time, consumers' needs were not in accordance with those of feather sellers, who sold by the parcel rather than the plume.[45]

With individual consumers barred from auction, the events were attended principally by feather manufacturers and wholesalers. Given the prevalence of Jews in these occupations, it follows that in London, as in the Cape, feather auctions were largely Jewish in composition (fig. 11). This is substantiated by the fact that ostrich feather auctions were routinely rescheduled if a given auction conflicted with the Jewish high holidays.[46] The industry as a whole was by and large discreet about the overrepresentation of Jews at feather sales, but it did not go unnoticed by observers of the industry. In his contemporary study of the trade Arthur Douglass observed, without referring directly to Jewishness, that an organized group of feather traders kept "ordinary" merchants from participating in London's feather market.

> By far the largest buyers [of ostrich feathers] are the resident representatives of the few great English manufacturers; where the ordinary merchant has tried exporting feathers it has generally resulted in a loss. The reason has generally been considered a mystery, but there is no mystery about it. These men have enormous connections in many parts of the world.[47]

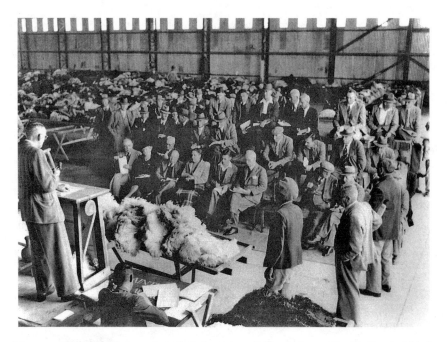

Figure 11. Ostrich feather auction, Oudtshoorn, 1948. Few Jews remained in South Africa's ostrich feather industry in the wake of the feather crash of 1914. Among those who persevered was the ostrich farmer and feather baron Max Rose, who stands at front right, with hands in pockets. Other Jewish feather merchants present include Jacob Wilck (leftmost seat, front row), Abraham (Abe) Berman (third from left, front row), Ephraim (Ephraini) Horowitz (second from right, front row), Isaac Nurick of Ladismith (seated second from right, second row), Chaikel Lazarus (fourth from right, second row), Derek Fish (seated in background, on left edge of tabletop), and, to the right of Fish, Abe Sindler, Julius Lazarus, and Solomon Markus. (Courtesy C. P. Nel Museum, Oudtshoorn)

Contacts local and foreign were indeed crucial to feather dealers in London, and these were abetted by the Jewishness of participants. This being said, the explanation Douglass gave hinted at rather more conspiracy than existed in reality. In fact, the connections that proved so critical to success in the ostrich feather market tended to be on the smallest rather than the largest scale: as in London more generally, the feather trade was dominated by "small masters" rather than industrial magnates.[48] The fact of being Jewish may have, on occasion, eased relationships between feather importers or manufacturers and would-be feather financiers (a number of dealings such as this are documented in Chapter 4). At the same time, those in the feather industry in Britain largely relied on familial contacts to broaden the base and scale of their operations. As the century turned and the feather boom exploded, large firms like I. Salaman and Company sent sons and sons-in-law to create and oversee operations abroad. Meanwhile, large-scale feather operations in North Africa and the Cape—including that of Max Rose, the "ostrich feather king of South Africa"—sent family members to London to create and oversee European operations.[49] Small-scale London-based merchants, wholesalers, and manufacturers, on the other hand, expanded titularly to include brothers, sons, and grandsons even when they did not maintain overseas branches. Extra-familial contacts were also eased by ethnicity. This was certainly true for the aforementioned Isach Hassan, a Tripolitanian Jewish feather merchant of Livornese origin who sold himself as a London-based auction shill to the South African Jewish feather exporter Isaac Nurick; we will pick up his story in the chapter that follows. In each case, the forging of intra- and extra-regional commercial alliances between Jews intensified the Jewishness of the industry.

Although Jewishness furnished opportunities to some in the feather industry, it never guaranteed prosperity. Like all in the trade, Jewish merchants' and manufacturers' success at auction depended on their own—and their partners'—commercial acuity and luck. Staying abreast of auction circulars, distributed by brokers after each month's auction, was one means of cultivating these qualities. These summaries were cited in local and international trade and agricultural journals in Britain, France, South Africa, and the United States, and were sent to loyal customers overseas.[50] Auction circulars detailed how many cases of feathers were offered at a given sale, specified how many were of North African (that is, southern Saharan or Sahelian) or Cape origin, and how many were sold or withheld for future auction. They also offered an accounting of how many British pounds sterling per pound each of roughly two dozen varieties of ostrich plumes commanded, commenting on notable trends such as the diminished appeal of Spadonas (young, immature wing feathers). Finally, auction circulars offered synopses of the mood at sale—whether it was brisk or faltering, aggressive or cautious—and reflected on the tenor of various national buying interests such as that of the Americans or French.

If the papers of I. Salaman and Company are any indication, these documents were critical tools for feather buyers. (For the same reasons, they are rich sources for the historian, who may use them to reconstruct serial data on the price that ostrich feathers commanded in London over a period of sixty years.) Circulars allowed feather buyers to track the vitality of the market and individual feather varieties, all of which was critical in determining whether one succeeded or failed. For this reason, representatives of I. Salaman and Company appear to have carefully analyzed and commented on their collection of auction circulars. The resulting marginalia reflects the firm's interest not only in the facts of an auction but in the perceived biases and reliability of the brokerage firms that handled them. A member of the Salaman family firm might, for example, decide that a Lewis and Peat circular "reflected the state of the trade best."[51] Or it might catalyze them to patronize an upcoming sale by Hale and Son. These asides are of relevance to the historian insofar as they emphasize that a feather buyer (or feather firm) needed more than familial, intra-ethnic, local, or overseas contacts. They also needed that ineffable feel for feathers that came only with time and experience: a long view of the market that allowed one to anticipate a trend, but also to sense whether a particular fashion was destined to be short-lived. This sort of instinctual and strategic know-how is evidenced most succinctly in a handwritten note that appears on a Hale and Son circular of 1875 preserved in the papers of I. Salaman and Company. On its top, a company representative (likely Myer Salaman) scribbled: "Don't be run up Hale may be 5 percent worse in January or may be 2 percent better buy for a *falling market* never mind if you do nothing Thirds cheap up to seconds will sell most likely get good large lots of them in preference to good feathers don't get excited."[52] To be able to anticipate and even appreciate volatility, to bid both judiciously and aggressively, to keep one's cool without losing one's edge: these, rather than the Jewishness of a given participant or the range of one's contacts, were a buyer's greatest assets at auction.

Depending on the purchaser, ostrich feathers sold at auction followed one of several routes. Some were sent directly, in an unprocessed (or "raw") state, to foreign markets, with the Americans and French being the largest consumers. In Paris and New York, in particular, extensive feather processing and resale industries existed. Other feathers were purchased by London-based manufacturing or wholesale firms—the vast majority of which were owned by Jews—and were processed and resold in the city. I will return to the story of I. Salaman and Company to reconstruct the workings of one such global wholesale operation, but first we remain with the feathers themselves, following as they pass from auction to factory, from a raw to finished state, and from the hands of Jewish men to the hands of Jewish women.

SWEATING JEWS: LONDON'S OSTRICH FEATHER HANDLERS

Britain's ostrich feather manufactories were overwhelmingly concentrated in a one-mile radius that spanned the City of London and the East End; they were particularly numerous on Barbican, Aldersgate, London Wall, Jewin, Cripplesgate, Bartholomew Close, and Fenchurch Streets. According to a British chief inspector of factories, the small-scale workshops in question were staffed by "Jewesses chiefly," most of whom were Eastern European in origin.[53] The roughly fifteen thousand Eastern European Jews who settled in London between 1880 and the eve of the First World War furnished a bountiful labor market to the feather trade. Immigrant Jewish women and girls especially had reason to be inclined toward this industrial niche, as many had experience in manufacturing in general and in the needle trades in particular. These Jews, like so many other women and immigrants who labored in London's "sweating" industries, worked at below-subsistence wages and were prone to myriad abuses.

Little about the individual women and girls in question can be reconstructed, but a great deal is known about the work they undertook and the conditions they faced collectively—as skilled and semi-skilled laborers in London's sweating system and as participants in a volatile global trading network. Women and girls made up the majority of London's ostrich feather workers, representing 73 percent and 17 percent, respectively, of the workforce as a whole (men and boys amounted, respectively, to 7 percent and 3 percent of the industry). The majority (63 percent) were employed in small-scale workshops with fewer than fifty people; smaller numbers were employed in shops with more than fifty hands (13 percent) and in shops of over one hundred (17 percent); a few labored in shops with more than two hundred or three hundred workers (1 percent each).[54] According to Trade Board representatives, the work conducted by these employees "requires deft fingers, care and patience and . . . the type of worker employed is usually smart and intelligent. It would therefore appear that the work, in the main, is skilled labour."[55]

In London, as in New York and Paris, the "treating" of ostrich plumes, which readied the raw feathers for sale, was an elaborate process. In each of these locales, the means of manufacture, the gendered division of this labor, and the "skill" each stage was thought to require differed. The most is known about such operations in New York (as we shall see in Chapter 4). But because these practices varied from place to place, a few words are warranted on its London manifestations.

When ostrich plumes passed from broker to manufacturer, they were still tied in the bundles created by North and South African feather sorters. The feathers were then separated and individually "strung" on lengths of twine. In London, feather stringing was done by women and girls by hand and was considered an "unskilled" job (here, as below, I echo notions of "skilled" and "unskilled" assigned by the Ostrich and Fancy Feather and Artificial Flower Trade Board in the course of its investigations of the industry).[56] Apprentices and other unskilled female workers then washed the feathers in machines designed for this purpose, passing them next to skilled male workers, who bleached and dyed the feathers manually. Feather dying was an odious and labor-intensive operation, with experienced dyers overseeing as many as eighteen boiling vats containing thirty pounds of feathers each; the complete dying process could take as long as ten days. After the dying was completed, unskilled male workers then rewashed the plumes by hand, after which they were sent to the youngest ostrich feather workers—girls and boys who were assigned to beat the plumes vigorously, thereby removing clusters of bleach and separating the individual barbs of each plume. The flue of each feather was then "scraped" by semi-skilled women workers, either by hand or by machine. This entailed thinning the flue with a piece of glass or other sharp implement to render it malleable for shaping. The remaining stages of feather manufacturing were considered the most painstaking by those in the American industry, but in London the stages that ensued were conducted by semi-skilled employees. These workers (all female, as in New York) sewed thin plumes together, by hand or by machine, giving them the appearance of a single full feather (a process known as "laying up"). Next the feathers were "curled," or shaped, and a portion were twisted onto boas. Finally, the resulting ornaments were stacked and packed for sale.[57]

Ostrich feather manufacturing was plagued by many of the conditions that afflicted London's sweating industries more generally, including abuse of the apprentice system, poor working conditions, and abysmal wages. Fortunately for the industry's blue-collar workforce, the ostrich feather trade appears to have been less plagued by seasonality than most others, as demand for the plumes (as opposed, say, to artificial flowers) persisted year round.[58] Though employment was steady when the market was strong, bulwarks faced those who wished to move into this industrial niche. The apprentice system demanded that some ostrich feather apprentices board and lodge with their masters on credit until they could repay the debt. This process took two to three years, including three months of free labor.[59] According to an inspector employed by the Select Committee of the House of Lords on Britain's Sweating System in 1888: "In the case of the ostrich feathers people [sic] where girls must be skilled to do their work, they go through a sort of apprenticeship, and yet it is no apprenticeship; they receive wages, small wages, to begin with, and get raised according to their proficiency." Asked by the members of the select committee if this represented a "hardship," the inspector answered in the affirmative, stating further that it was common practice in the trade that "an employer [contracts] work out of people at a very low rate of wage on the ground of their being learners and then, when he has used them as far as his purpose requires, discharges them."[60]

Additional hazards were endemic to ostrich feather manufacturing at the turn of the century. London's ostrich feather factories were ill ventilated and "tainted for want of change."[61] Many children labored in these spaces, routinely working until late at night.[62] In violation of labor laws, women and girls in the profession took work home "and did it at home till late at night or early the following morning before starting for their place of employment."[63] Before minimum wages were set by the Trade Board in 1919, feather handlers were "very badly paid," likely putting most apprentice and unskilled feather workers scarcely above the poverty line defined by Charles Booth's survey of 1902.[64] As no trade union catered to London's ostrich feather trade, workers had little means of effecting change in the industry; as late as 1919, 74 percent of the workforce was thought to be unorganized.[65]

A minimum wage scale for the ostrich feather industry was imposed by the state only after the feather slump, when the trade was but a shadow of its former self.[66] Even after this point, the Board of Trade vetted a seemingly endless series of requests for exemptions on behalf of manufacturers (nearly all of which were approved) who employed workers deemed too old or too young, or who suffered from, among other ailments, deformity, ill health, paralysis, ulcers, and poor eyesight. Often, these conditions appear to have had little effect on workers' ability to process feathers. The mother of a thirty-one-year-old female employee who was said to be "handicapped, by reason of being small in stature," for example, provided the Board of Trade with medical evidence demonstrating that her daughter was "quite fit to perform her ordinary work."[67] Fortunately in this instance the manufacturer in question was labeled "the bullying type" and the exemption denied, but the board approved most such requests. The resulting memoranda were stamped with the self-conscious warning "not to be communicated to press."[68]

London's ostrich feather workers were also vulnerable to a legal system that sanctioned employers' abuses. In 1882, for example, *The Times* of London reported that Abraham Botibol, a prominent Sephardi feather manufacturer, had been called before the solicitor at Guildhall for violating the terms of his apprenticeship of Honora Regan, a young female worker. Fortunately for Botibol, the solicitor "had no doubt Mr. Botibol wished to carry on his business in a respectable manner," and the summons was dismissed for lacking the appropriate stamp.[69] Some years later, *The Times* reported on the ill fortune of a second apprentice, forty-nine-year-old Mary Anne Baker, who was accused of having stolen five shillings' worth of ostrich feathers from her master. The feathers were discovered in Baker's lodgings, and the apprentice claimed that she had received them in lieu of pay. Given the fact that this incident occurred in the early months of the feather slump of the 1880s, when wages were less available to manufacturers than plumes, this was not an implausible defense. On the word of Baker's overseer, however, the apprentice was condemned to twenty-one days of hard labor.[70]

After the creation of a Trade Board dedicated to the feather industry, exploitive manufacturers and merchants were reprimanded for ill treatment of employees—at least when they were caught. Among the first to fall prey to the board's scrutiny was A. Botibol and Company, now represented by Cecil Botibol, likely the son of Abraham Botibol, whose encounter with Guildhall *The Times* had reported some forty years earlier.[71] In 1927 the board initiated an extensive evaluation of the firm, then considered "the biggest in the feather trade." Detailed interviews were conducted with Botibol's roughly fifty employees (all of whom were women), and twenty-seven were found to be underpaid, among them five learners. Cecil Botibol protested that he was "a very old employer in the trade, and that he treated his workers in the usual fatherly manner and paid them wages for high days and holidays." The employer argued further that because of the "uncertain nature of his trade which depended on the fluctuations of fashion," had he paid his workers a stable wage he would have been obliged to send them home for days at a time when there was a lull in the business. Undeterred by this self-defense, the Trade Board chose to formally charge Botibol both for underpaying his workers and for failing to keep proper pay records. Members of the board anticipated "a flood of oratory in mitigation."[72] The charge against A. Botibol and Company reached the magistrate at Old Street Police Court in December 1927.

It is striking how differently the grievance against Cecil Botibol was handled compared to that lodged against Abraham Botibol some forty years earlier. When Abraham Botibol was charged with violating his apprentice's contract, it appears that the court weighed the words of employer against those of employee, deciding in favor of the former. Forty years later, the Ostrich and Fancy Feather and Artificial Flower Trade Board conducted personal interviews with each of Botibol's employees, even going to the length of visiting certain potentially intimidated workers at home.[73] Cecil Botibol's wage records for the preceding two years were also demanded; those that he was unable to deliver (or, as the case turned out to be, that he had failed to keep in the first place) resulted in a fine. The extent of the investigation against his firm was so great that Botibol himself telephoned a member of the Trade Board and announced "genially that [the Trade Board] had an excellent case against him and he realized he would lose on all points."[74] This Botibol did, and as a result he was obliged to pay more than £234 in arrears to twenty-seven workers and £17 in fines, for failing to keep adequate wage records and to post current minimum wage notices.[75]

The state's oversight of the feather trade was the principal reason that the charges against Abraham and Cecil Botibol were prosecuted differently in 1888 and 1927. As in South Africa, in Britain the state was increasingly inclined to micromanage the ostrich feather trade as boom turned to bust. With the decline of the feather market, the industry seemed to pose more and increasingly pressing social, moral, and labor problems. Thus while Abraham Botibol's own word sufficed as defense in 1888, in 1927 even personal lobbying of the board by Cecil Botibol was insufficient to sway its representatives, even though Botibol the younger was a dominant force in the industry and had taken "a prominent role in the negotiations which led to the establishment of the Trade Board."[76] This is, perhaps, one sign that conditions for ostrich feather workers had improved with the passage of time. But it is possible, too, that as anti-alien and anti-Semitic sentiment surged in Britain, East End Jewish manufacturers —whom many social reformers and the state blamed for the sweating system and related social ills—were increasingly and singularly vulnerable to censure.[77] This was all the more likely to have been true in an industry seen as being "in the hands of Jews."

If the Botibols' encounters with the law suggest ways in which Britain's feather industry changed over time, they also point to an important continuity. In 1927, as in 1888, the global feather market was in a slump, and in both instances manufacturers meted out losses to employees. Feather handlers' vulnerability as sweated laborers was thus overlaid by a sensitivity to the volatile global market. The Trade Board recorded Cecil Botibol's explanation during the proceedings against him: "For some years he had been carrying on his business at a heavy loss mainly to keep his workers in employment. He could not afford to pay more wages."[78] One need not condone Botibol's ill treatment of his employees to recognize that there was truth to his claim. Ostrich feather manufacturers were squeezed not only by the increased wages, scarce skill, and high rents that the sweating system aimed to offset, but *between* the demands of the state, which aimed to legislate a stable local economy, and those of global consumers, whose desires for feathers ebbed and flowed.[79] Botibol father and son were linked, in other words, by the inherent fragility they shared as purveyors of luxury goods to a trans-hemispheric market, while their workers were pinioned by a punishing local and global economy. In this, the conditions those in the ostrich feather industry labored under had not changed over the period in question: rather, it was the state's relationship to them that was assuming a new form.

In its vigorous oversight of the feather industry, the Board of Trade was attempting—to borrow loosely from Judith Walkowitz's recent meditations on the domestication of cosmopolitan cultural forms in early-twentieth-century

London—to incorporate transnational economic forms into a national culture.[80] Such efforts appear to have aided feather handlers, but they would inevitably be jarring to feather merchants like the Botibols, whose business resided in the interstices of the metropolitan and global market. Our sense of the delicate position of London's ostrich feather manufacturers, wholesalers, dealers, and feather handlers comes into sharper relief as we return to the story of I. Salaman and Company.

WEATHERING BOOM AND BUST: I. SALAMAN AND COMPANY

When Myer Salaman entered the feather warehouses on Billiter Street in the summer of 1884, he was serving as the informal head of I. Salaman and Company, a position he had held for more than twenty years. Myer's father Isaac was the first member of the family to enter the ostrich feather trade. In 1816, when Isaac made his first foray into feather buying, he was twenty-six years old, a veteran of the British navy, and possibly disinherited by his father, Aaron Solomon, a well-to-do merchant with a country house in Edmonton.[81] (Isaac changed the spelling of the family name around this time, either due to an innocent mistake, to deemphasize it as recognizably Jewish, or to distance himself from his father.)[82] Two accounts of Isaac's life suggest that he served in the British navy at St. Helena, where he encountered distinguished relatives in St. Helena's Jewish community who shared the family name.[83] For a brief period, Isaac joined these relatives in South Africa, where he may have been exposed to the feather trade; thus it is possible, as Isaac's son Redcliffe Nathan would subsequently claim, that "in that sub-continent . . . the foundations of the family fortunes were laid."[84] Despite references to I. Salaman and Company developing business contacts in the Cape, however, there is no evidence of whether Isaac retained contact with the Solomons of South Africa, St. Helena, or Oudtshoorn, where more than one feather merchant claimed the family name.[85]

In 1863, when I. Salaman and Company was legally incorporated, the company was valued at £2,000, inclusive of "the whole of the stock in trade books manuals [and] plume bundles."[86] At this time, the company operated out of a ground floor shop at 69 Lamb's Conduit Street, Bloomsbury, with Isaac and his wife, Jane Raphael, living upstairs with their seven children (Betsy, Rachel,

Fanny, Aaron, Abraham, Nathan, and Myer). According to Myer's son, the shop was "visited by the great ladies of fashion who did not hesitate to pay £5 for a single feather."[87] Relatively speaking, however, I. Salaman and Company was still a small-scale operation. The business did not maintain offices abroad or, as it soon would, have subsidiary factories in London. And it appears that at this time, the business relied on no employees outside the family. Isaac's three daughters, Betsy, Rachel, and Fanny, themselves "worked in the business, even helping to dye the feathers they subsequently sold."[88] In the ensuing decades the firm rose rapidly. In 1864, one year after I. Salaman and Company was legally indentured, its assets had increased by 30 percent, and the amount of space the company leased doubled (after it acquired a lease at 15 Monkwell Street, in the City of London, where it would maintain an office for over fifty years). Isaac Salaman, now a widower "and in consideration of the natural love and affection which [he] hath for his seven children," legally transferred his business to his sons Nathan and Myer, yielding his 30 percent share of the business that the 1863 indenture had guaranteed.[89] The reconstitution of the I. Salaman and Company partnership came at roughly the same time as Myer's marriage to Sarah Solomon, a graduate of the Jewish Neumegen School in Kew and, according to her son, "one of the best-looking women of her circle."[90] Their marriage settlement suggests that the pair lived in elegant comfort, if not luxury. Their first home boasted servants' quarters, an extensive French mahogany bedroom set, a dining room furnished with eight mahogany chairs covered in Moroccan leather and a bearskin rug, and a kitchen stocked with a two-hundred-piece dinner service in blue and gold.[91] Myer and Sarah remained married for forty-three years and raised thirteen children.[92]

As I. Salaman and Company's successes grew, the firm closed its shop on Lamb's Conduit Road, converted to a wholesale operation, and moved its base of operations to Monkwell House in Falcon Square.[93] From roughly the mid-1860s on, then, I. Salaman and Company had no commercial relationship with feather consumers, at least in London. While it restricted its relationship to the public, I. Salaman and Company expanded its manufacturing operations. As of the 1860s, the firm oversaw the treatment of feathers in four manufactories in London. In addition to the manufactory at Monkwell House, these were run by the firms of Greener and Wiggell, E. and E. Kohn Ltd., and Julia Davis.[94] Additionally, I. Salaman and Company maintained business relations with at least two extensive overseas operations, in New York and Paris. Redcliffe Nathan Salaman credited I. Salaman and Company with maintaining depots elsewhere—in Buenos Aires, Cape Town, Durban, and Port Elizabeth—but there is no confirmation of the existence or significance of these operations. Nor do the available Salaman family papers offer evidence of I. Salaman and Company relying on family members or commercial associates in the Cape, despite the possible existence of distant relatives in Oudtshoorn.[95] Evidence of the company forming relationships with exporters or associates in North Africa is similarly absent; a personal letter scrawled by Harry Salaman to his brother George on the back of an ostrich feather auction circular of January 1876 refers to the latter's voyage to Cairo, but no mention is made of whether the trip benefited the business of I. Salaman and Company.[96]

More is known about the company's connections in London, Paris, and New York. In London, Myer and Nathan Salaman diversified their investments by engaging in aggressive real estate speculation. From at least the 1870s, the pair bought properties in the City of London, including, among many others, buildings in Falcon Square, Naked Boy Court and Barros Court, and on Castletown, Charlesville, Cheapside, Fairholme, and Palliser roads. Although Myer was occasionally "caught out" (as his son put it) by his tendency toward speculation, the real estate investments he made eventually sheltered I. Salaman and Company from the impending feather crash and ultimately "relieved Myer's children of the need to earn a living."[97]

Meanwhile, the firm maintained active commercial relationships in Paris and New York. These were logical sites for company branches: New York because it was America's ostrich feather manufacturing capital and thus a gateway to American consumers, and Paris because of the city's history as the doyenne of superior plume craftsmanship.[98] Until the feather market began to falter, it appears that the board of directors and trustees of I. Salaman and Company, Myer and Nathan among them, concerned themselves little with the day-to-day running of these foreign operations, delegating questions of management to representatives at each site. The Parisian branch of I. Salaman and Company was overseen by Myer's daughter Betty, her husband Charles Feist, and their associate August Guyot, while the financial management of the New York office was overseen by Lovejoy Nathan, who reported to I. Salaman and Company through the offices of Turq and Young.[99] Minutes from the monthly meetings of the company's board of directors recorded from 1907 into the 1940s suggest that little attention was given to these operations before 1907. Indeed, during this period, the directors concentrated their energies on debating how often and how much they and the trustees of the firm should be remunerated for their leadership of a flourishing business. The luxury of arguing over such matters as these proved short-lived. In the summer of 1914, founding board member Alexander Frederick Blaikley reported to the board that he had attended a general meeting of the company's trustees to warn that although the trustees had received a bonus of 5 percent per share in 1913, "trade for the current year was slated to be very bad," and such a bounty might not be forthcoming in the months ahead.[100]

Blaikley's counsel vastly underestimated the vulnerability of I. Salaman and Company's feather operations and the ostrich feather market in general. In 1915, it was drawn to the board's attention that the Parisian office of I. Salaman and Company was in debt to the tune of £70,000, due in part to bad investments but also to poor oversight of its feather operations. By 1919, the Parisian office was running at a loss and the interest on its debt to the main office alone exceeded £11,000.[101] The board of directors considered reconstituting the company, but its Parisian representatives demurred, arguing that feather sales were bound to increase after the conclusion of the war.[102] As time passed, however, it became clear that the Parisian office was a liability to the company, which decided to acquire the branch to annul its many debts.[103] This decision was met with great relief by August Guyot. The ostrich feather "trade in Paris was extremely bad," he told the board of directors, and when his contract with I. Salaman and Company terminated in two years' time he did not intend to stay in the business.[104]

The Paris office was not the only one of I. Salaman and Company's branches to feel the effects of dwindling demand. All but one of the firm's affiliated factories in London lost money in 1914, with the facilities at Monkwell House proving the most vulnerable.[105] Some of these partnerships were dissolved—I. Salaman and Company cut its ties with the affiliated company E. and E. Kohn Ltd. in 1917—and those that endured had a rocky future.[106] At the same time, financial hardship produced fissures in the commercial and familial relations of the Salaman family and the firm. As late as 1918, the company's board of directors maintained that the failures of its partner factories and operations overseas did not point to the evaporation of the feather market as a whole, but were merely products of improper business practices, among them messy bookkeeping, ill-monitored commissions, and the failure to take "adequate precautions . . . to ensure that the [resale] value of raw feathers estimated . . . not [be] exceeded in the course of manufacture."[107] One member of the board offered the unlikely claim that even in lean times "it would seem not unreasonable to expect a net profit of say 10 percent on sales of such an article as feathers."[108] Like so many in the industry, the company's management refused to concede—or could not imagine—that the ostrich feather market could simply disappear.

The feather crash that began in the early winter of 1914, and accelerated in Britain after the passage of anti-plumage legislation in 1921, took a profound toll on the London-based industry. During 1914 the *London Gazette,* which published notice of companies entering liquidation pursuant to the Companies (Consolidation) Act of 1908, included almost monthly notifications about the dissolving, "winding up," and liquidation of ostrich feather manufacturers, wholesalers, and merchants. A typical announcement read like this one, printed on August 21, 1914: "The partnership between Moses Waldman and Barnard Rose, Ostrich and Fancy Feather Dealers and Brokers under firm The Oudtshoorn Ostrich Feather Company, dissolved on 18th August by mutual consent."[109] These announcements, typically encapsulated in no more than a half inch of type, could only hint at the fortunes and fantasies upended by the feather bust.[110]

With ostrich feather manufacturers, merchants, and import-export firms facing bankruptcy and closure, blue-collar feather workers faced dramatic reductions in their hours and pay, or even layoffs.[111] Some voiced their desperation to the Ostrich and Fancy Feather and Artificial Flower Trade Board. Hoping for help in her pursuit of lost wages, seventeen-year-old Florence Thomasson explained to the board in 1927 that "things are very bad, me losing 2 days and a half a week which makes things very bad at home." Nineteen-year-old Edith Button, too, hoped the board would be able to assist her, for, as she wrote: "I am in poor circumstances and my mother is near the end of the money for my keep."[112] Though it is likely that these blue-collar workers were particularly vulnerable to the collapse of the ostrich feather market, to some extent their plight reflected that faced by the industry as a whole. When the board conducted its own surveys of the industry in 1919 and again in 1927, feather merchants spoke of the trade as "slack," or "small and declining," stating that "ostrich feather firms are . . . giving up the work."[113] Those that managed to hold on expressed interest in waiting out the slump, but all agreed that prospects were not promising. Ostrich feathers were now said "only to sell when they are made as unlike ostrich plumes as possible."[114]

I. Salaman and Company was unusual in its tenacity. In 1929 a journalist referred to a representative of the firm as "one of the few remaining feather merchants in London."[115] Even so, it is clear that company profits were ever dwindling. As late as 1922, I. Salaman employed no fewer than eight hundred people; seven years later fewer than fifty were in its charge.[116] In 1924, the Board of Directors resolved to sell off the company's property at Monkwell Street, where it had been housed for nearly sixty years.[117] With feathers no longer in demand as objects of adornment, I. Salaman and Company now served a rather less glamorous industry: the vast quantities of plumes the company had stored in affiliated warehouses in London were being exported to Germany, France, and the United States to be made into feather dusters.[118] Ten years later, the liquidation of the business had begun. It would take roughly four years for this to be accomplished; according to minutes of the Board of Directors, "the entire stock of feathers of I. Salaman and Co." was liquidated by the summer of 1943.[119]

The Salaman estate, padded by years of investment in London property, still managed to support members of the family for years to come. But by the postwar period, the feather division of I. Salaman and Company—like the fanciful plumes the company once sold—had become a symbol of a bygone era. In October 1953, the extended Salaman family attended a gathering addressed by Redcliffe Nathan Salaman, at that point the longest serving member of the company's Board of Directors. The notes for his address, scribbled on stationery from the University of Cambridge's School of Agriculture (where he headed a government-funded research project on the potato virus), concluded with this terse, elegiac description of the once great firm: "Liquidation Fashion War. Little now left: Feathers—Industry—Foresight—and generosity—has provided a source of strength and union to 3 generations. May the bond that unites us grow stronger into the years."[120] For the Salamans, as for so many Jewish descendants of the ostrich feather trade, feathers had become an inheritance, a memory, a pursuit so old-fashioned that its evocation drifted seamlessly into prayer (fig. 12).

Britain's Board of Trade was not rash to conclude that the country's ostrich feather industry had been "in the hands of Jews" before the First World War. The board's phrasing, however, which hinted darkly at practices monopolistic and conspiratorial, was both infelicitous and inexact. Jews were indeed well represented at all levels of Britain's ostrich feather commodity chain: as importers, wholesalers, large- and small-scale feather merchants, manufacturers, and feather handlers. At the same time, Britain's ostrich feather trade was never wholly in Jewish hands, and not only because non-Jews maintained a footing in feather commerce. Jews at all levels of the industry—from the wealthiest feather firms to the poorest feather handler—were enormously vulnerable to a volatile global feather market that could careen wildly out of hand. As most in the feather trade learned the hard way, taste could be catered to but never controlled.

Nor was the category of "Jews" as transparent as Britain's Board of Trade presumed. The Jewish feather merchants the board referred to were likely East End manufacturers associated—rightly as well as wrongly—with the evils of Britain's sweating system. This system, and the associated social ills of sexual violence, prostitution, vice, and an inflated thirst for luxury, had long been pinned on the flood of Jewish "aliens" of East European origin to Britain.[121] Jewish ostrich feather manufacturers did participate in the abuse of employees. But Jews were both perpetrators and victims of the sweating system. Although Jews were overrepresented in Britain's ostrich feather trade, they were an internally diverse group, differentiated by gender and class, by place of origin and sub-ethnicity, by their relative rootedness in England. Though Jews had a hand in London's feather industry, this industry could not be said to be in their hands, for "they" were a heterogeneous collective, bonded by commerce rather than kinship.

Cape Town, Tripoli, Algiers, Paris, New York: all were feather bourses, and some shared with London qualities that rendered Britain a vital site of the global ostrich feather trade. But no other city had all the qualities that pushed London to the feather trade's center stage. Indeed, the ascendancy of London as the world's ostrich feather hub depended on the failure of others of the

Figure 12. The abandoned premises of H. Bestimt and Company, Ltd.,
Feather Merchants, of 105 Sheperdess Road may be the last architectural trace of
London's historic feather industry. Likely a professional rather than a patronymic name,
the Yiddish *bastimt* may be translated as "certain."

market's historic nodes. As we shall now explore, the rise of trans-Atlantic feather sales eclipsed older feather trading networks that interlinked the economies of the Niger River Delta, the Sahara and Sahel, North Africa, and Europe. In these regions Mediterranean Jewish feather merchants, financiers, and exporters found the apex of the feather boom inaccessible—despite their historic expertise and commercial resilience. Among them was the London-based South African intermediary, Livornese, Jewish, Tripolitanian feather merchant Isach Hassan.

CHAPTER 3

The Trans-Saharan Trade: Mediterranean Connections

On February 5, 1914, the High Court of London issued a receiving order certifying that "Isach Hassan, of 101, Leadenhall Street, in the City of London, Merchant, and trading at Jarrow-on-Tyne under the name of W. H. and A. Richardson," was in bankruptcy. At this moment, the bulk of Hassan's assets were tied up in materials stored in and near the Port of Tyne, in northeastern Britain; the Jarrow Mill held £17,194 worth of Hassan's paper stock, while a £1,000 stock of esparto grass (a coarse grass grown in southern Spain and North Africa used in the manufacture of inexpensive paper) languished on the docks of the Port of Tyne.[1]

In cooperation with his father, Stanley Hassan, Isach Hassan worked as an importer of goods from North Africa and the southern Sahara. The men hailed from a prominent Livornese Jewish merchant family in Tripoli and, in addition to retaining important professional contacts in North Africa, they maintained bases of operation in London, Manchester, and Paris, where they operated under the name "Hassanisach." It would be an overstatement to suggest that the Hassans had offices in each of these locations: the London address cited on Hassan's bankruptcy filing referred to a public telephone exchange where they might receive telegrams, and Isach Hassan's business stationery mentioned no permanent addresses in Paris or Manchester. And yet the Hassan firm represented the residue of one of the most powerful Tripolitanian Jewish merchant families, whose wealth and social mobility were greatly bolstered by the ostrich feather boom of the late nineteenth and early twentieth centuries.[2]

Modern Mediterranean Jews were prominent in a feather-trading web that linked the economies of the Sahara, the Sahel, the Arabian Peninsula, North Africa, West Africa, Europe, and the United States. In addition to operating across the geographic breadth of this commodity chain, they occupied nearly all of its industrial tiers. Wealthy Moroccan, Livornese, and Sephardi Jewish merchants financed the conveyance of feathers to North Africa's ports via trans-Saharan camel caravan, across the Red Sea, and along the Nile. Poor Maghrebi Jews were responsible for sorting and packing feathers in Alexandria, Cairo, Tripoli, Algiers, and Tunis, thereby readying them for sales overseas. Mediterranean Jewish mercantile families, most of whom were of Livornese origin, oversaw the export of feathers from the major port cities of North Africa —Essaouira, Algiers, Tripoli, Benghazi, Alexandria, and Cairo—to Livorno, Marseilles, Paris, London, and other European ports.[3] And Yemeni Jews were said to monopolize the processing and trade of plumes in and from Aden; the bulk of the resulting goods were ferried across the Red Sea and down the Nile to Alexandria and Cairo, whence Livornese Jewish families oversaw their export to Europe.[4]

Jews had been prominent traders in the Mediterranean since ancient times, and some of the Jewish families involved in feather commerce at the turn of the twentieth century had operated continuously for generations.[5] Many of these families profited from the escalating appeal of the ostrich plume— indeed, for a time, entire communities seemed engrossed in its exchange. And yet Jews and non-Jews in the Mediterranean feather market would experience a regional feather bust even before the global feather market collapsed. Due to the emergence of new, more efficient east-to-west trading routes, by 1907 nearly all exportable plumes were redirected westward to the Atlantic coast. With the Mediterranean no longer serving as the region's principal feather conduit, traditional Jewish feather hubs like Tripoli were edged out of the global market well before a shortage of demand upended the feather trade.

The evolutions that remapped modern Mediterranean feather commerce resulted in financial catastrophe for many Jews in the industry. Others were able to respond to these developments fluidly: by segueing into new trading niches, by moving closer to feather sources in the southern Sudan, and by relocating their operations overseas. Strikingly, these reactions—like the actions of Mediterranean Jews who thrived in the early years of the feather boom—were enabled by the commercial skills and diasporic contacts Jews in the feather trade possessed because they were Jews and members of sub-ethnic Jewish diasporas.

THE "BARBARY PLUME" AND GLOBAL FEATHER COMMERCE

The geography of turn-of-the-century Mediterranean feather commerce was obscured by contemporary mythology, mainly because the nomenclature Europeans and Americans assigned to the much coveted "Barbary plume" betrayed ignorance of the complexity of Mediterranean commerce. So-called Barbary feathers did not originate on the Barbary Coast, but were gathered and hunted by settled and nomadic farmers in the semi-arid Sahel and along the southern edge of the Sahara; lesser quantities of plumes from East Africa and the Arabian Peninsula reached North African ports via Aden.[6] Ostrich feathers and eggs had been exported from these regions since antiquity, but commerce in the former goods intensified dramatically in the 1870s with the onslaught of the modern feather boom.[7] As European and American demand for plumes inflated their commercial value, more locals were drawn to ostrich hunting in the Sahel and southern Sahara. At the same time, the small-scale cultivation of ostriches began to proliferate in central Niger and in Sudan.[8]

The bulk of ostrich feathers destined for overseas export reached North Africa's ports by way of trans-Saharan camel caravan, transported with other commodities that were in demand, including gum, ivory, and gold dust. Myriad primary and secondary caravan routes crisscrossed North and West Africa in the early modern and modern period; some, particularly those with a primarily religious function, were oriented on an east-to-west axis, while others, especially ones that serviced overseas trade, ran south to north. The five principal trans-Saharan routes used in the feather trade ran south to north and included those linking Timbuktu to Essaouira (of which there were two, one through Tishit and the other through Toadeni), Kano to Tripoli, Bornu to Tripoli, and Wadai to Benghazi.

A contemporary scholar has suggested that, for "all major routes [of trans-Saharan commerce], markets and wholesale trade at every stage were administered by merchants and their representatives who worked together on the basis of ethnic ties."[9] The ostrich feather market was no exception, for it too depended on the smooth integration of a complex ethnic and commercial mosaic. Once ostriches were hunted and skinned in the south, they were purchased by three groups from the north: Ghadamasi merchants (from the commercial entrepôt of Ghadames), Swiri merchants (from the trading hub of Essaouira),

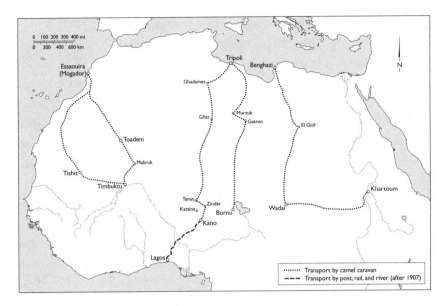

Map of the principal trading routes by which ostrich plumes were conveyed from the southern Sahara and Sahel to sites of export in North and West Africa

many Jews among them, and members of the Sanusiya Muslim Brotherhood, an economic and political power in the eastern Sahara. Ghadamasi and Swiri merchants operated on the three major trade routes that extended south from Tripoli and Essaouira, while the Sanusiya dominated commerce on the route from Benghazi to Wadai, though Jews, too, were represented on this route.[10] Each of these mercantile communities relied on representatives in villages and towns along trans-Saharan trade routes who would buy ostrich skins directly from hunters or through the intermediary of village heads, thereafter preparing for their export northward. As feathers were readied for export to North Africa's port cities, other ethnic groups were employed in turn. Ghadamasi merchants commissioned transport animals and armed escorts from the Tuareg people of the Sahara, who operated out of the main transit centers, Ghat and Aïr, and who also ran refreshment stands along the caravan route; Swiri merchants employed residents of Aït Baha as conveyers and traders of goods.[11] There is evidence that in an earlier period Jews led their own caravans between the Sudan and North Africa, transporting luxurious items of feathers, ivory, and gold northward, and linen, silk, velvet, and iron on their return to the south. By the late nineteenth century, however, they seem to have absented themselves from this process.[12]

Though ostrich feathers were shipped across the Mediterranean from Essaouira, Algiers, Tunis, Alexandria, and Cairo, it was Tripoli that emerged as North Africa's principal feather conduit in the late nineteenth century. In 1870, £16,000 worth of ostrich plumes were exported from the western Sudan to Tripoli; by 1874, the quantity had risen to £100,000, and by 1883 to more than double this amount. From the early 1870s to 1883, the value of feathers shipped from Tripoli to Europe had increased fifteen-fold: £292,000 worth of ostrich plumes were brought to Tripoli for export to Europe in 1883 alone.[13] During this period ostrich plumes were commanding higher prices in Europe, and trade in West and North Africa was also growing to keep pace with demand. At the height of the feather boom, ostrich plumes represented fully half of Tripoli's exports to Europe by value and nearly 80 percent of the city's imports from the Sahara. Though the value and quantity of feather imports to Tripoli slumped in the late 1880s—as they did throughout the global market—the plumes' value revived thereafter and remained robust as late as 1906.[14]

Tripoli came to serve as the southern Mediterranean's principal port of plume export in great part because of the actions of the Ottoman regime, under whose sovereignty the city fell. The Ottoman authorities in Tripolitania had for some time actively protected and encouraged feather commerce through this North African city. To ensure the port would remain a vital center of the feather trade and to hedge against French interests, the Ottomans conquered the crucial trans-Saharan entrepôt of Ghat in 1875. In the years that followed, new Ottoman administrative districts were introduced in the vicinity, notably in the Tuareg region. Simultaneously, the government offered economic privileges to merchants who utilized the Kano-Tripoli caravan route, which traveled through Ghat.[15] For a time, these measures prevented most of the city's export firms from relying on new east-to-west trading networks that ferried feathers from the southern Sudan by way of Kano downriver to the Atlantic, and thus out of the reach of Ottoman tax authorities.

Finally (and most importantly from the perspective of Tripoli's Jewish feather exporters), the Ottoman state protected so-called foreign merchants operating on its terrain. According to agreements dating to the early sixteenth century, "foreign" merchants living in Ottoman territory were under the protection of foreign consuls—principally those of France—and were consequently subject to reduced taxes and customs duties. Because most Tripolitanian Jews in the feather trade were Livornese and Italian subjects, they too were eligible for foreign protection, even though in most cases their families had lived in Tripoli for centuries.[16] As a result, many Tripolitanian Livornese Jews acquired Italian or French protection while others sought to acquire protégé status from British and American governmental representatives.[17] The economic advantages afforded by these relationships greatly enhanced Jews' success as feather exporters in Tripoli. As far away as Constantinople, this symbiosis of Ottoman policy and Jewish mercantile practice (and the unlikely fact of African Jewish ostrich feather merchants) was heralded in the Ladino popular press.[18]

The constructive impact Ottoman policies had on the feather trade are illustrated by comparison with two other cases. Both Essaouira and Algiers might have become centers of North African feather exports at the turn of the twentieth century: Essaouira because of its historic importance to the plumage trade, and Algiers because of the French colonial government's desire to capitalize on the industry in the future. However, in neither case were the relevant authorities able or willing to foster feather commerce. As Daniel Schroeter has shown vividly, the Moroccan port of Essaouira had long been a crucial nexus of the intra- and extra-regional feather trade, in part because the royal court had subsidized and protected traders as a way of consolidating power. Yet by the late nineteenth century, the Moroccan royal palace was deeply in debt to the French and the British as a result of the Spanish-Moroccan War. Using this debt as leverage, French and British administrators pressured the Moroccan state to liberalize its taxation system, overturning the traditional relationship between the sultan and the local mercantile elite. Such policies had the effect of promoting European trading interests but were a death knell to the commercial vitality of overseas traders in Essaouira and other Moroccan centers.[19] Jewish fortunes were dragged down with the flagging state even though in Morocco, as in Ottoman Tripolitania, many Jewish mercantile families had begun to serve as protégés and consular agents of European or American powers.[20] Many Moroccan feather merchants thus faced bankruptcy even as the value of Barbary plumes was on the rise; largely as a result, the modern feather boom eluded most merchants in the erstwhile feather hub of Essaouira.

Algiers might also have been a center of modern feather commerce, as the French colonial authorities—like the British and the Ottomans—were eager to capitalize on the plume trade in and through their territories. As early as the mid-nineteenth century, French consular agents, civil servants, and agricultural economists began to debate whether the state ought to facilitate intensive ostrich farming in Algeria, Senegal, or other territories under French control. As early as 1859, the Société d'Acclimatation of Paris offered financial rewards for the successful domestication of the ostrich in French North Africa.[21] Other representatives of French interests proposed intervening in the feather trade more aggressively, by redirecting trans-Saharan caravan networks toward Algiers, where it could be controlled and taxed, or by conquering crucial trading entrepôts.[22] The French state was at first responsive to these suggestions. In 1894 it conquered Timbuktu in order (among other reasons) to maintain oversight of regional trade, and in 1907 it conducted an inquiry into the viability of domesticating the ostrich in French Sudan.[23] The results of this test were positive, but the French resisted either subsidizing intensive ostrich farming or attempting to reroute the geography of the feather trade to their advantage.[24] Perhaps their reluctance was due to "want of an enterprising spirit among the colonists," as one American consul claimed, or perhaps the French, like the British, eschewed trans-Saharan trade as unsafe, expensive, and, because of its importance to the slave trade, inherently unethical.[25] Whatever the causes, France's interest in capitalizing on the ostrich feather industry remained largely undeveloped, at least relative to what the British achieved in the Cape and the Ottomans in Tripolitania. As a result, Algiers failed to become a crucial hub in the modern ostrich feather market.

MEDITERRANEAN JEWS AND THE BARBARY PLUME

Mediterranean Jews' prominence in the ostrich plume trade dates at least to the early modern period. In the seventeenth, eighteenth, and early nineteenth centuries, Jews facilitated the export of feathers from North Africa (and, in smaller quantities, the Eastern Mediterranean) to southern Europe, particularly the ports of Livorno, Venice, Trieste, and Marseilles. Other European cities imported plumes as well; Jewish family firms in Tripoli, for example, oversaw the exports of plumes to Spain, where they sold them to members of the aristocracy in the heart of the Jewish quarter.[26] It was Livorno, however, that predominated as the world's early modern ostrich feather entrepôt and as the hub of Mediterranean Jewish feather commerce. Before London's ascendancy to the feather industry's center stage, fully 75 percent of ostrich plumes exported from North Africa traveled first to Livorno. There the trade in plumes was said to be handled by four or five ostrich feather firms that commanded large profits.[27] From the perspective of Jewish history, the emergence of Livorno as the world's first global feather capital is not surprising. This Mediterranean port was the center of an expansive early modern mercantile network in which Jews were preeminent. In addition, a Livornese Jewish mercantile diaspora—consisting mostly of Jews of Portuguese origin—was then spreading across the Mediterranean, with members settling and conducting trade in all of the region's principal ports.[28]

This mercantile geography evolved in direct response to the ascension of London in the global feather industry. The ongoing transformation was noted by industry observers in 1858:

> Leghorn [Livorno], after the decline of its commerce with the Levant, remained the great entrepôt of ostrich feathers, and did business in that article to the amount of about 1,200,000 francs annually. But . . . London has gradually become the principal center of that branch of trade, and Leghorn now only does business to about half the preceding amount.[29]

As demand for and the price of plumes skyrocketed and London's centrality to the global trade in plumage was cemented, Livorno's importance to the industry declined. By around 1860 the vast majority of ostrich feathers were shipped from North Africa's ports directly to the British capital, and the number of Mediterranean Jewish family firms in London and Paris began to grow accordingly.[30]

As the modern feather boom accelerated, Mediterranean Jewish feather merchants expanded their operations in North Africa, West Africa, across the Sahara, and in Europe, staking their financial fortunes on the enduring value of the ostrich plume. In the late nineteenth century, settled Jewish feather merchants were said to operate throughout southwestern Morocco, in Taroudant, Iligh, Goulimim, and Oufran, along the edges of the Sahara, and in cities like Tafilalt and Marrakesh, while itinerant Jewish feather merchants conducted business in the eastern regions of Morocco, where they commanded enormous profits.[31] In Ottoman-controlled Tripolitania, large-scale Jewish feather merchants could be found in the port cities of Tripoli and Benghazi, while Jewish itinerant merchants visited regional market towns along the Mediterranean coast and in the Tripolitanian mountains.[32] According to one scholar of North African Jewry, in Tripolitania, "the trade in ostrich feathers was wholly in Jewish hands."[33] In Tripoli alone, two hundred Jewish families owed their living to the trade in feathers in the last years of the nineteenth century (fig. 13).[34] Jews dominated the export of feathers from Cairo and Alexandria, and they likely played important roles in the sale and sorting of ostrich plumes from the Arabian Peninsula that took place at transit stations along the Nile—notably at Asyut—and between the Red Sea and Cairo.[35] Finally, Yemeni Jews traveled from Aden to Ethiopia and Somalia to purchase feathers they would process at home, ultimately reexporting them to Britain and Egypt.[36] In the words of a European observer writing in 1857:

> The Jews are almost everywhere the purchasers [of ostrich feathers]; since it is they who venture afar, visiting the most distant markets or the most remote tribes from European centres. Furthermore, they know better than anyone the customs, language, and means of exchange suited to the style of the Arabs.[37]

In addition to serving as prominent feather buyers, Jews financed the conveyance of feathers from the southern Sahara and Sahel to port cities in the north. Because trans-Saharan trade tended to operate on credit, the role of financiers was particularly crucial to the smooth functioning of the feather industry. For much of the nineteenth century, commercial firms in Tripoli and Essaouira, many owned by Jews, advanced Ghadamasi merchants goods imported from Europe—primarily English calico but also beads, mirrors, paper, spices, perfumes, tea, sugar, copper, and other goods—to sell on their return voyage south to Timbuktu, Kano, or Bornu. After the passage of six months to a year—the time it typically took a trans-Saharan caravan to complete a round trip—these firms would be repaid in ostrich feathers and other commodities that were subsequently carried northward.[38] Significantly, Jewish financiers usually did not bankroll the entire route from Tripoli to Kano. Instead, they supported Ghadamasi merchants' voyage as far as the commercial entrepôt of Ghat, after

Figure 13. Jewish-owned feather manufactory in Tripoli, ca. 1900. It is likely that the two men in Western attire (second and fourth from left, back row), and possibly the men standing beside them (at left and third from left, back row), are the firm's owners, and that the others are their employees. (Courtesy Or-Shalom Center, Bat-Yam)

which those merchants financed the remainder of their trip themselves. This dynamic changed in the 1870s as the value of ostrich feathers began to rise. With plumes commanding ever higher sums in Europe, it became desirable for Jewish mercantile firms in Tripoli to finance the passage of goods all the way to Kano, thereby maximizing their profits. At the same time, feather investors extended their loans to a period of three years.[39] To put this another way, as a result of the emergent ostrich boom, Tripolitanian Jewish firms were dealing informally in ostrich futures: extending larger quantities of credit for longer periods of time, staking their fortunes on the enduring and escalating value of feathers.[40]

Jewish blue-collar workers, meanwhile, predominated in the handling and processing of feathers in Essaouira, Tunis, Tripoli, Alexandria, Cairo, and Aden.[41] Due to local trading practices, the labor of this industrial workforce differed dramatically from that of colored sorters in the Cape or Jewish feather processors in New York and London. Workers in the latter contexts handled feathers that had been cut or plucked from live birds; by contrast, feather handlers in North Africa were responsible for plucking plumes from the skin of dead birds, subjecting the feathers to a series of treatments thereafter. What explains this difference in regional practice? In the ostrich hunting and rearing regions of the Sahel and southern Sahara, it was standard practice to kill an ostrich for its plumes, a practice that eventually decimated the Saharan ostrich population.[42] Before there was widespread awareness of the bird's impending extinction, the killing of ostriches for their feathers was thought to afford two advantages. Transporting the hide of a skinned beast intact allowed merchants in the north to profit from the sale of the bird's skin as well as its plumage; it also concentrated all aspects of feather handling in North Africa's ports (and, to a lesser extent, in Aden).

According to a French consul in Tripoli, writing in 1879, in that city feather plucking and sorting was something of a local Jewish industry:

> When the [trans-Saharan camel] caravans arrive in Tripoli, the feathers are still stuck to the hide of a skinned bird. They are delivered in this state to certain Jewish workers whose job it is to pull them out and then proceed to sort them by color and size and finally to classify them . . . after which they are arranged into distinct packets of varied value. This work constitutes a sort of local industry. But due to its simplicity it could be practiced anywhere else.[43]

As with so many things, the cultural politics that undergirded feather sorting were not so simple as they appeared. Feather sorting might have been practiced elsewhere or by other groups, but in practice this was a Jewish trade, undertaken even within the boundaries of the Jewish quarter.[44] Astonishingly, when it became financially advantageous for the higher grades of ostrich plumes to be exported from the Sahara by parcel post and trans-Atlantic steamship via Lagos, as it did after about 1907, the feathers were transshipped from London back to Tripoli for processing.[45]

Wherever feather sorting occurred, it was a dirty, unhealthy, and stigmatized job. In the Cape Colony, London, and New York, this task was undertaken by those of the most modest means; in some contexts, sorters doubled their risk of contracting tuberculosis as a result of their labors.[46] That it should be the terrain of Maghrebi Jews in North Africa is a reminder of the widespread poverty—and, perhaps, subordinate social status—this population faced at the turn of the twentieth century. Maghrebi Jews were poised to fill this occupational niche not only because they were poor residents of port cities; in addition, they would have been able to use their expertise from the processing and tanning of animal skins, both highly significant occupations for the North African and North African Jewish economy.[47]

What little we know of the quotidian work of Jewish feather sorters comes from William Coffin, an American consul stationed in Tripoli in the early twentieth century. Like many American followers of the global feather trade, Coffin's interest in feather commerce was motivated by self-interest. The consul's own ambition was to introduce American-made cotton cloth and yarn to North Africa: as a result, he conducted detailed surveys of the state of trade in the region. According to Coffin's account, "Arab" (likely Ghadamasi) merchants delivered feathers to Tripoli sorters in mixed bundles. Thereafter: "The feathers are washed and sorted here, but are not dyed or curled. They are washed in soapy water, and when still wet are beaten. A handful of them are taken by the stems and slapped against the floor with a force that to the uninitiated would seem to be enough to break them into pieces."[48] Relying on skilled sorters was critical for feather merchants, explained Coffin, for in the course of the cleaning, sorting, and packaging of ostrich plumes, 10–20 percent of the feathers could be destroyed.[49] Plucked and sorted, having traveled many miles and changed hands many times, the ostrich feathers were at last ready for export overseas.

What can be said of the Mediterranean Jewish feather merchants or families who oversaw the export process? According to a study conducted by the Alliance Israélite Universelle, there were fourteen large and thirty-five medium-sized European export houses in Tripoli owned by Jews in 1890.[50] Of these, three were prominent in Tripoli's feather world: the houses of Hassan, Arbib, and Nahum. All of these Jewish mercantile families were of Livornese origin and, like most of the wealthiest Jewish businessmen in Tripoli, foreign subjects.[51] The houses of Hassan, Arbib, and Nahum all maintained offices in Europe as well as Tripoli; as we have seen, the Hassan family had commercial toeholds in Manchester, London, and the Port of Tyne, as did the Arbib family in Manchester, London, Venice, and Paris. In Paris, the Arbib and Hassan families, along with the Livornese Jewish Guetta family, dominated feather imports.[52] In Tripoli itself, the Hassan and Arbib families owned no less than three separate firms in the late nineteenth century, while the Nahums and Arbibs even owned the boats they used to ship goods to England.[53] Archival evidence suggests that the Hassan family attempted to become shipping agents as well.[54] Crucially, all of these families appear to have traded in commodities other than ostrich feathers. The Nahums made much of their fortune in alfalfa, the Hassans in esparto grass, and the Arbibs in ivory, cloth, Murano glass, and antiques. Commercial diversification such as this was prudent in times of success and quite necessary when a single commodity's appeal waned.

Familial contacts, it is clear, proved crucial to the success and expansion of Jewish feather firms. For example, after Eugenio Arbib and his cousin Enrico moved from Tripoli to Britain in the 1860s, family members in North Africa served as their overseas business partners. Eugenio and Enrico also brought cousins and nephews from Tripoli to Britain to serve as apprentices; ultimately these young men, armed with newly acquired British citizenship, would return home to create new branches of the family business.[55] Consider, also, the case of Dinar Ohana, the most prominent Jewish ostrich feather merchant in Morocco. Differing from most Moroccan Jewish feather traders, Ohana's operations thrived into the twentieth century. This was due in large part to his relationship with his uncle Abraham Corcos, who, together with his brother Jacob, represented one of the most important Jewish mercantile families in Essaouira. Corcos was appointed United States vice consul in 1862 and thereafter granted Ohana financial protection and the coveted status of protégé. These actions insulated Ohana from the steep taxes and tolls newly imposed by the state that drove so many Moroccan traders out of the business. As a result of Ohana's familial and business relationship with Corcos, he flourished as a feather merchant even as other Moroccan traders saw their export operations flounder.[56]

Acts of familial allegiance such as this proved crucial to Mediterranean Jewish feather exporters in all the hubs of regional commerce. Though the importance of such allegiance is difficult to quantify, its symbolic magnitude is suggested in a story retold by Nahum Slouschz, a Franco-Jewish Orientalist who conducted research on North African Jewry in the 1920s. According to Slouschz, the following "published statement illustrates the spirit of" Tripoli's Jewish feather merchants.

During the panic in the ostrich feather trade, a merchant was ruined. To meet the demands of the creditors he brought them even the jewels of his wife. The father of [Jewish feather merchant] M. L. had lent seventy-five thousand francs to one of his nephews, who had established himself in business somewhere in Africa. The latter lost his entire fortune in speculation. M. L., uneasy about his loan, telegraphed his nephew, but received no reply. Months passed. He gave up the money as lost. Then, one day, he received a thick sealed envelope. He opened it, and found seventy-five thousand francs accompanied by a simple note in Judeo-Arabic: "Mine I have lost, but yours is sacred."[57]

Slouschz's tale highlights much of what was unique about the Mediterranean Jewish feather trading diaspora: it was contingent on familial fidelity, conditioned by risk, sustained by credit, geographically peripatetic, and last but not least, navigated in Judeo-Arabic.

The importance of shared language to the Jewish feather traders of the Mediterranean reminds us that, when it came to building commercial allegiances, the specifics of identity—not so much ethnicity, necessarily a broad category, as sub-ethnicity, were as crucial an element of human capital as was Jewishness in itself. Most Jewish feather traders—including those of Sephardi and Livornese origin—were speakers of Judeo-Arabic, and they tended to keep their account books in this language as well.[58] So important was knowledge of Judeo-Arabic to the smooth operation of the feather industry that non-Jews in the trade, including European merchants and Muslim chiefs, corresponded in the language through Jewish interpreters and secretaries.[59] A propensity for multilingualism also allowed Jews to serve as intra- and extra-regional brokers. Knowledge of Arabic and other local languages permitted negotiation with trading partners in North Africa, the Sahara and Sahel, and East Africa, while knowledge of European languages—some of which was preserved within families, some of which was acquired in schools funded by the European Jewish elite—was essential for overseas trade.

Having explored the involvement of Jews across the geographic breadth and industrial length of the Mediterranean ostrich feather commodity chain, it is useful to consider how Jews' prominence in this commercial niche was perceived by non-Jews in the industry. One late-nineteenth-century industry observer who was struck by Jews' visibility at every tier and across the geographic breadth of the Mediterranean ostrich feather trade suggested that

Jews seemed "to be everywhere" when it came to the feather trade, a statement of interest both for its insight and for its indelicacy. Jews were, indeed, well represented in all the geographic locales and across all tiers of this industry, but to many observers, this fact appeared the result of conspiracy rather than historical conditions. This argument was made most often in reference to the Jews of Tripoli, where many Jewish families were tied to the late-nineteenth-century feather trade.[60] For example, Felix Matthews, American consul-general to Morocco, argued in 1881:

> The competition among the Jews and the almost entire monopolization of this trade [in ostrich feathers] by those people has enhanced the value [of feathers], for by contriving to exclude the Christians as much as possible from this commerce, they are often induced to trade beyond their capital, overstocking the market, making a forced trade, and throwing the profits which before were reaped by the Europeans into the hands of the natives.[61]

Such cries of monopoly were echoed by others. Six years after Matthews recorded his views, a second American consul, Cuthbert Jones, expressed worry about what he perceived as the informality of extra-regional trade. Merchants in Tripoli, Jones noted, were given large and extended credit by English banks that also served as their brokers. Tripolitanian merchants thus exported esparto grass and imported cotton goods (among other articles), all the while never dealing in cash. This arrangement, entirely lacking in "honest competition," according to Jones, made American entry into regional trade all but impossible.[62]

Americans were not alone in feeling edged out of the feather market. French civil engineer Jules Oudot, author of an influential study of the feather trade written in 1880, described Tripoli's Jewish feather merchants as "strangling," "robbing," and "lying." According to Oudot, Jewish "exploiters" had also turned the commercial houses of London and Paris against Muslim caravan leaders who wished to conduct overseas business. Precisely how this malfeasance was operated Oudot was not certain: either Jews convinced European buyers to refuse competitors' feathers, he hypothesized, or they extended prices so low that caravan leaders would be "forever discouraged from selling their merchandise without going through middle-men."[63] Oudot's vitriol extended even to the Jewish blue-collar feather workforce, who, he argued, chronically falsified their bundles by weighing them down with "all measure of strange matter and sand."[64]

Other sources expressed similar caution. Speaking, for example, of how difficult it could be for an outsider to break into the Mediterranean feather industry, Julius de Mosenthal, an Anglo-Jew who wrote an extensive study on the ostrich feather trade in 1879, was warned by an industry insider that only the most experienced buyers should expect to succeed. Even before feathers were exported from North Africa's ports, Mosenthal's informant counseled, the plumes changed hands many times and were classed and reclassed, sorted and resorted, "for the purpose of deceiving the buyer as to the real contents of the bundles," which were "fraudulently packed" so "that the inexperienced buyer is often completely victimized."[65] A Parisian commercial journal offered similar advice to its readers: "The trade in ostrich feathers requires a good deal of experience, as it is easy to be deceived in the quality when they are not prepared."[66]

Accusations that the feather trade was steeped in trickery or that Mediterranean Jews maintained a chokehold on it may have had some basis in reality, particularly when it came to overseas trading. In North Africa, as in the Cape and London, non-Jews found feather exports impenetrable, insular, and highly competitive. Consider the case of the Muslim trader Mabruk ben Omar, sponsor of a caravan that connected western Sudan and Tripoli. With the support of the French consul, Mabruk unsuccessfully attempted to "break clear of the middlemen who had a monopoly of the marketing of ostrich plumes in Tripoli by dealing directly with London and Paris importers."[67] Was his failure—and that of countless other French and American merchants and government representatives—an indicator of a Jewish monopoly? Mabruk and his French collaborator answered this question in the affirmative, as, likely, would have Oudot and Mosenthal's informant. However, all of these parties were admittedly self-interested: each aspired to capitalize on the feather boom or guide others to similar successes. Accusing Jewish feather merchants of monopoly, then, was not simply a means of explaining why Jews succeeded as feather exporters: it was also a way of understanding why European and American consuls general, civil engineers, and merchants found it so very difficult to circumvent or overtake the existing feather market.

Concerns about Jewish monopolistic practices also betrayed an ignorance of the myriad intra-ethnic, intra-religious, and diasporic trading relationships that were essential to the feather trade. What Mabruk and others may not have appreciated is that successful feather merchants needed more than plumes to succeed. They needed regional and extra-regional contacts in the south as well as in the north and across the Mediterranean: they benefited from historical expertise and connections in the various hubs of the trade and London in particular. Perhaps most important, they required a sense for the pace and tenor of the volatile feather market that could only be acquired over time.

Although the importance of such assets eluded European, Muslim, and American observers of the industry, their value was eminently clear to Jewish traders. Nowhere was this formulated more succinctly than in a letter that a group of Tripolitanian Jewish merchants wrote in 1880. The merchants, banded together under the name Delegates of Commerce of Tripoli, were determined to contradict the accusation by American consul Cuthbert Jones that trade in Tripoli was monopolistic. In their dispatch, the merchants emphasized that "their commercial advantage stemmed not from dishonest practice, but from a knowledge of local customs, languages, and business practices, all of which were necessary to the merchants here to be able to do business with peoples so different from Europeans."[68] As these merchants knew firsthand, across the Mediterranean Basin Jews in general and Livornese Jewish merchants in particular were in unique possession of all these specific forms of human capital.

Such credentials did not have everlasting value. In the Mediterranean, as in all the regional hubs of global feather commerce, the plumage trade was capricious. In this context, however, it proved even shorter lived than elsewhere. In contradistinction to the Cape, London, or New York, the Mediterranean branch of the global feather trade was stymied before 1914 and not by dwindling demand or global oversupply. Instead, a rather more local collapse of trans-Saharan and trans-Mediterranean feather commerce culminated in the first decade of the twentieth century. The causes of this process are manifold and include the increasing insecurity of trans-Saharan commerce, the emergence of new trading routes, and the encroachment of European control. Combined, these factors rendered trans-Saharan feather commerce obsolete, catalyzed the "fall" of Tripoli as a hub in the global feather market, and resulted in the movement of the majority of Jews out of the industry in this region. The following section explores these processes, considering how Mediterranean Jews involved in the feather trade weathered this cataclysmic shift in centuries-old regional commercial practices.

THE END OF TRANS-SAHARAN FEATHER COMMERCE AND
THE FALL OF TRIPOLI AS GLOBAL FEATHER HUB

What caused the Mediterranean ostrich feather trade to disappear nearly a decade before the global feather bust of 1914? By the early twentieth century the caravan route that linked Kano and Tripoli—the last and most important trans-Saharan route used in the feather trade—was becoming increasingly unviable. Traders on this path were ever more vulnerable to attack, both because the French occupation of a number of trading towns had provoked intra-ethnic disputes and because the proliferation of rifles in the region abetted banditry. What's more, new alternative trading routes threatened the preeminence of the trans-Saharan caravan. By 1903, the cost of sending goods by freight from Kano to Lagos and thence south overland and by river to the Atlantic coast had become comparable to that of trans-Saharan travel. Some years later, a rail line linking Kano and the port of Baro promised to reduce the cost of transshipment via the Gulf of Guinea by a third or even half.[69]

An additional factor that contributed to the feather trade's demise in the region was the intrusion of European influence. Non-Jews as well as Jews in the industry experienced some aspects of this process negatively: both were forced to contend with new political boundaries, which fractured traditional trading networks and routes and resulted in the proliferation of taxes and tolls. Other manifestations of colonial influence were particularly palpable to Jewish traders. Beginning in the nineteenth century, the European powers began to impose or encourage the abrogation of advantageous treatment long afforded certain "foreign" merchants, many Jews among them. As we have already seen, this process unfolded initially in Morocco, after the royal palace liberalized its taxation structures under pressure from the British and the French.

Like the Moroccan regime, the Ottoman regime was also pressured by Britain and France to liberalize its economic and legal structures in the course of the nineteenth century. These outside demands, combined with domestic pressure for reform, resulted in the sultanate's adoption of an almost century-long process of legal reform.[70] When it came to the commercial realm, the Ottoman regime proved inconsistent in its willingness to change: even in the face of other juridical reforms, many so-called "foreign" merchants who lived on Ottoman soil continued to benefit from the financial protection of the regime into the twentieth century. State protection notwithstanding, Jewish merchants in Otto-man Tripolitania were nonetheless sensitive to the economic repercussions of European colonial influence. As the nineteenth century came to a close, French merchants and consuls in the region proved increasingly unwilling to affix the advantageous status of protégé on Livornese Jewish merchants they had begun to view as competitors.[71] Given that the discrepancy between taxes applied to local and foreign merchants was enormous, the loss of protégé status proved debilitating to many.[72] Largely as a result, those in the Mediterranean branch of the feather trade found themselves increasingly unable to offset the soaring expenses associated with new taxes and tolls—despite the fact that they were operating in a booming global market.

As a result of these factors (among others), the quantity of feathers ex-ported from North Africa began to wane even before European and Ameri-can consumers turned against feather wearing. By 1904, Tripoli was exporting roughly a tenth of the feathers it had twenty years earlier. Three years later, the trade in plumage across the Sahara and in Tripoli itself had all but ceased.[73] Having maintained a place of preeminence in the trans-hemispheric feather trade for centuries, the city of Tripoli was essentially falling out of the global market.

Some Jewish feather merchants found themselves paralyzed by these devel-opments. In the years after 1907, the number of bankruptcies filed by Tripoli's merchant community soared. Others in the industry proved resilient. Many Jewish merchants left Tripoli and even North Africa altogether, for Khartoum, Kano, Paris, and other locales.[74] According to an article in 1924, the collapse of the Kano–Tripoli trade route produced an entirely new community of Tripoli-tanian merchants near the Parisian Porte St. Denis: this diasporic community alone boasted over twenty mercantile firms.[75] Given that the Parisian feather market was already more or less cornered by the families of Arbib, Guetta, and Hassan, these new émigré firms were unlikely to deal in plumes. Perhaps they, like other Tripolitanian Jewish merchants, moved into or increased their investment in other commodities, among them esparto grass, skins, and pea-nuts.[76] All these responses to regional change showed the inherent plasticity of the Mediterranean Jewish commercial diaspora. Many of the skills that allowed Mediterranean Jews to excel in feather commerce ultimately proved transferable.

It is likely that Jewish blue-collar feather workers were less flexible in the face of crisis, but little is known of how they, as a group, responded to the collapse of trans-Saharan commerce. Fortunately, we are able to trace the path of one such individual overseas. Sometime after the arrest of Mediterranean feather commerce, a blue-collar worker from Algiers took leave of her family and home in order to seek employment in the Parisian industry. A "pretty girl of twenty-four," this "Mademoiselle M." was interviewed in 1913 by Elizabeth Sargeant, a social reformer conducting a study of the Parisian artificial flower and feather industries on behalf of the American Russell Sage Foundation.[77] According to Sargeant's account, Mlle. M. was highly skilled, very serious, and inclined to spend "nothing on frivolity." She shared a small room with another young woman, spent little on food, and relied on her parents for her clothing. Abstemiousness notwithstanding, Mlle. M. proved unable to support herself.[78] Despite the existence of a feather workers' union in Paris, she, like most female workers in the industry, was simply not paid a living wage: ostrich feather workers in the city earned as little as 43 percent (or as much as 65 percent) of their peers in the artificial flower industry, on average.[79] The story of Mlle. M. is striking in two respects. This woman's move to Paris hints that she shared a measure of geographic and social flexibility with those who operated at higher echelons of the feather industry. On the other hand, the contacts and elasticity she possessed did not outweigh her class. As in so many other cases, Jewishness was but an ingredient of human capital that individuals brought to the feather trade, and it alone could never determine success.

While some responded to the collapse of trans-Saharan and trans-Mediterranean feather commerce by emigrating overseas, others remained in the region and even tried to shift their base of operations closer to the feather source of the southern Sudan. Such was the path taken by S. Raccah and the London and Kano Trading Company. S. Raccah was a Tripolitanian Jew of Livornese origin whose family had conducted overseas trade in and through Livorno since at least the early eighteenth century (by the end of this century, the Raccahs, along with roughly a dozen other Livornese Sephardi families, had come to dominate trade between North Africa and Marseilles).[80] His own mercantile career began in the late nineteenth century, when he became associated with a Tripolitanian export firm with agents in Manchester that may or may not have dealt in plumes. With trade between Kano and Tripoli on the wane, Raccah chose to become "an independent middleman" in Kano and moved into the lucrative trade in peanuts. Over the course of the ensuing decade, Raccah came to handle more than a third of the Sudanese peanut crop, eventually exporting more of this commodity from Kano than all other European export firms combined (these had amalgamated into the United Africa Company several years before Raccah moved into the business).[81]

According to W. K. Hancock, a historian who interviewed Raccah in the 1940s, the trader's success could be explained by three factors: "low overhead charges, audacity, and hard work." Raccah employed few workers and, with their help, circumvented the local outstations through which most Europeans bought their goods. He relied on brokers in Europe rather than utilizing middlemen in the Sudan, and secured inexpensive shipping rates from a Livornese Jewish shipping firm. He reported to no one, eschewed the "buying limits" that European firms respected, and, not incidentally, worked fifteen hours a day. On the basis of these facts, Hancock concluded that Raccah's was at once "the story of an exceptional man" and "an emphatic variation upon the familiar West African theme" by which "hard-working and venturesome British merchants had time and time again fought the combinations and agreements and struggled upwards from small beginnings to established eminence."[82] There is perhaps truth to Hancock's claim, and yet the fact that Raccah was a Livornese Jew was also crucial to his success. Like so many Jewish merchants before him, Raccah relied on contacts across the Livornese and Tripolitanian Jewish diasporas that ran the full length and geographic breadth of the supply chain in which he operated. As much as any other factor, these contacts allowed Raccah to circumvent local middlemen and their fees, hedge against graft, and work with speed, autonomy, and efficiency.

There is no evidence that Raccah traded in plumes as well as peanuts in the years after he moved to Kano, though given that his business endured into the 1940s, this is not an unlikely scenario. Regardless, Raccah is relevant to our story insofar as he demonstrates how Jews involved in trans-Saharan and trans-Mediterranean commerce reacted to the shifting geography of regional trade in the first decades of the twentieth century. His story resonates with that of certain feather trading firms. The London and Kano Trading Company, for example, came to ferry a dizzying array of goods between Kano and Liverpool in the years after the Kano-Tripoli trading route collapsed. In addition to dealing in ostrich feathers, the company handled peanuts, hides, horns, gum, and champagne.[83] Because it was located close to the feather source, the London and Kano Trading Company was able, as was Raccah, to capitalize on the sustained demand for plumes even after so many North African firms had ceased to deal in the commodity. Buoyed by others' failure, the company continued to export feathers until 1916, when the feather crash and the First World War at last attenuated its operations.

In the roughly five years that the London and Kano Trading Company remained in operation, commerce in Barbary plumes was extremely limited. These feathers continued to command high prices in London's auctions, but the quantity available for sale was ever dwindling. The diminutive size of this branch of the global feather market is nicely illustrated by the following coincidences. Among the London and Kano Trading Company's principal feather suppliers was the emir of Katsina—the same dignitary who, in 1912, plied Russell Thornton's expedition with the Barbary birds they so desperately sought.[84] More striking still is the fact that a portion of the Kano and London Trading Company's plumes—shipped from Kano to Baro and thence across the Atlantic to Liverpool—was among the merchandise that a nearly bankrupt Isach Hassan stored under the name Richardson in warehouses in the British Port of Tyne.[85] The trans-Saharan feather trade had undergone cataclysmic changes in the early twentieth century, evolving to such an extent that it now stretched along the Atlantic rather than the Mediterranean. When all was said and done, however, the overseas exchange of Barbary plumes remained an incestuous operation over which a relatively small number of Jews and non-Jews presided.

The unexpected relationship between the London and Kano Trading Company and Isach Hassan returns us to the figure with whom this chapter began. As trans-Saharan feather commerce dwindled and Tripoli's importance to the global trade in plumes along with it, Hassan, too, adapted to the shifting global geography of the feather trade. This was achieved, in part, by the forging of commercial relationships in the feather source of Kano. But Hassan employed other tactics as well, including nurturing commercial alliances in the world's new heart of ostrich feather production, the Cape. To this end, Hassan courted a new (but, to us, familiar) partner in the feather world: the Russian, Jewish, South African feather merchant Isaac Nurick. In a series of letters exchanged by these men between 1911 and 1914, we find evidence of Hassan's efforts to transfer his skills to the trans-Atlantic market, thereby insulating himself from (and, he hoped, capitalizing on) the deteriorating state of trans-Saharan and trans-Mediterranean feather commerce. In so doing, Hassan bridged the three contexts we have thus far explored—South Africa, London, and the Mediterranean—at the same time facilitating alliances across the Mediterranean and Ashkenazi Jewish commercial diasporas.

ISACH HASSAN, FEATHER GO-BETWEEN

By the time Hassan brokered relations with Nurick, he had been working in London's feather industry for over twenty years, a period in which the Hassan family had extensive operations in Tripoli and overseas. Hassan had announced his services as an ostrich feather merchant in the pages of Kelly's Post Office Directory as early as 1883, but his name did not reappear in subsequent editions, leaving the nature of his business during this period murky.[86] Details of a meeting between Hassan and Nurick—if indeed they did meet in person—have eluded the historical record. What has been preserved is Hassan's first collaborative proposal, written in the summer of 1911. Hassan wrote Nurick with the suggestion that he be employed to "push the prices" of Nurick's feathers at auction. Apparently Nurick was not quick to agree, for Hassan wrote again several months later offering further details of the proposed arrangement:

> *The protection of your feathers*
> I await your decision. The conditions that I consider fair are that I protect your feathers and charge you ½ percent, and any lot left on my hands will be put in next sale [*sic*] and any profit or loss to the dividend. This is necessary, because by protecting your feathers I have to bid up and naturally a few lots must fall to me, and if they remain for my a/c [account], the loss might be more than the ½ percent you pay me commission.
>
> I do not propose this for the sake of my ½ percent, but for the sake of our friendship and I am willing to do it for you *for nothing* but any lot falling to me must be all for your a/c. In this way I make no profit and no loss.[87]

What Hassan was proposing was that he be paid half a percent of Nurick's earnings at a given auction in return for bidding aggressively on Nurick's feathers, which could be identified in brokers' catalogues by Nurick's mark. There was a risk that Hassan would inadvertently become the highest bidder, in which case, Hassan proposed, Nurick should pay for the feathers himself and "recycle" them by selling them at the next auction. Nurick appears to have accepted the terms extended by Hassan and he was assured almost immediately by Hassan that the arrangement was proving advantageous. After one subdued auction, for example, Hassan reported to Nurick that without their assistance his feathers would have sold for 10–15 percent less than they did.[88]

Flush with this success, Hassan unsuccessfully tried to lure Nurick "and his friends" into either utilizing or co-founding a shipping company for which (in Hassan's words) "I will be the agent of all the shippers who join us, and I hope that we will have the control as the others will not be able to compete: and I hope to save them some money in brokerage etc."[89] Hassan, it would seem, hoped to emulate the operations of the Nahums—another Livornese Tripolitanian Jewish family prominent in the feather trade—who used their own ships to convey goods from North Africa to Britain. Nurick shied away from the proposition, however, and there is no evidence that Hassan's venture ever was realized.

The quasi-legal nature of Hassan and Nurick's business relationship guaranteed that good relations would not endure. Hassan soon complained that he was not willing to pay cash for feathers "accidentally" acquired through vigorous bidding. He wished, instead, to have the cost of these feathers charged to a joint account in the names of Nurick and Hassan that was to be held by the brokerage firm Hale and Son. This arrangement required that Nurick and Hassan alert Hale and Son to their collaboration, thereby involving at least one person at the brokerage house in their shill. That person was Mr. Hale, whether father or son we do not know. In return for accommodating Nurick and Hassan's partnership, Hale seems to have secured a promise that Nurick would use Hale and Son as his exclusive broker.

Business relations among Nurick, Hassan, and Hale soured quickly. Hassan inevitably overspent at auction and when he attempted to "return" the mistakenly purchased feather lots to Hale, Hale refused to hold them against a joint Nurick-Hassan account, instead holding Hassan alone financially responsible.[90] To Hassan this was a financially and professionally risky arrangement. He had more to lose than a drop in the value of any inadvertently purchased feathers:

the regular attendees of London's ostrich feather auctions were able to recognize lots that made a second appearance at auctions on Mincing Street and were prejudiced against feather buyers who handled recycled goods. Remarked one observer of instances such as this: "The old hands in many cases know when it is so, and pass their remarks freely."[91]

Meanwhile, Hale had a vested interest in the success of Nurick's feather sales. At Hassan's urging, Hale began to bid against Hassan on Nurick's lots, with the knowledge that he, too, could "recycle" any feathers he was obliged to purchase at a future auction.[92] With this arrangement in place, Hale was extending three sources of credit to Nurick for feathers that he or his associates had bought or sold at auction: one account was in Nurick's own name, one was jointly appointed to Nurick and Hassan, and one was jointly appointed to Nurick and Hale. This annoyed Hassan, who felt he was losing commission at Hale's expense.[93] In the meantime, Hale piqued Nurick by attempting to counsel him about what feathers to buy, when, and in what quantity—judgments Nurick felt were his own to make. In anger, Nurick appears to have stopped employing Hale and Son as broker and Hassan as co-conspirator. A year passed before the two men would write again.

Hassan resumed his correspondence with Nurick at a moment when the global feather market was beginning to fall on hard times. In two letters written one day apart, Hassan pleaded with Nurick to take responsibility for some of the £400 debt that had been incurred when Hassan bid up Nurick's lots.[94] To sweeten the deal, Hassan offered Nurick presumably unwanted tips about feathers in vogue. A final letter, written just months before the ostrich feather market collapsed, reports that Hassan was unable to return to business, and that Hale and Son would soon be reporting the final status of the Nurick-Hassan account. Hassan's last recorded words to Nurick were stubbornly optimistic: "I trust we may soon be able to get this squared up."[95] In fact, nothing could have been further from the truth. The next time Nurick, Hassan, and Hale and Son had reason to communicate, it was through their respective liquidators, with both Hassan and Nurick demanding their debts be honored. The bottom had fallen out of the ostrich feather market, and neither Hassan nor Nurick would deal in plumes again.

Though ultimately Hassan and Nurick met the same financial fate, in the years before the feather crash the risks these two men faced differed because they were operating in different regional contexts. At the time of their correspondence, while some observers of the industry were accurately predicting an imminent feather crash, the value of Cape feathers was as high as it had ever been. The so-called Barbary plumes, too, commanded high prices at auction. But the quantity of such feathers available for sale in London was minuscule, and neither the Hassan family nor most Mediterranean Jews who had a historic toehold in the industry were managing to capitalize on existing demand. Thus although Hassan himself was not undone by the collapse of trans-Mediterranean feather commerce, when his correspondence with Nurick began he was already something of a ghost. In attempting to capitalize on the soaring value of Cape feathers, Hassan was living proof of the extinction of the trans-Saharan and trans-Mediterranean feather trade. In this sense, Hassan's correspondence with Nurick is immensely bittersweet. Hassan's letters reflect the resilience of one Mediterranean Jewish merchant, but they also remind us that Jewish mercantile culture in the Mediterranean was threatened. Plumes were not the last highly valued luxury good traded by Mediterranean Jews on the international market, but they were among them; with the collapse of the region's ostrich feather market, a centuries-old Jewish regional economic practice was becoming obsolete.

Hassan's relationship with Hale and Nurick is illuminating in one other respect. It reminds us that although the ostrich feather trade at the turn of the twentieth century was a global one, stretching across myriad geographic, political, and social contexts, the buying and selling of plumes was nonetheless something of an intimate affair. Observing, evaluating, and even wooing one's competitors was a necessary part of business, despite (or perhaps because of) the fact that they might reside thousands of miles away, speak another native tongue, or have a radically different genealogy. That so many in the industry were Jews may have eased this intimacy, the cultural boundaries of sub-ethnicity notwithstanding.

As we saw in the Introduction, it was a representative of the Hassan family who provided the essential link to Russell Thornton's Trans-Saharan Ostrich Expedition in the spring of 1912. According to Thornton's unpublished memoirs, his party of South African poachers made two stops on their way to West Africa: in London they were outfitted by Putnam and Mason of Piccadilly, and in Paris they met with a Jewish-Arab trader named Hassin, who served as a crucial informant.[96] There is little doubt that this "Hassin" was a member of the Tripolitanian Jewish Hassan family. Indeed, two pieces of evidence suggest that Isach Hassan and Thorton's Hassin may have been one and the same. Both men maintained offices in Paris; both were intimate with the same West African feather supplier, the emir of Katsina. In the British Port of Tyne, it must be remembered, Hassan stored feathers exported by the London and Kano Company on behalf of the emir. Hassin's counsel to Thornton's crew, meanwhile, greased the wheels required for the explorers to acquire 156 Barbary birds from the same dignitary.

One need not be convinced that Hassan and Hassin are one in order to be struck by how neatly these episodes illustrate the centrality of Jews to the modern trans-Saharan feather trade. That a Livornese Jew from Tripoli should serve as the critical intermediary to a South African explorer poised to smuggle contraband across imperial boundaries serves as a reminder that Jews were uniquely familiar with—and adept at navigating—the feather world. At the same time, if Hassin's encounter with Thornton hints at Mediterranean Jews' success as feather traders, it also echoes the implosion of trans-Saharan and trans-Mediterranean feather commerce, still a fresh development at the time of these men's encounter. When Hassin and Thornton had their secret meeting in Paris, none in the feather world knew that the international market for ostrich feathers faced imminent collapse. But those with a mooring in the Mediterranean feather market were already aware that their regional economy would never regain its footing. In this climate, for a feather merchant to diversify his investments—by moving into the trade of esparto grass or peanuts, for example—was an obvious means of hedging against risk. Similarly, for Hassin to traffic in information that might imperil a mercantile network he himself had a stake in was but a means of using knowledge and human capital to his advantage. If Mediterranean Jews were, as a group, well poised to pursue plumes, some proved adept at retreating from them.

In certain respects, Mediterranean Jews in the feather trade were not so very different from their American Jewish peers. In the American context (as in all others thus far explored), Jews of varied backgrounds and classes brought distinct elements of human capital to the feather industry. Like Mediterranean Jews, American Jews at all tiers of the ostrich feather industry exhibited versatility and geographical flexibility in the face of a volatile global market. They too struggled against the economic sway of London's feather market; they too forged ties with nascent feather sources. To explore these endeavors, we leave the Mediterranean for the strike lines of immigrant New York and the budding corporate farms of the American West, Southwest, and South.

CHAPTER 4

The American Feather World

In late October 1888, forty women employed by the New York–based ostrich feather manufacturing firm of Lowenstein and Gray went on strike rather than accept a dramatic reduction in wages. By evening, the strikers had chosen to be represented by the Working Women's Union and the organization had dispatched a representative to meet with the management of Lowenstein and Gray. Lowenstein expressed his willingness to pay his workers their original wages "provided his girls return to work as non-unionists," but they demurred, declaring "they would never leave the union."[1] Their actions—and the callousness of their employers—proved infectious. In the months that followed, workers at almost every ostrich feather manufactory across the Lower East Side joined their strike. The work stoppage lasted five months and pitted at least a thousand mostly female ostrich feather workers—many of them Russian Jewish immigrants or the children of Russian Jewish immigrants—against their mostly Jewish employers, the ostrich feather manufacturers of New York.[2]

Pay cuts were a recurring threat to ostrich feather workers in 1888, and the strike that began in October was not the first work stoppage the industry had witnessed.[3] Since 1886, the global ostrich feather trade had encountered a severe suppression in demand and, consequently, a 75 percent drop in prices. At the same time, American tariffs on imported ostrich feathers had not been reduced or lifted, and many manufacturers, the firm of Lowenstein and Gray among them, meted out their financial hardship on their employees. When the strike against Lowenstein and Gray reached the New York State Board of Arbitration in early December 1888, ostrich feather manufacturer Isidore Cohnfeld testified that "the raw material in the feather trade had come down about 90 percent in prices, the prices to the jobbing trade had been reduced 75 percent, and the wages of the girls had been reduced 50 percent within the past six years." These wages, he continued, "rose and fell in proportion to the rise and fall of the values of the goods in the market."[4] Experienced feather workers, for their part, testified that four years earlier they had earned $25–30 a week and averaged $1,200 a year: in 1888, by contrast, the same feather handler could count on only $12 a week during the busy season, an average worker $7–8 for the same period, and the least remunerated a mere 45 cents a day. When the workers complained to their employers that "girls could not make a living wage under the reduction," Lowenstein and Gray claimed they preferred to reduce wages rather than discharge half their staff.[5] Cohnfeld, who also dramatically reduced employees' wages, justified his actions by comparing a well-manufactured ostrich plume to a fine painting and the feather industry to the world of art: "A Micael Angelo [sic] might get scores of thousands of dollars for one painting and a simple 'brush slinger' might not get 50 cents. So one girl could do her work much better than another, and would deserve much better pay."[6]

The girls, boys, men, and women who made up New York's ostrich feather workforce faced labor conditions similar to those of the many thousands of workers who undergirded the garment, fashion, and millinery industries of New York's Lower East Side. They worked in unsanitary spaces for long hours and were pressured to take work home: most were paid low wages, without the guarantee of equal compensation for comparable work. To understand fully the position of New York's strikers, however, one must also appreciate how profoundly the American market for ostrich feathers was shaped by global conditions—and why it proved so difficult for workers at all levels of the industry to circumvent these conditions. New York's ostrich feather handlers labored at an impossible intersection: between the global economic market for feathers and attempts by their employers to harness the American potential to reduce the economic fluctuation that adversely affected all in the trade. These endeavors included petty attempts to reduce employees' wages, but extended to ambitious efforts to develop ostrich farms in the American West, Southwest, and South that might emancipate American consumers from an imported commodity—in the process earning its producers and processors a fortune.

If New York's ostrich feather workers were squeezed between the conditions of a global market and the ambitions of their employers, the New York feather industry itself was situated between London and those arid regions in the United States where American, South African, and British feather manufacturers and financiers (Jews prominent among them) funded corporate ostrich farms. New York's feather market was, on the one hand, "pushed" by London. In London the volatile prices of ostrich feathers were set, and because ostrich feathers reached American consumers via London they were heavily taxed by the American authorities.[7] (These tariffs, which were widely viewed as gratuitous, provoked the New York representative of I. Salaman and Company to sue the American government.)[8] On the other hand, New York's feather market was "pulled" by California, Arizona, Georgia, and other homes of the budding ostrich industry. These would-be suppliers of plumes promised to wrench the American feather worker free of the volatile international market and New York's ostrich feather manufacturers free of heavy tariffs imposed by the federal government.

Those who supported the endeavors of America's first ostrich farms at the turn of the twentieth century—the farmers, financiers, and managers, the allied feather manufacturers and sellers, the governmental representatives who allocated them resources—were gambling on one simple fact: that consumer demand for plumes would persist. Representative Carl Hayden of Arizona, sponsor of a successful bill in 1913 for the appropriation of funds for ostrich farming, assured his colleagues in the House: "No one need have any fear for the future of the ostrich industry. The feather is undoubtedly the most beautiful ornament of its kind, and as such is independent of fashion."[9] This proved a woefully nearsighted argument. Months after Hayden delivered his impassioned speech, ostrich feathers fell from consumers' good graces; soon thereafter, the vast majority of American ostrich farms and feather manufactories would close in debt. No amount of managing the supply side of the ostrich feather commodity chain, it seemed, could offset the importance of demand.

The ostrich feather workers' strike of 1888–89 proved a failure for corollary reasons. Six months after their work stoppage began, New York's ostrich feather workers returned to work, forced to accept the wage reductions that caused them to go on strike, with the most energetic protesters denied their former positions.[10] Ostrich feather workers blamed their employers for this failure, as for their initial ill treatment, and these complaints were undeniably sound. But another reality existed as well: employers in the ostrich feather business inevitably passed their own vulnerabilities on to their employees. Ultimately, none in the American ostrich feather industry—neither blue-collar workers nor manufacturers, neither ostrich farmers nor their financiers—could resolve the volatility of the global ostrich feather market or ensure that the demand for plumes would endure.

If the global nature of ostrich feather commerce had an impact on its American participants, the prevalence of Jews at all levels and in all the geographic hubs of this industry furthered the trans-hemispheric character of American feather commerce. At every level of the trade, Jews were visible in America's ostrich feather industry. Regardless of what tier of the industry a Jew occupied, his or her being Jewish was not an incidental fact but, instead, a productive force. At the blue-collar end of the workforce were ready numbers of Jewish immigrants from Russia (and Russian Jewish women and girls, in particular), well poised to move into feather work not only because they were poor, unskilled immigrants, but because many had a background in industrial labor or the needle trades.[11] Diasporic contacts among Jewish feather buyers and manufacturers, meanwhile, facilitated feather commerce between the United States, South Africa, and Britain. Finally, Jewish financiers facilitated the evolution and expansion of the ostrich feather industry in the American West, Southwest, and South because they had ties to manufacturing in New York and markets abroad. Jews were thus central to the American ostrich feather industry because of the crucial skills and contacts they brought to it and because of their overseas connections with other Jews.[12] This is demonstrated neatly in the story of Alfred Mosely. A British-born South African Jewish diamond merchant enmeshed in the power structure of the Cape, Mosely cooperated with a relative in London and a Jewish ostrich feather manufacturer in New York to fund an entrepreneurial ostrich farm outside Atlanta, Georgia. Understanding the value and meaning of Jewishness to commercial alliances such as this, brokered by Jews to sustain, alter, and expand the global feather market, is a central task of this chapter.[13]

HOW AN OSTRICH FEATHER IS LIKE A "MICAEL ANGELO": PLUMES AND POLITICS ON THE LOWER EAST SIDE

In 1890, *Frank Leslie's Popular Monthly* featured an article about the ostrich business. Its writer showed an appreciation for the allure of feathers, as well as an understanding of the darker side involved in their production.

> One feels that the gorgeous feathers from some large factories are saturated with tears and sighs, and haunted by the shades of ruined souls. . . . The finished ostrich plume is one of the most beautiful ornaments which may be used to deck the hat of fair lady or brave knight, and it is sad to reflect that some of its associations are anything but pleasant. Its beautiful form and glowing color might excite in us pleasurable emotions always, if we were not compelled to feel that those forms are in some cases produced by workers whose humanity has been nearly crushed out of them, and whose life's blood has been dissipated in the varied tints and hues of the plumes.[14]

In the decades that bracketed the turn of the twentieth century, New York's Lower East Side served as America's center of ostrich feather manufacturing and of garment production generally. Most ostrich feather manufactories were clustered on or near Broadway between Houston and Canal Streets, amid the countless factories, sweatshops, and workrooms that supplied the country's garment industry.[15] (Industry sub-specializations could be found elsewhere in the city; the sewing together of ostrich plumes, known as willowing, was a micro-industry that flourished on the Upper East Side.)[16] In New York's ostrich feather factories, bundles of plumes were received from London, and a mostly female and largely Jewish and Italian workforce shuttled their contents through a cascade of treatments; the feathers were strung, dyed, washed, dyed again, dried, thrashed, trimmed, finished, parried, willowed, fashioned, and curled. Thereafter, the finished plumes left manufactories, passing either to "jobbers"—wholesalers who supplied milliners with the feathers, fabrics, flowers, ribbons, and lace used to adorn hats—or to fashion and millinery retailers, who sold them to the public. With the feather workers in New York, the supply side of the global ostrich feather trade reached its penultimate stage; these workers were also the last ostrich feather specialists to handle the plumes before they reached consumers.

No study ever identified the ethnic breakdown of New York's ostrich feather trade or specified what percentage of workers were immigrants or foreign born.[17] The existing evidence, however, suggests that the industry was disproportionately Jewish. One child of this world, whose father founded the first American ostrich feather duster firm, the P. R. Schuman Duster Company (renamed Schuman Feathers in 1990), has commented simply that "it was a Jewish industry."[18] This point was also advanced in popular press accounts of the day, which casually referred to the trade as Jewish. In fact, many Italian women were employed as ostrich feather workers, and their numbers seem to have risen over time.[19] Yet, throughout the feather boom, Jews appear to have supplied the public face of the trade. Perhaps this was because Jews' prominence in global feather commerce had seeped into the American popular consciousness; perhaps it was evident that Jews, and not Italians, were represented at all levels of the American industry, as novice and experienced feather workers, as factory foremen and -women, and as factory owners and manufacturers. Or perhaps the early organizing efforts of Jewish feather workers, who tended not to be joined on the picket lines by their Italian co-workers, indelibly marked the industry.[20] (There were also reasons for Jewish feather strikers to want to eclipse their Italian colleagues, as Italian ostrich feather handlers not only proved less amenable to organizing but were more likely to conduct work at home, and for low wages, than their Jewish peers.)[21]

Whatever the precise percentage of Jews in the trade, it is clear that the "Micael Angelos" behind the work stoppage of 1888–89 harbored concerns that were not specific to their ethnicity but, on the contrary, were in certain respects typical of the countless blue-collar workers employed in New York's Lower East Side. To begin with, the ostrich feather industry employed a largely female workforce, and concern about low wages for women was rife. When girls first entered ostrich feather manufacturing, they served as unpaid apprentices for two weeks, after which they might face a period of several months at two to three dollars a week. These sums, which fell far short of what a single woman required for essential expenditures, were also far less than female workers were likely to earn in comparable positions in the "sister industries" of fancy feather or artificial flower making.[22] (The "fancy feather" trade dealt in all feathers except those of the ostrich, and specialized in the plumage of wild birds.) The ostrich feather workforce was also akin to sister industries in its reliance on young laborers. Most female ostrich feather workers—like most women in the American workforce of the period—were between the ages of sixteen and twenty-five, although a significant proportion were between ten and sixteen.[23] In this trade, as in so many others, the Russian Jewish immigrant labor force was disproportionately represented by "daughters."[24]

The strike of 1888–89 suggests that ostrich feather workers were also prone to random reductions in wages, as were so many workers in Lower East Side industries. Indeed, one of the central grievances of feather strikers was that the management of New York's leading ostrich feather manufactories had conspired to create a Manufacturers' Mutual Protective Association. Though the members of this group denied it was formed with illegal intentions, it functioned as a cartel whose principal purpose was to set caps on feather workers' salaries that undercut those on the union price list.[25] The ripples caused by this oligopsony spread quickly through the industry. Henry Motley, an ostrich feather manufacturer who testified before the Board of Arbitration that attempted to settle the strike, explained that although his firm (Wood and Company) was in favor neither of reducing wages nor joining the manufacturers' association, it was compelled to reduce workers' pay in imitation of other manufacturers simply to remain competitive.[26] Motley's concerns were echoed by other owners. The *New York Times* reported that, of the manufacturers who testified before the Board of Arbitration, "Some sought to evade questions put them by Lawyer Post [counsel for the strikers], but every one of them admitted that he would be willing to pay the rates of wages as put down on the union price list, provided the other manufacturers in the trade paid them too."[27] The notion that employers were misanthropes by necessity surely provoked ire among their employees. But to manufacturers prone to a volatile international market, wages may well have appeared one of the few expenses over which they had control.

The conditions faced by workers in New York's ostrich feather factories were also typical of the garment industry as a whole. Like so many of the spaces occupied by the millinery, textile, fur, and ready-to-wear industries of New York's Lower East Side, ostrich feather workshops were notoriously unhygienic environments (fig. 14). They were hot and crowded, and workers were prone to "the constant inhaling of tiny bits of feather fluff that are detached during the processes."[28] Writing in 1911, an inspector for the New York Board of Health

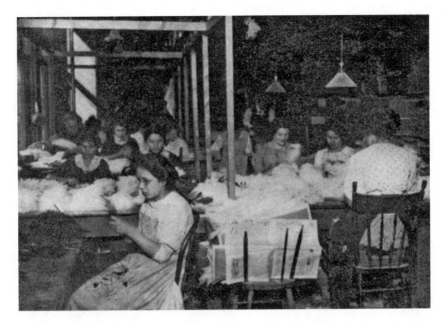

Figure 14. Processing plumes in New York. Women and girls, mostly first- or second-generation Eastern European Jews or Italians, dominated feather work in the Lower East Side, America's center of feather manufacturing from the 1880s to the First World War. (Photograph by Lewis W. Hine, "A Feather Factory," from Mary Van Kleeck, *Artificial Flower Makers,* 1913, courtesy Russell Sage Foundation)

noted that in areas densely inhabited by ostrich feather manufactories, "the streets and stoops were full of ostrich feather refuse, the stairways littered and the air full of feather particles."[29] The persistent ambient dust generated by feathers made ailments of the nose, throat, and ears ubiquitous among workers: fully 94 percent of ostrich feather employees examined by a doctor in 1913 were determined to have rhinitis, a chronic inflammation of the mucous lining of the nose, while 81 percent were judged to suffer from pharyngitis, a chronic throat inflammation.[30] One ostrich feather worker complained of being "choked up at the end of the day," while others attested that "the dust and the small particles which flew from the feathers when they were sewing hurt their throats and 'often gave girls consumption.'"[31] Nor was it easy for women in the industry to afford or find access to the health care they required. Wrote one New York factory investigator,

I have seen a girl in the descumating [*sic*] stage of scarlet fever (when her throat was so bad that she could not speak above a whisper) tying ostrich feathers in the Italian district. These feathers were being made for one of the biggest feather factories in the lower part of the city. She told me herself she had been sick with scarlet fever for ten days, but had been upstairs in a neighbor's rooms working for over a week.[32]

Perhaps the only good thing that could be said about an ostrich feather manufactory was that it lacked the incessant and excessive noise that plagued other sweatshops of the period.[33]

New York's ostrich feather factories resembled those of the garment district in another respect, as well: they observed a strict occupational segregation by sex.[34] To explain this point, and to enumerate the work conducted in these mills, it is worth describing the labor of feather workers in some detail.[35]

The first stages of feather manufacturing were completed by men. Men and boys cleaned dirt and guano from the plumes with an acid solution, clustered the feathers in threes, and strung them, fifty clusters at a time, on strong twine. The resulting "string" could weigh ten pounds. The strung feathers then went through six or seven laundering cycles, including being dipped in a bath of ammonia and soaked overnight in a bleach solution. Bleaching was followed by a second round of washing and starching, after which the strings were "beaten and flung in a peculiar manner backward and forward, until the starch has dried and dropped out of the feathers." One observer described what followed:

> Now the cleaned bleached, opened white feathers are ready for the fingers of the girls. So far they have been entirely in the hands of men. Men gather them in the desert or on the plain, sort and pack them for export, work the ships in which they are brought to port, handle them at the custom-house and at the wholesale dealer's, and so on as just described in the process of manufacturing. Men usually untie the clusters from the string, when the feathers are thrown on a heap on the broad table before the girls, where they show no sign of having recently been dragged through so many waters charged with many varieties of chemicals, but are simply feathers whose dirty faces have been washed clean.[36]

The girls and women who next attended the feathers shepherded them through an elaborate series of preparations. First the plumes were cut, the feathers' tips trimmed, and quills and shafts pared with pieces of glass (fig.

15). Plumes were then "fortified" with a wire, which replaced the less malleable quill. Thereafter, the feathers were dyed any one of a hundred colors, boiled, steamed, and readied for willowing and, finally, "curling." At the willowing stage, the trimmed, pared feathers were laid together in groups of four to seven and carefully stitched or knotted together to give the appearance of a single full plume. Some industry observers spoke of willowers as the most highly skilled of feather workers. According to one such account, written relatively early in the feather boom, willowing was the first stage of ostrich feather manufacturing that required artistry.

> This part of the work requires the best skill the worker can command. The manufacturer's profit or loss can be reckoned from this very moment. If the preparer has had experience, and uses judgment, she may make from two to four dozen more tips out of a pound of feathers than a less careful or skillful worker would do. If a dozen tips sell for $18, then the loss would be thirty-seven to seventy-two dollars on a pound. When the work is on feathers worth $400 a pound the value of a careful, painstaking, experienced woman of clear head and quick judgment is almost beyond estimate. Fortunes are made on the skillful labor of a few such workers, and many a firm has gone to ruin through the wasteful work of incompetent preparers.[37]

This description of the willower's art, written in 1890, little resembled the realities that would face the countless young girls and women who gravitated toward the feather trade at its apex. By 1908, at which point the value of individual plumes was higher than ever before, the sub-specialization of willowing was dominated by Italian homeworkers (most of them girls and young women), who experienced the worst of the ostrich feather industry's abuses. In 1911, a representative of the New York Board of Health reported that while wages for willowers had once been high—with the experienced worker earning fifteen cents for tying one set of knots per inch—in recent seasons their pay had decreased, until, by 1910, homeworkers were paid but three cents an inch for their labors. According to these rates, one woman and two children could labor for a day and a third on a single plume—whose preparation required as many as 8,613 knots—earning no more than three cents, jointly. Complained one young female willower, presumably an Italian immigrant, "Pretty soon, the bossa, he wants us work for nothing."[38]

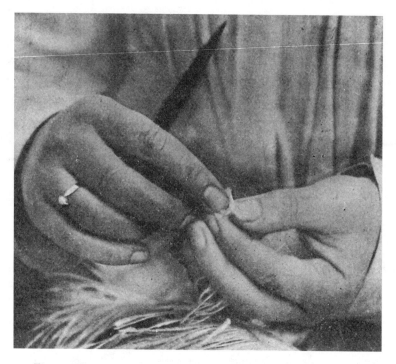

Figure 15. Processing plumes in Paris. This difficult and dirty stage of
feather manufacturing, always carried out by girls and women, involved the use of
a knife or piece of glass to thin and soften the flue for subsequent shaping.
(From Edmond Lefèvre, *Le commerce et l'industrie de la plume pour parure*, 1914)

Better rewarded were curlers. Curlers transformed straight, uneven plumes
into the fanciful sculpted feathers associated with the ostrich. Because of the
importance and difficulty of curling—a technique that was rarely taught, as
were other stages of feather preparation—curlers were the highest paid ostrich
feather employees: the most experienced could earn the astronomical sum of
fifty dollars a week, and their labor was considered "the most expert work in
the whole process of the manufacture of ostrich feathers."[39] One chronicler
of this art, who aspired to usher young girls into the profession, wrote: "A
first class curler is a prize in any factory. . . . A good curler need never want
for employment. Even when a cyclone of labor strikes sweeps away all the
other workers, the curler is the very last to go, if she goes at all."[40] After the
curler finished her craft, the feathers were ready for sale. Entirely transformed

from the scraggly form in which they reached New York, the plumes left the ostrich feather factory wrapped in tissue paper and gingerly packed in boxes two feet long.

Given the value placed on "first class" feather workers—Cohnfeld's "Micael Angelos"—why did the feather workers of New York not realize their demands during the strike of 1888–89?[41] According to the *New York Times,* the failure of the strike was due to the limited funds of feather workers and the temporary union they created. This was not an unfair interpretation, but it did not get to the heart of the matter. Strikes had been widespread in New York's garment industry in 1886, the year of the "Great Upheaval," but the American labor movement was still young and struggling, and female strikers faced even more obstacles than their male peers.[42] Furthermore, by the end of the 1880s the general strike movement—and the Jewish strike movement in particular—was entering a temporary depression, provoked by legal rulings against the use of boycotts and the defeat of pro-labor reformer Henry George, who ran a vibrant (if unsuccessful) third-party bid for mayor of New York in 1886.[43]

Ostrich feather workers had difficulty maintaining their strike for two additional reasons that tell us a great deal about the American branch of the global ostrich feather trade. First, despite being situated in the heart of the garment district, the American ostrich feather trade was a small and, in certain respects, isolated strand of the millinery, textile, and ready-to-wear industries, and these factors proved debilitating to ostrich feather workers when they attempted to organize. A profound fissure divided American ostrich feather workers from those in the two trades that most resembled theirs: the fancy feather and artificial flower industries. This fracture was prompted by the nature of the commodities in question. In contrast to fancy feathers and artificial flowers, ostrich plumes were in demand all seasons of the year, and ostrich feather manufacturers preferred to employ trained and experienced workers who specialized in—or would learn to specialize in—the product.[44] Fancy feathers, by contrast, were popular in spring and summer, rendering the industry busiest between the months of May and October, while artificial flowers were most popular in autumn and winter, which meant that this industry was busiest between October and May. The near-perfect asymmetry in these schedules led manufacturers to fuse the two industries, all but eliminating any slow period for their workers and factories.[45] Because their workers shared concerns about work schedules and wages, the artificial flower and fancy feather industries served, for all intents and purposes, as a single industry whose workers could organize as a unit. Because seasonality was a central concern for workers in other industries, it further behooved fancy feather and artificial flower workers to attempt to organize with milliners, wire makers, and neckwear workers, and such alliances appear to have facilitated unionizing.[46] It seems that ostrich feather workers never joined these unionizing efforts, while at the same time proving unable or unwilling to sustain a union of their own.

The fact that workers in the artificial flower and fancy feather industries shared a concern over seasonality and homework also had an effect on their visibility, which arguably abetted their unionizing activities. From 1910 to 1930, numerous inquiries into conditions faced by artificial flower and fancy feather workers in manufactories and homework environments were conducted in New York and Massachusetts, the principal centers of the American millinery trade.[47] This scrutiny was prompted by a study in 1913 that identified the artificial flower industry as both a site of and a metaphor for the most grotesque abuses of child labor.[48] Ostrich feather workers, by contrast, by and large escaped the gaze of reformers, the government, and, subsequently, historians: while ostrich feather workers were occasionally mentioned in studies of other trades, their anomalousness was recognized consistently by the authors involved, and no focused study of the industry or its workers was conducted. It is also true that at the time the New York ostrich feather workers initiated their early work stoppages, the city's socialist Yiddish press, which would have a profound impact on labor organizing in the years to come, was yet in its infancy.[49]

The impact of anonymity on protesting workers is difficult to gauge, but the importance of visibility is somewhat clearer. Perhaps the most prescient reading of this phenomenon was offered by an ostrich feather manufacturer whose workers initiated what proved to be a successful strike (likely in the summer of 1888). Of his acquiescence to employees' demands, this boss explained: "I can hold out against the feather workers . . . I can hold out against [other] manufacturers; I can hold out against public opinion; but I cannot hold out against all three."[50] With their limited resources, unionist pool, and visibility, ostrich feather workers could make temporary gains in the struggle for fair labor conditions. Permanent changes—particularly in times of economic hard-ship—were far harder to achieve.

If market conditions created a rift between feather workers and those in comparable industries, ostrich feather manufacturers had their own reasons for wanting to stand apart from the fancy feather trade. In the last decades of the century, as the bird protection and anti-plumage movements grew in power and popularity, ostrich feather manufacturers went to great pains to emphasize that "their" feathers were not taken from wild birds and, in any case, that their removal did not injure the bird. This argument was accepted by the Audubon Society and other vociferous supporters of bird protectionism, who never aimed to include ostrich feathers in anti-plumage legislation.[51] The popular press, too, acquiesced to the disaggregating of the fancy feather and ostrich feather trades. By the last years of the nineteenth century, journalistic accounts of the industries were increasingly inclined to paint the fancy feather trade as a shadowy and barbaric operation and the ostrich feather trade as organized and legitimate. The fact that Jews were so prominent in the ostrich feather trade seemed to reinforce this point, for (or so it was argued) Jews' very visibility as international brokers rendered them ill-disposed to the sort of underground economy on which the fancy feather trade was imagined to rely. In the words of one commentator, writing in 1886: "There is a sharp distinct line drawn between the ostrich feather trade and that in fancy feathers. The former has for years traveled in clearly defined channels. There is the great depot of supplies at Cape Town, South Africa, thence through the trade sales in London and so on to the world. In this country and especially in this city [New York], the [ostrich feather] trade is in the hands of a few houses conducted by Jews."[52]

In sum, a spectrum of highly localized conditions that undergirded New York's ostrich feather industry distinguished—and, in certain senses, alien-ated—its blue-collar workforce from others with which they might have been expected to ally. These conditions may be counted among the factors that led to the failure of the strike of 1888–89. A second set of circumstances more germane to this study was also critical in thwarting the strikers' effort. All who participated in the American ostrich feather industry, from the lowest-paid wage laborers to the most successful manufacturer, were highly sensitive to the volatility of international feather sales. (This was certainly true relative to workers in other garment industries, as most produced merchandise that was more elastic in form and function than feathers.) Indeed, volatility catalyzed the feather workers' strike and predisposed its outcome. The strike of 1888 was, on one hand, precipitated by a slump in international ostrich feather commerce that had begun two years earlier, after the price that raw plumes commanded at auction in London began to dip. The slump, which would last nearly a decade, proved disabling at every stage along the global ostrich feather commodity chain and in every region where the plumes were obtained, traded, manufactured, or sold.[53] On the other hand, the strike failed partly because the feather workers' employers, themselves debilitated by a down market, were unable to offset the cost of experienced labor, no matter what pressures were applied on them. In this light, we may conclude that the ostrich feather manufacturers who testified before New York's Board of Arbitration were likely being truthful when they claimed to feel the financial squeeze of this temporary feather bust. Their economic susceptibility was passed along the feather chain to blue-collar workers who themselves had no direct involvement in overseas trade.

The Italian and Jewish girls, boys, women, and men who worked as ostrich feather handlers on the Lower East Side of New York faced a distilled set of risks that arose from the international composition of their industry. These risks may have been especially paralyzing for these wage earners, but in substance they were no different from those that afflicted the industry as a whole. Feather exporters in the Cape and of the Mediterranean Jewish diaspora, feather wholesalers in London, feather manufacturers in New York: all were prone to the inherent volatility of the ostrich feather market, and few proved resilient once the market crashed. But as the supply side of the ostrich feather commodity chain neared its end, individual workers were less and less likely to reap significant financial reward when times were good. Thus the feather handlers of New York were doubly cursed: they were vulnerable to volatility without benefiting from boom.

By participating in a work stoppage, feather handlers were attempting to stabilize their own experience of the global feather market. They were not alone in their quest for novel solutions to this problem. At precisely the same time as New York's feather workers were organizing, others in the industry were concocting possible correctives to the industry's volatile and international nature. To explore these strategies, and to further ground the experience of

New York's ostrich feather workers in a global context, we explore the role of Jewish feather financiers and manufacturers in developing ostrich farms in the American West, Southwest, and South.

THE AMERICAN OSTRICH FARM IS HATCHED

On February 7, 1913, the Honorable Carl Hayden of Arizona rose to address his colleagues in the House of Representatives. Hayden's goal was to appropriate funds "for all necessary expenses for experiments in the feeding and breeding of ostriches and for investigations and experiments in the study of the industry," perhaps in the form of its own Agricultural Experiment Station. His appeal was informed and detailed. He described the precipitous growth of South African ostrich farming since its inception half a century before. He detailed the tremendous sums Americans were investing in ostrich feather imports: two years earlier, he reported, over $5 million worth of ostrich feathers had flowed into the United States. Finally, Hayden dwelled on the work of those entrepreneurs in California, Arizona, Arkansas, and Florida who had moved into ostrich farming—without, he noted, the benefit of the many advantages the South African government provided its own. Hayden waxed further that the use of ostrich plumes for adornment was immune to moral judgment, as "the ostrich remains preeminent as the bird against which there is no suspicion of ill-usage in yielding up its plumage." To the applause of his colleagues, Hayden concluded his case thus: "Whoever wears an ostrich plume is adorned with an emblem of justice; whoever wears the feather of a slaughtered wild creature bears a badge of cruelty. The ostrich feather fulfills every legitimate need in the way of adornment—adornment obtained without shedding the blood of innocents—and, if for no other reason than this, the industry deserves encouragement by the American Government."[54]

American ostrich farms seemed a sound investment at the turn of the twentieth century. Once the market had recovered from its late-nineteenth-century slump, demand for ostrich plumage seemed unquenchable; the price a feather commanded was ever on the rise; and, according to some optimists, American-bred plumes were poised to exceed South African and Saharan feathers in quality. The government had already offered support for this promising industry, sponsoring an ambitious fact-finding mission on the viability of domestic farming as early as 1882 and, some three decades later, approving Hayden's bill.[55] It seemed, in short, that the country had all the ingredients required to transform the ostrich feather industry into a profitable and fully domestic operation. As one enthusiastic journalist reported: "When the American woman can buy only the ostrich feather of the American ostrich, the most sanguine hope of Edwin Cawston, the pioneer California ostrich farmer, will have been realized; two million dollars each year will then remain in the country instead of going to London, and another magnificent industry will have been added to the already vast resources of the greatest of all republics."[56]

The pages that follow trace the history of the Cawston Ostrich Farm, a subsidiary operation it ran in Georgia, and its competitors in Arizona, focusing on the involvement of Jews in the expansion of America's ostrich industry. This study will resonate with students of American agriculture, the American West, and of southern California, in particular, touching as it does on familiar themes. It is striking, for example, that the impetus to farm ostriches arose from the desire of corporate farmers and agricultural industrialists to remain competitive in the international market for agricultural produce; ostrich farming emerged in California at precisely the same time as the state's farmers watched American wheat prices being driven down by suppliers in Argentina, India, Russia, Canada, and Australia, thereby alerting them to the importance of diversification.[57] The growth of ostrich farming was also made possible by climatological conditions that fomented fierce struggles over the development and distribution of water in southern California. Relative to other new agricultural crops that the region's farmers were beginning to specialize in (among them oranges, pears, and raisins), ostriches required minimal water. Thus, cultivating the birds allowed farmers to remain more or less aloof from the bitter struggle over irrigation that afflicted other agricultural entrepreneurs.[58] Finally, it is noteworthy that much like growers of other agricultural produce of the period, ostrich farmers bemoaned the influence of financiers and manufacturers in the Northeast and other urban centers, on whose capital, equipment, and expertise they depended. The attempt to build an ostrich industry in the West, Southwest, and South thus reiterates what we know of the regional interdependence of American agriculture at the turn of the twentieth century, and the tensions this interdependence engendered.[59]

If the story of American ostrich farms resonates with the American agricultural historian for one set of reasons, it is germane to us for another. The expansion of the Cawston enterprise—like many other aspects of the industry that we have already seen—resulted from the investment and assistance of Jewish collaborators. The management of the Cawston Farm depended on two such associates: a Jewish ostrich feather manufacturer from New York by the name of J. A. Stein, and the aforementioned British-born South African–based Jewish financier Alfred Mosely. Other ostrich farms formed alliances with other Jews in the feather world: the Arizona-based Western Land and Cattle Company, for example, employed a New York feather merchant named O. B. Fish to store and vend its plumes. To their collaborators in the American West, Southwest, and South, Fish, Stein, and Mosely served as liaisons to the feather worlds of New York, London, and the Cape. They also promised to function as sources of expertise, trans-hemispheric contacts, and capital. From Fish's, Stein's, and Mosely's perspectives, on the other hand, a successful partnership with American ostrich breeders could allow them to tame and possibly even reorient the global ostrich feather commodity chain to their advantage. In this, the ambitions of these men were not so divergent from New York's striking feather workers, who also tried to insulate themselves from an unpredictable market. These were risky efforts; with the feather crash looming, they would also prove ill-fated.

Edwin Cawston was one of several entrepreneurs who imported ostriches from the Cape Colony to southern California in the 1880s.[60] His farm, initially called the Washington Garden Ostrich Farm, was inaugurated in 1885 or 1887 with 18 Cape birds; by Cawston's own account, the animals (and 32 more that did not survive) were whisked out of South Africa even as a bill was being signed forbidding the export of live ostriches and eggs from the Cape Colony.[61] Thanks to the intensive farming practices of Cawston and his peers and to the ostrich-friendly climates of California and Arizona, his birds—and those of other early ostrich entrepreneurs—bred an astonishing number of progeny. In 1896, roughly 700 ostriches lived on American soil: in 1910, this number had risen to more than 5,300, and by 1913 to 8,000. In 1911, the value of the birds in Arizona's Maricopa County, where fully 80 percent of the country's ostriches were farmed, was minimally less than that of horses or cattle.[62] Astonishingly, the vast majority of these birds could be traced to Cawston stock.[63]

As the Cawston Farm grew, its birds were bred on multiple sites, notably in Norwalk, Los Angeles County, but the farm consolidated its operations on a ranch of roughly two hundred acres in San Jacinto in March 1909.[64] The administrative base of the Cawston Farm was in South Pasadena's Lincoln Park neighborhood, where, in 1900, Cawston and his partners purchased eleven plots of land framed by three boulevards—Pasadena Avenue, Arroyo Drive, and Monterey Road—and serviced by the Santa Fe Railway, the Pacific Electric Railway, and the Union Pacific Railway.[65] The choice of Pasadena for the home of this budding ostrich empire was deliberate. Pasadena had emerged as an agricultural colony of the orange industry, and this "earthly paradise" displayed the fantastic wealth of those who profited by it.[66] The success of California's fruit industry was no doubt a model to Cawston and his peers (as it was, not coincidentally, to agricultural financiers and engineers in South Africa), and the wealth of its pioneers something to emulate—perhaps, even, something to exceed.[67] For in certain respects ostrich feathers appeared easy to grow and prepare for market, at least relative to other agricultural produce under cultivation in California at this time. Ostriches required little water or space, the plumes themselves were compact and easy to package and ship, and, more significant still, they were not perishable, did not require refrigeration, and were not prone to decay or to bug infestations.

Yet penetrating the global feather market did not seem to be the initial priority of the Cawston Farm. The Washington Garden Ostrich Farm (soon renamed the Cawston Ostrich Farm) was to serve as the nucleus of a "zoological and botanical display" to which other animals would be added.[68] Thus the Pasadena site was developed into a show farm advertised on the electric railways, automobile liveries, and tallyho stables that shuttled tourists to the site, as by the hotel industry, whose members promoted it as an up-and-coming local attraction.[69] The farm's own promotional literature described the show farm as "a semi-tropical private park, abounding in handsome arborial [sic] growths, flowering plants, decorative shrubbery and grassy lawns," all of which featured "beautiful specimens of Asparagus Plumosis . . . oak trees draped in ivy, delicate ferns clinging to the roofs of buildings and to the branches of tall trees . . . ornamental terraces, artistically contrived retreats, airy promenades, the aviary of rare birds and many other inviting allurements."

The Cawston Farm's main attractions, of course, were the birds themselves, 150 of which wandered "amid natural surroundings."[70] These "natural sur-

Figure 16. Promotional postcard from the Cawston Ostrich Farm. In addition to producing feathers for sale, the Cawston Farm functioned as a tourist destination. The ad, like the industry, tried to emulate the success and allure of the orange. (Courtesy Huntington Library, San Marino, California)

roundings" appear to have included a collection of miniature pyramids roughly five feet tall that were apparently meant to emphasize the birds' "Oriental" roots; presumably the fact that ostriches never roamed in the vicinity of Egypt's Nile Valley didn't diminish the display's appeal.[71] Postcards produced and sold by the farm picture tourists observing an ostrich-pulled carriage, the incubation of ostrich eggs, the clipping of plumes, and birds fighting and being fed oranges—which, to the horror of South African breeders, seem to have been a component of the California ostrich diet (fig. 16).[72] Such exotic displays made the Cawston Farm—like other new agro-tourism ventures in the American West—a popular destination.[73] In the 1904 fiscal year, admission fees earned the Cawston Ostrich Farm over $13,000 and sales of souvenirs and eggshells an additional $2,600. Cawston's board of directors anticipated that this figure would grow 10 percent per annum.[74]

The Cawston Ostrich Farm was not envisioned solely as a for-show operation. As early as 1893 the farm was shipping feathers to New York for manufacture and sale, with "the very finest retailed in California at ten dollars a plume."[75] By 1904 the farm had formed relationships with individual sales-men and shops that featured the Cawston name, and at roughly the same time, the farm's board of directors contemplated moving into manufacturing and the wholesale trade. The firm's leadership expected that "agencies can be established in every city in the United States," each of which would return to the farm a profit of 10–20 percent (or, in the optimistic mindset of the farm itself, upward of $2,000–$50,000 per year, per store).[76] For this to be the case, however, Cawston Farm would be required either to manufacture its own feathers or intensify their manufacture off-site. In either case, it needed a liaison to the feather manufacturing world that commanded the expertise, contacts, and experience that the Cawston administration lacked. Filling this role was J. A. Stein.

J. A. STEIN, FEATHER MEDIATOR

At the turn of the twentieth century, J. A. Stein owned an ostrich feather manufactory at 54–58 East Ninth Street, New York City. Stein's was an extensive manufacturing operation, prominent enough to warrant a tour by a journalist covering the ostrich feather industry for *Scientific American.* The resulting article tells us little that would distinguish Stein's operation from others of its day (aside from attesting to its impressive scale), but it does provide a hint that the manufacturer may have already established a rapport with the Cawston Farm. While guiding his visitor through the plant, Stein took pains to emphasize that, although "at first the feathers supplied to the market from [the Cawston Farm] were below the average, . . . [o]f late years careful breeding and a more careful selection and care of the birds have produced a marked improvement, and to-day the feathers received from California are fully up to the standard."[77] This was an ambitious and controversial position for an American ostrich feather manufacturer to hold in 1901, and it likely would be advanced only by someone with ties to the farm in question.

Although Stein's formal relationship with the Cawston Farm at the time of this interview remains unclear, it is evident that by 1912 he had become the farm's New York representative. By this time, he was overseeing the New York–based manufacture of Cawston feathers, supplying the farm with expe-rienced feather workers, courting investors, advising the farm about the nature and future of its operations, and, increasingly, financing the business when it fell on hard times. The papers of the Cawston Ostrich Farm make clear that the feather division of this business could not have succeeded—to the extent that it did—without Stein. Indeed, it is evident that many of the challenges posed to the management of the Cawston Farm arose from the business being located so far from New York City, the center of American feather manufacturing. Why was it so difficult to create an autonomous ostrich feather operation in the American West? Why did Stein—and Jewish feather workers in New York—prove indispensable to the Cawston Farm?

Answering these questions requires fleshing out the Cawston Farm's own history. After existing as a show and breeding farm for nearly a decade, the firm's management embarked on an aggressive new venture in 1909, moving into retail sales. This involved incorporating the company a second time; the associated certificate specifies that the mission of the Cawston Farm was to continue to breed and propagate ostriches, as it always had, but also to "build, erect, equip, operate and maintain manufacturing plants and such other structures as may be deemed necessary or expedient for the making, manufacturing, or sale of feathers, feather fans, feather boas, and all other by products."[78] This shift in direction was eagerly anticipated by the management of the farm, which could not have realized that feather sales would ultimately prove a financial drain on the company.

None of this could be known, however, when the Cawston Ostrich Farm embarked on independent manufacturing and wholesale operations. Beginning in 1909, the Cawston Farm engaged in vertical integration, opening a manufactory on its Pasadena site and a retail store on South Broadway Street in Los Angeles.[79] Two undated lists of the Cawston Farm's workers show the business employing at least thirty-eight people in the Pasadena Factory and Repair Shop, including as many as twelve sewers, five curlers, and four dyers.[80] A photograph of the factory's staff suggests that the majority were women, while a list of employee names hints that perhaps as many as half were Jews: possibly, as we will see in a moment, Jewish women brought from New York for this purpose. (Also hired by the farm was a Chinese dyer and two Japanese workers, one a gardener, the other a janitor. The ethnicity of other employees was not specified in company records.)[81] According to the farm's promotional literature, these workers labored in "the largest [factory] of its kind in America

. . . under ideal climatic conditions, drawing its supply of raw feathers direct from the farm."[82] Signs on the side of the feather manufactory announced the building to be "fire proof" (thereby drawing attention to its geographic and professional distance from New York competitors) and boasted that it housed $100,000 worth of feathers.

Internal accounting by the Cawston Farm documented that by introducing manufacturing on site, the business increased its profits on feathers, boas, and other feather goods by at least 30 percent, at least in the short term.[83] By 1911, Cawston plumes were available for sale in branch stores in Los Angeles, San Francisco, Chicago, and New York, and were being sold to individual consumers by mail order.[84] The feathers commanded high prices—even higher, by some accounts, than imported plumes—and they were lauded at world's fairs in Omaha, Buffalo, St. Louis, Jamestown, Paris, and Seattle.[85] Soon wealthy American women became targets of Cawston sellers, who exploited the fact of their domestic production to increase sales.[86] Buyers like these may also have responded well to the farm's self-promotion techniques, as the company embarked on an energetic advertising campaign, pouring over $12,000 into magazine promotions in 1912 alone.[87] Other Cawston enthusiasts anticipated the farm would soon be the key to a thriving American industry that not only had thrown off the shackles of South African suppliers and London middlemen but was poised to move into overseas exports. In one journalist's words: "The boy is now alive who will behold the wharves of San Francisco, Los Angeles, and San Diego some day laden down with bales of ostrich feathers for import to foreign lands, while through the Panama Canal en route to New York will go quantities for distribution to the crowded centers of the distant east."[88]

And yet there were obstacles to the Cawston Farm's success. Even as the company was breaking into feather wholesaling, there were signs that its plumes were faring poorly on the market, and that the profitability of an in-house manufactory was limited. The ostrich feather merchants responsible for passing feathers on to consumers were, in the first place, divided on the quality of domestically raised plumes, even though by buying and reselling California stock, feather merchants stood to save the 15 percent and 25 percent tariffs, respectively, levied by the government on imported untreated (or "raw") and manufactured feathers. According to one journalistic account, feather merchants perceived "the difference between the California and South African ostrich feathers . . .

as marked as the difference between California and Burgundy claret," adding: "Merchants have not given a hospitable welcome to the American bird. They insist that the contribution of ostrich feathers from California ranches are a mere bagatelle in the trade, and that if it were not for the duty of 15 percent imposed on South African feathers in the rough the Pacific Coast ostriches would cut no figure at all."[89]

Promotional literature produced by the Cawston Farm countered such claims aggressively. "Even the best African feathers are injured more or less by their long sea voyage in damp holds of vessels, close packing and months of storage," explained one pamphlet of 1903.

> The ostrich goods sold in retail stores represent a large profit, which is divided among the gatherers of the feathers, the importer, the dyer and finisher, the wholesaler and retailer. In buying from the Cawston Ostrich Farm you get goods direct from the producer, at producer's prices, thereby not only saving several profits, but securing new, fresh goods of a vastly superior quality. The feathers of foreign birds are often dressed carefully and in a manner which gives them a good appearance, but in reality they lack the life and durability of the sturdy, well-nurtured feathers of the South Pasadena Ostrich Farm. Time alone will prove the vast difference in quality between the cultured product of our Farm and the half-starved imported feather.[90]

Literature like this, produced by the farm in abundance, made an eloquent case for California plumes. And yet, even according to the leadership of the Cawston Farm, such advertising "produced absolutely no results."[91] The majority of consumers and wholesalers were resistant to American feathers and the higher prices they commanded. This prejudice would prove debilitating to ostrich farms other than Cawston's. At the time it was "busted high, wide, and handsome" in 1914, the Pan-American Ostrich Company of Maricopa County, Arizona, held 1,120 acres of land and 2,700 ostriches. Yet its management had been able to turn an annual profit only once between 1906 and 1914; this profit, calculated at $7,257.36, was minimal compared with the company's overall losses, which were at least $50,000.[92]

Why did it prove so difficult for the American ostrich farm to subvert the intercontinental feather market? Why were American plumes more expensive than imported ones? In the case of the Cawston Farm, there were, first, seemingly unnecessary start-up expenses. All the requisite dye and chemicals used in a feather manufactory, including iron liquor, logwood, and peroxide, cost from 15 to 200 percent more in California than in New York.[93] Second, since the Cawston ranch did not purchase feathers on a month-to-month basis, as did most feather manufacturers in New York, it proved highly vulnerable to seasonal or periodic trends in consumption; because it produced its own plumes, the farm, quite by necessity, had considerable stock on hand at all times—by one account, as much as $250,000 worth. With the volume of Cawston feather stock dictated by the farm's bird stock rather than consumer demand, the company was more vulnerable to a volatile market than were New York's feather manufacturers. Third, experienced feather workers did not abound in southern California. The Cawston Farm was obliged to bring employees from New York, and this proved an expensive and risky undertaking. One prominent figure in the company admitted that "frequently . . . when they get here they are not first class operators."[94] Even when imported feather workers did not live up to the company's standards, the farm had to fight to retain them, as the region offered no experienced workers to take their place. To keep these feather workers from returning home, the company was obliged to provide them with year-round work at wages comparable to what could be earned in New York regardless of how steady was the demand for plumes.[95]

Finally, controversy rocked the farm's management. In 1911, Edwin Cawston permanently left California for his hometown of Torquay, England.[96] Although Cawston's reasons for abandoning his entrepreneurial venture are unclear, the profound legacies of his departure are irrefutable. Before bidding his farm farewell, Cawston, the majority stockholder in the Cawston Ostrich Farm, cashed out the entirety of his stock, leaving the business in dire financial straits. Upon his departure, a prospectus for reshaping the company was produced by a group of solicitors in London who seem to have brokered the company's transition to new leadership. The representative of this group was E. P. Cawston—possibly Edwin Cawston's son Edwin Junior, who resided for a time in South Africa as well—himself an investor in the ostrich industry.[97] E. P. Cawston described his concerns about the financial implications of Edwin's abrupt departure in a letter to Herbert Vatcher, general manager of the Pasadena farm. The farm's best strategy, E. P. Cawston advised, was to form "a new Company with a million dollar Capital to take over the old Company." He continued:

What weighs most with me is that the scheme under which a new Company is formed gets rid of the necessity of explaining how it is that so much of the present stock is on offer. The sale of practically the whole of the stock of the largest proprietor is a nut that will take some cracking whereas the flotation of a new company in which a substantial amount of stock is already subscribed would be a much more promising proposal. Do you not think so?[98]

In accordance with this dubious advice, the Cawston Ostrich Farm was incorporated for a third time in 1911, a move that seems, at last, to have soothed what local nerves might have been frayed by Cawston's departure.[99] Papers testifying to this incorporation, filed with the British Board of Trade, named E. P. Cawston "Director" of the farm.[100] The role of director appears to have been exclusively titular in nature. The president of the Cawston Ostrich Farm would soon confide to Stein that "the Farm has never at any time been placed on a proper financial footing since Mr. Cawston took from it all of its available funds in the way of excessive dividends."[101]

The financial turmoil left in Cawston's wake, combined with the economic challenges of breaking into retail, prompted at least one member of the board of directors to propose that the company abandon feather manufacturing altogether. Such was the instinct of Ernest Vatcher, who in 1912 outlined the above dilemmas to his brother Bert, then general manager of the Pasadena site. (Their father, Herbert J. Vatcher, had been one of Cawston's first collaborators, and he served as secretary, treasurer, and general manager for the farm in Pasadena from 1906 to 1914.) The solution Ernest Vatcher seized upon was for the Cawston Farm to "close down the factory and buy our manufactured stock from Stein"—that is, that the farm would send all its raw plumage to Stein for manufacture, after which he would distribute the finished goods to branch stores and consumers under the Cawston name.[102] This was a sound proposal, and there is evidence that the Cawston Farm did outsource some of its manufacturing to Stein, sending him as much as $20,000 worth of raw plumage in a single shipment.[103] However, the pride and ambition of the Cawston Ostrich Farm's management prevented Vatcher's plan from being adopted wholesale. Had his suggestion been heeded, the farm would have been considerably more insulated from the impending feather crash than it ultimately proved.

Though surely Vatcher was not aware of the fact, precedent for his suggestion existed in the history of the global ostrich feather trade. In other regional contexts, historical expertise proved more important than geographic proximity in determining the path of the ostrich feather commodity chain. As we have seen, before the collapse of the Kano-to-Tripoli camel caravan route, ostrich feathers from the Sahel and southern Sahara were ferried by camel caravan to port cities in North Africa to be prepared for export to London by a mostly Jewish workforce. However, once it became expedient for higher grades of the plumes to be sent by post west to the Atlantic coast and thence to London, the feathers were transshipped back to North Africa for processing. The emergent ostrich feather industry of the American West was different from the older feather trading networks of West and North Africa in countless respects. But these stories are tied together by the persistent importance of historic mercantile hubs and the skilled workers that sustained them. One could dream of a self-sufficient Californian (or, indeed, American) ostrich feather industry, but breaking free of established commercial circuits and contexts could prove a nightmare.

With feather sales less than robust, the managers of the Cawston Farm embarked on two entrepreneurial ventures in cooperation with Stein. First, they attempted to bulk up their stockholders' list, aggressively courting investors. H. J. Vatcher Jr., who had been with the company since its inception, became the single largest shareholder by far: by 1928, he held 62 percent of the company's 8,682 shares. Most of the roughly 130 other shareholders owned fewer than 50 shares each, and all owners of 100 or more had personal ties to the company.[104] The proliferation of Cawston Farm stock seems to have served the company rather more profoundly than its investors. Dividends averaging 9.25 percent were paid when feather sales were brisk, but only then. When times were hard for the farm—which may have been more often than not—the company's stockholders became its backers.[105] This prompted Fred Ralsten, one of the company's larger shareholders, to complain to the farm's president in a letter of 1914, "I bought this stock little thinking I would be obliged to 'dig down' again so soon. At the time Stein and you both seemed to think you were doing me a great favor in taking my $3,300. I can't afford to lose the original much less this $1,502. . . . No more assessments please!"[106]

Shareholders were being asked to "dig down" in 1914 because the Cawston Ostrich Farm was severely affected by the devastating feather slump that commenced in that year. The high costs of materials, the lack of competent work-ers, the farm's geographic isolation from New York: all this might have been overcome or, indeed, offset by the expense that untaxed plumes saved manu-facturers. A shift in international fashion trends, on the other hand, could not be avoided or counterbalanced. Global trading realities thus dealt the most devastating blow to the Cawston Farm. In the summer of 1914, Jonathan Dodge, then president of the company (as well as president of the First National Bank of South Pasadena), wrote a letter to all shareholders outlining the company's misfortunes.

> The Ostrich Feather business has been the poorest this Season at any time for the past fifteen years. On account of fixed contracts and expenses, it has been impossible to take care of our current claims with the income on hand. You will recall that after the payment of our last Assessment, this company was still in debt for approximately the sum of $50,000, which debt has not decreased during the past year, but has increased to approximately the sum of $90,000. We will arrange our finances so that we will not be bothered and harassed by pressing debts, and further, greatly reduce the expenses of the company.[107]

In fact, it proved all but impossible for the Cawston Ostrich Farm to avoid its debts. The company's liabilities of $90,000 included nearly $30,000 owed to Stein alone. Stein forgave $10,000 of this to the farm after receiving a heartfelt appeal from Dodge in June 1914. "I want to say that at all times we have deferred to your opinion and judgment," the fretful president wrote Stein: "I want to say also that you have on your part, done everything that we have requested, and we appreciate the loyal and generous support and consideration that you have given our Board of Directors."[108] Dodge's letter proffered sev-eral desperate solutions to the woes of the business: perhaps, he wrote, Stein would consider buying the farm, which he had tried "very, very hard" to sell. If not, the company might assess its stockholders or even take a mortgage on Dodge's own home. Possibly fearing that Stein would follow the lead of the farm's founder by demanding payment and deserting the operation, Dodge concluded by pleading with his collaborator:

> Now Mr. Stein, you and I and [Cawston Ostrich Farm director] Mr. Coulston have enough money in this business that it is imperative that we stand together and pledge our efforts to carry the concern through until fall. We will have

to adopt whatever method we can; as it seems now that the things we desired most to do were the things that were impossible. The disappointment has been a great one to me as no doubt it has been to yourself, and if I have erred along business lines, I am perfectly willing to stand my share of criticism. This business will succeed better with the support of all of us than it will if we divide and each works for himself, and I solicit a united effort on the part of yourself and that balance of us for a strong pull together along any lines that you may finally suggest as best to be pursued. I know that you are physically exhausted and that you are seeking rest, but before you go, I trust that our matters will have your attention and favorable consideration.[109]

Dodge's plea to Stein attests to the increasing strain faced by partners in a deteriorating business. But it was also informed by the ethnic and geographic orientation of the feather trade. To the Cawston Farm, Stein was more than a financial backer: he was a commercial liaison in New York experienced in global plume commerce. That he was Jewish was not incidental. Given the ethnic makeup of the feather trade, it was almost guaranteed that the New York associate of a California ostrich farm would be Jewish. Although the papers of the Cawston Farm never referred to Stein's Jewishness, it is clear from the company's interaction with him that his expertise, in all its nuances, were keenly appreciated by the business.

Far-fetched as this point might at first appear, it is substantiated by the uncannily parallel correspondence that existed between a second New York Jewish feather merchant and the management of the Western Land and Cattle Company (the reconstituted Pan-American Ostrich Company) of Maricopa County, Arizona. For over ten years, this company relied on O. B. Fish, a New York dealer of (at turns) egret, heron, and ostrich feathers to store, evaluate, and vend their plumes. Fish was in possession of as much as 2,769 pounds of the company's feathers at a single time, and in one frenzied year he sold more than $10,000 worth of plumes for the firm.[110] Just as the leadership of the Cawston Farm pleaded with Stein as the feather market soured, so representatives of the Western Land and Cattle Company came to beg for Fish's loyalty. "After the long time we have done business I have come to rely entirely on your judgment as to what should be done," went one such dispatch by a company director: "I would be satisfied if you handled the matter just as if it was your own entirely, whatever the result."[111] One need not turn Stein and

Fish into commercial martyrs to recognize the vital role played by these Jewish merchants in the construction of America's ostrich farms. The fact of these feather merchants' Jewishness was not incidental to their utility but was, in this context, a crucial credential. This was because Jews in the feather trade tended to have ties to Jewish industrial insiders in other feather markets that non-Jews in the industry lacked. In a global industry highly sensitive to volatility, personal relationships like these were necessary building blocks of success.

Stein did not buy the Cawston Ostrich Farm, as its president suggested, but he remained loyal to the entrepreneurial venture, responding to Dodge's letter with a $10,000 loan. But a month later Stein, like all of the firm's stockholders, was bled for a heavy assessment of $8,000.[112] Sometime thereafter, likely in mid-July 1914, Stein "sold out, losing a lot of cash."[113] At the time of his break with the company, the Cawston Farm owed Stein at least $50,000. Perhaps because he aimed to see this debt realized, his turned out to be a temporary goodbye to the Cawston Farm. Meanwhile, taking Stein's place as the principal backer of the enterprise was a South African British Jewish financier by the name of Alfred Mosely.

ALFRED MOSELY AND THE GLOBAL FEATHER GAME

Before delving into Mosely's own history, it is necessary to chart the fate of the Cawston Farm during and just after the feather crash. Over the course of 1914 the Cawston Farm's obligations mounted. "The store game has proved an absolute failure," wrote investor and company administrator Fred Ralsten in the summer of 1914. "And the mail order business for this last spring—why, we didn't even take in enough money to pay for the advertising!"[114] By this time, the ranch at San Jacinto had been sold to dairy farmers and a trust deed of $23,000 stood against the outfit's property in Pasadena.[115] The following winter, the company was dispossessed of its space on Fifth Avenue in New York—which it had occupied for five years—after failing to pay rent for six months.[116]

Many American ostrich farms, feather manufacturers, and buyers declared bankruptcy or had permanently or temporarily folded their operations by the late winter of 1914. Ostrich farms in the West and Southwest were reported to have deliberately sabotaged their birds' health, or even to have released them

into "the Arizona wilds."[117] In the ensuing decade, the number of feather factories (including both ostrich and fancy feather establishments) in the United
States fell from 239 to 131, and the number of wage earners employed in them
plummeted from roughly 4,500 to 1,700.[118] The failure of the industry as a
whole was becoming an object of humor in the popular press. With the commercial value of ostriches collapsing, one journal jibed that with Thanksgiving
on the horizon, the birds should be eaten (not then a sanctioned practice),
adding: "Heaven help him who gets the neck."[119] A cartoon titled "Locked
Out!" published in *Life* magazine in December 1914 satirized the feather bust
thus: locked out of his crude "African" hut stands an elegantly dressed but
clearly befuddled ostrich, complete with top hat and glasses. The caption
explains the bird's dismay—in his great hunger, he had swallowed his key.[120]
Like so many cartoons that dotted the American and European press of the
period, this image contained a distinct measure of anti-Semitism. It hinted
that the propriety of the ostrich feather merchant—like that of the bird whose
feathers he sold—was little more than a disguise, a temporary mask belying
the middleman's irrepressible appetite for profit.

While many in the feather trade suffered bankruptcies or severe debt in the
months after the market began its precipitous plunge, the Cawston Farm managed to remain in operation by relying on its reputation as a showplace. The
company even emblazoned its name on an extravagant exhibit at the Panama-
California Exposition of 1915. Here the roughly 180,000 visitors in attendance
could enter a phantasmagorical pyramid adorned with faux hieroglyphs, framed
by towering sphinxes, and marked with the confusing sign "Home of the
Cawston Ostrich Farm."[121] Popular as the display was, it could do little to
reverse the company's dire financial standing. The year 1917 saw the Cawston
Farm settling a legal claim with the Sun Drug Company, from whom the farm
had procured a two-year lease on South Broadway Street in Los Angeles six
years earlier (the space was used for the manufacture and retail sale of ostrich
feathers).[122] This settlement lost the farm a considerable sum, but it was better
than the alternative, as the rental of this space ensured that the farm was "in-
curring a loss of approximately $100 a month." The legal firm advised that "it
is fair to assume that in the absence of some marked revival in the market for
your product you would continue to incur a very substantial loss."[123] In 1920 the
farm claimed just over $2,000 in liquid assets but faced $40,000 in liabilities.

These included a debt of more than $2,000 to I. Salaman and Company, which suggests that the Cawston Farm may have resorted to purchasing inexpensive imported processed feathers and passing them off as its own.[124]

Strikingly, certain of the farm's principal players held out hope for the resurgence of the feather market and the Cawston operation. Wrote one investor to another: "My idea would be to forget the farm until [the] ostrich returns to style and then form a pool and take over all the stock. You realize that when [demand for] ostrich is good this company makes lots of money and quickly. . . . I have two or three large real estate deals on at this time, but, as I say, it is rather hard to wean myself away from the feather game."[125] The feather game did, indeed, seem to have a certain gravitational pull. Others involved in the Cawston enterprise saw the company's financial downfall as temporary. The Cawston ranch no longer possessed all of its birds and had lost its breeding land, but it still commanded a well-known name, managers' expertise, and the Pasadena site, complete with manufacturing facilities. Were demand for plumes to suddenly rise, all this could be put to good use. And so the Vatchers, Stein, and Dodge all kept a watchful eye on the feather market, waiting for a resurgence in the fashionability of ostrich plumes. In 1919, it seemed their prayers were to be answered.

In the spring of 1919, fashion watchers predicted a return of ostrich feather wearing. One such article, titled "Ostrich Coming Back," announced: "Ostrich, used in a variety of ways, is gradually coming back into favor, and before long dealers expect to see a very good volume of business on this long dormant article."[126] Indeed feather wearing did seem to be experiencing something of a renaissance. Mrs. Cornelius Vanderbilt, host to one of the largest and most widely reported-on social functions of the year—the wedding of her son, Cornelius Vanderbilt Jr.—sported a "small high hat covered with green ostrich feathers" at the event.[127] In New York's Hotel Astor, two thousand buyers watched in awe as the Retail Millinery Association paraded its 1919 fall fashion show before a "special curtain of ostrich feathers on a background of tennis netting" that had been created with $100,000 worth of ostrich plumes.[128] As consumers' demand for the feathers grew, the industry galvanized to accommodate their needs. In July 1919, the first auction of ostrich feathers imported directly from South Africa was held in New York City, at the warehouse of the New York Fur Auction Sales Corporation. Regular auctions were promised for the future, and at least initially these events offered American manufacturers feathers at prices that were greatly reduced relative to those they might encounter in London.[129]

The Cawston Ostrich Farm's erstwhile management was not inclined to let this opportunity pass them by. With the price of ostrich feathers on the rise, they saw an opportunity to pull themselves out of debt and, perhaps, to profit. In a bold entrepreneurial move Bert and Lillian Vatcher invested in a ranch outside Atlanta and moved nearly all of the Cawston Farm's remaining birds there in April 1919.[130] Financing this operation was Alfred Mosely.

Mosely was a British-born and -educated Jew who had made his way to the diamond mines at Kimberley in the early years of South Africa's mineral revolution. He earned a considerable fortune in this enterprise, eventually joining the De Beers diamond syndicate.[131] Mosely's expertise in the diamond business enabled him to serve on the board of the London-based Exploration Company, created in 1886 by two California mining engineers interested in purchasing and selling international mines and mining rights. The Exploration Company thrived and ultimately expanded its operations as an "import-export agency for capital and expertise," which played a crucial role in facilitating the movement of engineers, ideas, and technologies between California and South Africa.[132] Agricultural engineers from California were particularly valued in the Cape for their knowledge of their home state's fruit industry and the novel irrigation techniques it spawned.

It was by way of the fruit business, too, that Mosely likely encountered California's budding ostrich industry. Well before he tried his hand in the feather game, Mosely was sent to California by the diamond magnate Cecil Rhodes (then prime minister of the Cape Colony) to study irrigation and other agricultural techniques that might benefit Rhodes's fruit farms.[133] Conducting research on California's inchoate ostrich farming enterprise appears not to have been a mandate of this journey, but it is likely that Mosely visited one or more of the area's farms. In 1890, the year Mosely explored California, the Cawston Farm was a major tourist destination: this farm and others like it were also potential competitors of those in the Cape, a fact that would have rendered them of profound interest to a representative of South Africa's agricultural industry. Unfortunately no documentation attests to how Mosely spent his time in California, or whether he forged connections with the management of the Cawston enterprise. Still, Mosely's earliest adventures in California highlight the extent to which the development of American ostrich farming was embedded in the economics of colonialism, on one hand, and, on the other, in the global competition to supply European and American consumers with the luxury items they craved.

Twelve years after Mosely toured California on behalf of Rhodes, he embarked on a second exploration of the American industrial landscape, this time sponsored by the British Board of Trade. The Mosely Industrial Commission, as it came to be known, brought roughly two dozen delegates to the United States in 1902. Each was allowed, according to Mosely, "to investigate his special industry without hindrance as to time or expense."[134] These explorations led the commission to praise American industry with sycophantic ardor. In Mosely's and his colleagues' renderings, American industry was highly efficient, technologically sophisticated, and generous to the workingman—a model for British manufacturers and industrialists. In summarizing the findings of the delegates, Mosely advised his British colleagues:

> I can only say that if we are to hold our own in the commerce of the world, both masters and men must be up and doing. Old methods must be dropped, old machinery abandoned. Practical education of the masses must be instituted and carried out upon a logical basis, and with efficiency. The bulk of our workmen are already sober and intelligent but with many of them there is urgent need for them to become more sober, more rational; more ready to adopt new ideas in place of antiquated methods, and improved machinery whenever produced, and to get the best possible results from a day's work. Manufacturers for their part must be prepared to assure their men a piece price that will not be "cut" when the latter's earnings exceed what has hitherto been considered sufficient for them. Modern machinery must be introduced, co-operation of the workmen sought, and initiative encouraged in every possible way. Without such a modernized system we can not hope to compete with countries like the United States.

Mosely was soon an active investor in California's ostrich farming industry, hoping to capitalize on just the sort of industrial innovation he urged on his British peers.

Mosely's initial foray into the American ostrich industry did not involve the Cawston enterprise. In 1917 he was said to be "controlling" the British American Mercantile Company, an ostrich farm based in El Centro, California. At this time—a lull in the feather market—this firm was reported to be shipping the astronomical quantity of two hundred pounds of ostrich feathers to New York every day. This was according to a member of the Cawston management, who visited British American Mercantile in 1917, admired its birds (which he found "far superior" to Cawston's own), and to whom his farm contemplated selling both stock and farming acreage.[135] This encounter must have laid the foundations for Mosely's cooperation with the Cawston Farm. Two years later, Alfred Mosely—in cooperation with his brother and associate George Mosely, an import, export, and shipping agent based in London—refinanced and assumed responsibility for the bulk of the Cawston Farm's debt.[136] This freed the Cawston executives to devote their energies to the enterprise in Atlanta. This arrangement was viewed with great enthusiasm by Bert Vatcher, who gushed in one letter that the "Mosely crowd not only [has] lots of money but are [the] squarest people."[137]

Mosely was peripherally involved in the running of the Atlanta Ostrich Farm as well. This ranch, like the Cawston Farm, was meant to function as both a show and breeding farm. It was also seen as the key to the revival of the Cawston ranch, as all raw plumage from Atlanta was to be sent to Pasadena for manufacture. In the words of Bert Vatcher, the Atlanta Ostrich Farm promised to "turn black stock into cash."[138] This time, Vatcher felt, success was assured. To a good friend he prophesied, "You will never catch Bert in the ostrich business the next time the market drops."[139] Overseeing the Georgia farm was Lillian Vatcher, who temporarily moved to Atlanta for this purpose. Joining her was a manager, Mrs. C. Bradley, and a Mr. McDevitt, who may have served as the farm's president. Stein was involved in this project too, not as a financier—he was said to be "not in funds" at this time—but because he hoped to reclaim debts owed him. Bert Vatcher, for his part, was certain that the Atlanta venture would allow Stein to "clean up materially."[140]

George Mosely visited the Cawston and Atlanta operations in 1919, and Alfred Mosely's funds allowed Bradley and Bert and Lillian Vatcher to pay frequent visits to New York in 1919 and 1920, during which they met with Stein and assessed the state of the market.[141] After one of these visits, conducted just before the farm was opened to the public (in May 1919), Bert Vatcher wrote his wife in the most optimistic of terms. "While in New York I visited most of the raw stock dealers and manufacturers," he extolled, "and I never saw, at least for the last five years, the ostrich people so enthusiastic and optimistic about the future of this industry."[142] Vatcher outlined his sanguinity in another letter to a lifelong friend.

> As you know, I have been in the feather game practically my whole life, and I have seen the ups and down; and it would please you to know the feeling of the ostrich feather people in New York, with reference to the future of this industry. Raw stock is increasing by leaps and bounds, and it is a question of getting the raw stock and the labor to put it out. . . . I hear almost daily from the Cawston Farm and the reports are very pleasing—our business is running a great deal stronger than last year, and the prospects for this fall could not be brighter. . . . [T]he Ostrich Feather people in New York could not have stronger confidence in me than they have already displayed and I am going to see that they never regret it. I have had, as you know, an up hill road to travel the last few years, and I appreciate what my friends are doing for me and only hope that some day I can show my appreciation in the right way.[143]

At first, Vatcher's enthusiasm did not seem exaggerated. Between four thousand and twenty thousand visitors were expected at the opening of the Atlanta Ostrich Farm. Two months after the event, the value of raw feathers produced by the joint Cawston operations was increasing rapidly, according to Vatcher.[144] The cache of Cawston goods, once considered inferior to South African plumes, was buoyed by the acute shortage of Cape ostriches, as many of South Africa's farmed birds had been destroyed in the wake of the 1914 slump. Demand was high and supply finite, leading many to believe that "Ostrich feathers will soon be in a class with diamonds as luxuries."[145] To pad the company's stock of feathers, the Cawston Farm even invested in $4,000 worth of plumes from the Western Land and Cattle Company, leaving the historian to imagine a commercial interaction between Stein and Fish—whose New York offices were located within three blocks of each other—that has eluded the archival record.[146]

Yet despite the rebounding of the ostrich feather market, the Atlanta Ostrich Farm was by no means on firm footing. In the summer of 1919 Lillian Vatcher admitted to her husband Bert that she was unable to pay the farm's bills and had "come to the conclusion I must not pay any more of those due unless it is absolutely necessary, as I will certainly run short of cash for the running expenses."[147] Among those owed was Stein, whose debt had only increased.[148]

Meanwhile, McDevitt proved a singularly inept manager, and under his watch the farm began "going to the dogs."[149] By the spring of 1921 the farm's ostriches were "in very bad condition and the Farm fast on a downward path." Not wishing to be involved with the enterprise "when it is in such a bad condition," George Mosely withdrew his and Alfred Mosely's support for the endeavor.[150] Without the Moselys' backing, the Cawston Ranch was culpable for the Atlanta farm's expenses. These the management was able to pay for a time, but this was not a sustainable commercial relationship.[151]

More damaging, the 1919 vogue for feathers didn't last. In 1921 O. B. Fish reported to his collaborators in Arizona that the commercial value of ostrich plumes was so low that "it hardly pays to bundle the goods," proposing, instead, to sell them to the "Duster man."[152] His suppliers appear to have been more optimistic than he, for his proposal was rejected; a year later, Fish reported to them that "customers these days are wanting to buy a few pounds of goods now and then at about twenty-five cents on the dollar." Thanks to a short-lived trend in trimming kewpie dolls with the cheapest grade of ostrich plumes and selling them at county fairs and summer resorts, Fish's own business came to depend on buyers in search of "cheap doll yardage." Like so many in the feather trade, Fish did not have the stamina to wait for another bull market. The spring of 1924 found him pondering a switch "from the feather business to Chinese Rugs," which to him appeared "very much better . . . considering the outlook."[153]

There is no documentation about when the Atlanta Ostrich Farm was disbanded, but the dissolution of the Cawston Farm can be reconstructed. The operation's site in Pasadena was subdivided in 1923, and a selection of its plots sold for $8,000 to William Ellis Lady, a longtime stockholder in the company.[154] Four years later, Bert Vatcher was still placating disgruntled stockholders and trying to settle the company's debt, which included $42,000 arrears against the farm and more than $215,000 in liability against the Cawston business.[155] The remaining property in Pasadena was put on the market in 1928, as was the Vatcher family estate, which was on the grounds of the erstwhile farm. Vatcher hoped prospective buyers would maintain the ostrich show farm, and he assured one such buyer that upcoming conventions of the Shrine Conclave, the Elks, and the American Legion in Pasadena would guarantee a constant stream of visitors. But, Vatcher was quick to add, the land had live steam and power and its buildings could be easily converted into a candy or jam factory.[156] After the farm's sale, the legendary Cawston birds were donated to the California Zoological Society. Following them was Herbert Vatcher, who served as the society's vice president.[157] Fittingly, the legacy of Cawston birds' feathers stretched farther. As late as the 1940s, the plumes of roughly 1,200 Cawston ostriches were still being stored in a Los Angeles warehouse. Valued at $100,000, the plumes were bought by a budding Jewish feather merchant from New York for just $300. By the 1970s, this merchant, Joe Weinstein, had become the largest-scale feather dealer in Los Angeles.[158]

Reaching as it does into the realms of American agriculture, industry, and labor, as well as the West, Southwest, and South, the history of the American ostrich industry may be evocative to readers for reasons that have not been addressed here. Seen from the perspective of a Jewish historian, it is a dynamic and in certain respects familiar tale. The story of the American ostrich feather industry allows us to root Jews in the American industrial countryside and situate this narrative in a trans-hemispheric context.[159] As feather workers, merchants, financiers, and commercial go-betweens, New York's ostrich feather handlers, like Stein, Mosely, and Fish, embody the commercial links Jews experienced and forged in and between regions of the United States, and across oceans, political boundaries, and global markets.

We have seen how feather commerce linked Jews across disparate regions of the United States, but also Jews of different classes, countries, and hemispheres. In tracing the ethnic constitution of a global commodity chain, this is a history of Jews—and American Jews, in particular—circumscribed by the logic of consumption, a logic that is geographically uncircumscribed. Arguably such an approach is well suited to the American context, as Jews in this country were historically involved in so many industries—one thinks of the liquor, diamond, garment, scrap metal, banking, and motion picture businesses, among others—that spanned the continent and relied on regional and diasporic networks abroad. In this light, a global history of American Jews' involvement in the ostrich feather trade is at once exceptional and evocative, a case study that sheds light on an idiosyncratic world that itself simultaneously reveals the transnational foundation of modern Jewish and modern American life.

CONCLUSION

Global Stories

In the wake of the ostrich feather crash of 1914, a bankrupt Jewish merchant left his home and family in disgrace, traveling thousands of miles to a new country in hopes of rebuilding his life. The man settled in a city where one of his grown sons resided and in which he had commercial ties. The son, who had left his homeland as a teenager, was a successful medical professional, husband to a Gentile wife and the father of baptized children. Because of the dishonorable circumstances that surrounded his family's recent fate, the feather merchant's son disowned his father and chose not to tell his own children about his past. His children were thus unaware that their father was by birth a Jew or that their grandfather was alive and residing in the same city. Years passed, and the feather merchant, unable to rebuild his business, lived in near poverty. When times were particularly hard, he called on his son for alms. The son did help his father, but generosity was offset by insult; the son's children, innocent of the identity of their grandfather, habitually mocked the disheveled Jewish beggar who came to their door.

This story was related to me by a grandchild of the feather merchant: a Jewish cousin of the non-Jewish children who unknowingly affronted their grandfather. My informant considered this a delicate piece of family lore, one that should be conveyed only with great discretion and, perhaps, never to family members. But my informant was unaware that the historical record would prove one crucial fact of her story errant: the feather merchant's grandchildren, it turns out, were born after their grandfather's death, so they could have served neither as witnesses nor irritants to his impecunious condition.

What does this counterfactual history tell us—what does it try to tell itself? In truth, both the factual and the imagined elements of this tale are evocative.

Together, they highlight the fleeting nature of success and expertise and the transnational nature of so many turn-of-the-century Jewish lives. Fitting, too, is that this is a story about shame spawned by economic failure: a breakdown felt all the more acutely because it came on the heels of success. To a historian of modern Jewish culture, the humiliation that shrouds the real and imagined elements of this story bespeak more than a sensitivity to personal financial calamity or the rejection of father and faith. This shame is also born of speaking freely of the commercial lives of Jews, particularly if they are speculative, unorthodox, or globally oriented, and perhaps additionally if such a narrative threatens to pass outside Jewish circles—traveling, in this case, from a Jewish to a non-Jewish cousin.

It has been a goal of this book to eschew the indignity that popular and scholarly sources have directly or indirectly associated with Jews' involvement in modern global commerce. This ambition has been shaped not in the interest of taboo-breaking in and of itself, but, rather more modestly, because so many of the commercial practices undertaken by modern Jews were undertaken for clear historical reasons: even, or perhaps especially, if they were speculative, unorthodox, and global in nature. That these reasons do not include Jews' primordial attachment to profit or capital should scarcely warrant mention, were it not for the fact of a centuries-old literature—some but not all of which is anti-Semitic—that has argued otherwise.

Jews were hugely overrepresented in the global exchange of luxury goods at the turn of the twentieth century because they were members of modern Eastern European, Mediterranean, and Anglophone Jewish diasporas. As a result, large numbers of Jews possessed contacts across oceanic, cultural, and political divides. Migration brought Jews to port towns, new colonial markets, and metropoles in Europe and the United States. In all of these contexts they filled novel mercantile and industrial niches. This was possible not only because the Jews in question were transplants, but also because they possessed marketable and portable skills. Some had experience conveying such agricultural goods as grain, leather, or fur from rural to urban markets; others had background in industrial work; and still others already had a footing in trans- and extra-regional trade and could segue with ease into the exchange of new commodities. Even Jewish poverty was relevant, for it readied an enormous industrial labor pool across the globe.

These factors, among others, prompted modern Jews to move into the exchange and processing of a wide variety of consumable goods. Once in these industrial roles, their experiences differed widely from place to place and from one commodity chain to another. This was because the roles Jews filled in a given commercial niche—and, no less, the impact of a given commercial niche on its Jewish participants—depended on the various social and political systems in which they were formed. Thus, for example, a South African Jew's racial identity could hinge on the industry in which he labored, seemingly independently of class, provenance, or immigrant status. Mediterranean Jewish merchants benefited unevenly from extra-regional commerce in the modern period because the Ottoman state was able and inclined to support these endeavors while the Moroccan state was not. Jewish-owned firms in London that dealt in colonial produce multiplied in number, size, and reach as their city acquired the status of global trading hub. And the existence of steep American tariffs on imported ostrich plumes prompted some Jewish merchants and financiers to cultivate feather supplies in the American West, Southwest, and South, an enterprise that might have unfolded in French West Africa but, due to the lackadaisical attitude of the French imperial regime (among other factors), did not.

Even after I have rehearsed some of the reasons for Jews' prominence in the trade of modern luxury goods, on one hand, and for the divergence in their experiences across commodity chains and contexts on the other, a single fundamental question remains. What new insights are generated by a history of Jews and modern global commerce? I propose four answers to this question.

First, by thinking about global commerce we may better appreciate the material ties that have sutured many modern Jews to one another—and, no less, that bind together many aspects of modern Jewish history. Indeed, when it comes to weaving an integrated history of modern Jewries, commerce proves a particularly resilient thread. Perhaps this is due as much to the novelty of this topic as to its inherent fiber; Jewish intellectual history, for example, is a field ambitious in reach and limitless in possibility, but it is, for the moment anyway, yoked to its imagined European, Ashkenazi, and elite male foundation. Jewish social history, meanwhile, is quite rightly moored by the perceived importance—even the omnipotence—of the local. The story of Jews' involvement in global commerce, by contrast, is uniquely and usefully peripatetic. By necessity, histories in this vein reach into diverse geographic and social contexts and across lines of class, gender, and sub-ethnicity, all the while emphasizing the global (and multidirectional) flow of bodies, culture, and capital that brings these contexts together.

If by thinking about global commerce we deepen our understanding of modern Jewries, it is no less true that by thinking about Jews we develop a more nuanced and vivid understanding of global commerce and the modern world. For all the recent interest in consumption as a modern practice, we know little about global supply, that dimension of modern commerce in which Jews were so strikingly overrepresented. Nevertheless, this history is crucial, complicated, and unexpected. One of the more striking aspects of the story of trans-hemispheric commerce is the visibility and influence of ethnicity and sub-ethnicity to its constitution. This finding is surprising partly because it has not commanded the attention of scholars of modern Jews—or scholars of consumption, colonialism, or world history—and partly because of its very conspicuousness for the historical actors involved. Yet attention to Jews' involvement in a single historical commodity chain vividly demonstrates how global supply was actualized on the quotidian and individual level.

Third, a history of Jews and global commerce may move us away from the tropes that have framed, unified, and chronologically structured modern Jewish history—the leitmotifs of community and practice, emancipation and liberalism, modernization and secularization, politicization and embourgoisement. I am interested in circumventing these themes not because they are exhausted, but because they are tried and true, and perhaps, a bit tired. In their place, I center an object—an object that is far less insubstantial, frivolous, or culturally neutral than first appears. A feather cannot topple treasured historical tropes. And yet a feather, like other commodities or material practices whose relationship to modern Jewish history warrant further inquiry, can point to an alternative historical path: one that evades flashpoints much meditated upon; one that spans regions and cultural contexts whose relationship to one another are unimagined; and one that opens up new historical vistas. For our purposes, the pursuit of feathers does not necessarily promise a soft landing onto a smoother historic landscape; it does entail drifting out of certain conventions and into new conceptual and spatial terrain.

Fourth, as a cultural history of economic practices—and an economic history of culture—this study suggests that the boundary between these fields might have outlived its usefulness. A history of Jews' involvement in the global flow of goods suggests that Jewishness and commerce could have been shaped in dialogue, rather like Jewish and political identities were dialogic in so many modern contexts. Derek Penslar has proposed that in some historical instances, "Jews knew they were Jews because of the economic bonds between them."[1] Here I suggest something slightly different. Jews involved in various echelons of the turn-of-the-century ostrich feather commodity chain embarked on commercial adventures in part because of the particular skills, expertise, and contacts they possessed as Ashkenazi, Sephardi, Maghrebi, and Anglophone Jews—and as rich or poor, immigrant or native-born, South African, Mediterranean, British, or American women and men. I have described these skills, expertise, and contacts as elements of human capital, but perhaps it is historically more precise—though politically more risky—to call them elements of modern Jewish capital. In certain industries and times, Jewishness provided the crucial economic thread that knit together global markets.

NOTES

⁓ ⁓

ABBREVIATIONS

AJUSA	*Agricultural Journal of the Union of South Africa*
CPN	C. P. Nel Museum and Archive, Oudtshoorn
GLMS	Guildhall Library Manuscript Section, London
HL COF	Huntington Library Manuscripts, Cawston Ostrich Farm Collection, San Marino, California
LRO	Liverpool Record Office, Liverpool
NASA CTA	National Archives of South Africa, Cape Town Archive Repository, Cape Town
TNA	The National Archives of the United Kingdom, Kew
UAL WFS	University of Arizona Library, Papers of William F. Staunton, Phoenix
UCT BC	University of Cape Town Manuscripts, Cape Town
ULC RNS	University Library Cambridge, Redcliffe Nathan Salaman papers, Cambridge

PREFACE

1. This and all subsequent translations and references to Feldman's book (unless otherwise mentioned) refer to a wonderful recent English language translation and annotation: Feldman, *Oudtshoorn* (1989), 121–22. For the original work: Feldman, *Oudtshoorn* (1940).

INTRODUCTION

1. This quotation comes from expedition member F. C. Smith's unpublished manuscript, "The Union's Ostrich Expedition to North Africa." This manuscript, and further correspondence on the topic, were directed to and preserved by the amateur historian George Aschman of Oudtshoorn, who began (but did not complete) a history

of ostrich farming in the 1940s. Smith's essay is undated, but Aschman's notations on the piece suggest that he received it in April 1944. CPN, Aschman, George [hereafter ASC] 27/16–21 Aschman, George, "Thornton Expedition."

2. Lefèvre, *Le commerce et l'industrie de la plume*; Mosenthal, *Ostriches and Ostrich Farming*.

3. CPN, ASC 27/1 Aschman, George, article clipping, Professor J. E. Duerden, "Ostrich Farming: Crossing the North and South African Ostrich," journal unspecified, February 21, 1910.

4. Lefèvre, *Le commerce et l'industrie de la plume*, 349, 42, 45. In her 1930 study of the ostrich industry, Margaretha Wormser estimated that in 1905, Britain absorbed 31 percent of Cape feathers, Germany 11 percent, and Austria, Hungary, and the Netherlands less than 8 percent each. The United States and France purchased the rest with the bulk destined for the United States. Wormser, "The Ostrich Industry," 47. The American press approximated the value of annual imports of ostrich feathers at $2–3 million at the turn of the century: "Ostrich Raising," *Current Literature (1888–1912)* 31/6 (1902): 710; R. E. Bicknell, "An American Ostrich Farm," *Current Literature* 24/5 (1898): 460.

5. Board of Trade and Industries (South Africa), "Report No. 55: The Ostrich Feather Industry"; Stein, "Falling into Feathers."

6. Data on ostrich feather exports from Tripoli and elsewhere in North Africa has been presented in a series of scholarly works, including Baier, "Trans-Saharan Trade and the Sahel"; Baier, *An Economic History of Central Niger*; Fituri, "Tripolitania, Cyrenaica, and Bilad as-Sudan Trade Relations"; Johnson, "Calico Caravans"; Lovejoy, "Commercial Sectors in the Economy of the Nineteenth-Century Central Sudan"; Lovejoy and Baier, "The Desert-Side Economy of the Central Sudan"; Newbury, "North African and Western Sudan Trade." A brief but thorough discussion of the evolution of this historiography is offered in the Lovejoy study cited here.

7. Hayden, "Speech: The Ostrich Industry."

8. My sense of this expedition relies on a number of sources. In addition to Smith's accounts, these materials include an account of the expedition published in the 1912 *South African Agricultural Journal* that summarized two presentations by Thornton, one to members of the Cape Parliament and another at the Old Town House of Cape Town, both of which took place in May 1912. The archival papers of George Aschman, of the C. P. Nel Museum, also contain a manuscript of an article that was eventually published in the journal *Spotlight* in 1951: CPN, ASC 27/13, H. J. Davin, "Three South Africans Risked Their Lives in Quest of the Golden Feather." Finally, this account draws upon Rob Nixon's summary of Thornton's unpublished memoir, the original of which proved inaccessible: Nixon, *Dreambirds*, 78–87. On Smith and Bowker: "Ostriches from the Soudan: Mr. R. W. Thornton's Story," 807.

9. CPN, ASC 27/1–15 and 27/16–21 "Aschman, George documents: North African Expedition, 'Thornton Expedition.'"

10. "Protecting African Birds"; Oudot, *Le fermage des autruches en Algérie*. According to a

study of 1912, ostrich feathers were exported from the Algerian river valley of M'zab, located in the northern Sahara. There is, however, little evidence of feather commerce being conducted elsewhere in Algeria. Gsell and Delamare, *Exploration scientifique de l'algérie*, 259.

11. CPN, ASC 27/13, Davin, "Three South Africans." By one account, American ostrich farmers had acquired Barbary stock some years earlier: "The City in Brief: Rare Nubian Chicks."

12. CPN, ASC 27/13, Davin, "Three South Africans"; CPN, ASC 27/1–15, "Aschman, George documents: North African Expedition, 'Thornton Expedition'"; CPN, ASC 27/16–21, Smith, "The Union's Ostrich Expedition to North Africa."

13. These experiments were conducted at the Grootfontein School of Agriculture by Professor J. E. Duerden, the only scholar worldwide to hold an academic position in ostrich research. Though the feather market crashed before his experiments were completed, Duerden nonetheless proceeded. His results were published in, among other sources, Duerden, *Ostrich Feather Investigations.*

14. "Ostriches from the Soudan: Mr. R. W. Thornton's Story," 813.

15. CPN, ASC 27/1–15 and 27/16–21 "Aschman, George documents: North African Expedition, 'Thornton Expedition.'"

16. UAL WFS, Box 6, Folder 6, O. B. Fish to W. F. Staunton, September 15, 1921; TNA, LAB 11/697/TB134/2/1927, "Revision of Scope."

17. CPN, ASC 27/16–21 Aschman, George, "Thornton Expedition," F. J. Smith to George Aschman, December 4, 1944.

18. This is according to Joseph Jacobs, who conducted a statistical study of London Jewry of the period. The only full monopoly Jews commanded at the time, according to Jacobs, was over the trade of coconuts. Other of the "chief Jewish monopolies" included the trade of oranges, esparto grass, canes, slippers, sponges, umbrellas, furs, meerschaum pipes, and valentines. These figures are derived from London directories of the period, the records of the Board of Guardians, and membership lists of the Jewish Working Men's Club and the Lads' Institution: Jacobs, *Studies in Jewish Statistics*, 37–38. These figures are usefully summarized in Lipman, *Social History*, 79–82.

19. The quotation is from Phillips, *Song Pilgrimage*, 316. Chapter 3 contains a brief description of the Yemeni Jewish monopoly over Aden's ostrich feather trade.

20. Hajjaj-Liluf, "Ha-kalkalah ve-hatmorot."

21. On occasion work in these fields hints that Jews consumed or operated as whites, Europeans, Londoners, and so on, but rarely as or because they were Jews. Two notable exceptions to this trend are: Auslander, "'Jewish Taste'?"; Heinze, *Adapting to Abundance.* Sociologists, anthropologists, and geographers have been far more sensitive to the importance of Jewishness (and kinship more generally) to commerce, but tend to disavow the importance of sub-ethnicity, on one hand, and the particularities of individual commodity chains on the other. Among other relevant sources: Bonacich, "A Theory of

Middleman Minorities"; Bonacich and Appelbaum, *Behind the Label*; Chirot and Reid, *Essential Outsiders*; Curtin, *Cross-Cultural Trade in World History*; Gmelch, "Groups That Don't Want In"; Perinbaum, "Social Relations." For a more detailed exploration of the usefulness of this literature for historians: Slezkine, *The Jewish Century*, 4–39.

22. On the notion of "homo economicus judaicus" in European and European Jewish thought: Gutwein, "Economics, Politics, and Historiography"; Karp, *The Politics of Jewish Commerce*; Mendes-Flohr, "Werner Sombart's 'The Jews and Modern Capitalism'"; Penslar, *Shylock's Children*. Among the excellent studies of modern Jewish economic practices—which are, as a whole, too numerous to mention here—are Feldman, *Englishmen and Jews*; Graetz, *The Jews in Nineteenth-Century France*; Green, *The Pletzl of Paris*; Heinze, *Adapting to Abundance*; Hyman, *The Emancipation of the Jews of Alsace*; Kahan, *Essays in Jewish Social and Economic History*; Kaplan, *The Making of the Jewish Middle Class*; Kosak, *Cultures of Opposition*; Morawska, *Insecure Prosperity*; Mosse, *Jews in the German Economy*; Rozenblit, *The Jews of Vienna*; Stanislawski, *Tsar Nicholas I and the Jews*.

23. A step in this direction has been taken in a recent edited volume in which the history of Jews' involvement in New York's garment industry is included in a larger collection of work on globalization. The contributions to that volume that focus on Jews are, however, themselves not focused on global trends: Soyer, *A Coat of Many Colors*. See also Feldman, *Immigrants and Workers*; Glenn, *Daughters of the Shtetl*; Green, *The Pletzl of Paris*; Green, *Ready-to-Wear and Ready-to-Work*; Kosak, *Cultures of Opposition*.

24. Chaudhuri, "Shawls, Jewelry, Curry and Rice"; Isaacman and Roberts, *Cotton, Colonialism, and Social History*; Lemire, *Fashion's Favourite*; Maskiell, "Consuming Kashmir"; Ramamurthy, "Why Is Buying a 'Madras' Cotton Shirt a Political Act?"; Roberts, *Two Worlds of Cotton*.

25. Benatar and Pimienta-Benatar, *De Rhodes à Elisabethville*; Ferguson, *The House of Rothschild*; Guershon, "Kippur on the Amazon"; Henriques, *Marcus Samuel*; Meyer, *From the Rivers of Babylon to the Whangpoo*; Stansky, *Sassoon*; Yogev, *Diamonds and Coral*. Jews' involvement in related trans-hemispheric commercial networks moored in the colonial world include: Gartner, *The Jewish Immigrant in England*; Van Onselen, "Jewish Marginality."

26. On the modern period: Slezkine, *The Jewish Century*, especially pages 4–39. Still definitive are S. D. Goitein's masterful studies of Jewish traders of the medieval Mediterranean; Goitein, *A Mediterranean Society*; Goitein, *Letters of Medieval Jewish Traders*. Among the sources on Jewish traders and the early modern world: Bodian, *Hebrews of the Portuguese Nation*; Cesarani, ed., *Port Jews*; Cohen, *Jews in Another Environment*; Israel, *Empires and Entrepôts*; Israel, *European Jewry in the Age of Mercantilism*; Israel, *Diasporas Within a Diaspora*; Schorsch, *Jews and Blacks in the Early Modern World*; Trivellato, *The Familiarity of Strangers*; Yogev, *Diamonds and Coral*.

27. Kurlansky, *Cod*; Kurlansky, *Salt*; Moxham, *Tea*; Pendergrast, *Uncommon Grounds*; Pollan, *The Botany of Desire*; Rappaport, "Packaging China." Two exceptions to this trend are Sidney Mintz's work on sugar, which highlights the centrality of African slaves' stories,

and Andrew Zimmerman's recent work on the global cotton industry: Mintz, *Sweetness and Power;* Zimmerman, "A German Alabama in Africa."

28. Ramamurthy, "Why Is Buying a 'Madras' Cotton Shirt a Political Act?" 741.

29. Vadala, "Une Colonie Tripolitaine."

30. Feldman, *Immigrants and Workers;* Green, *The Pletzl of Paris;* Kahan, *Essays in Jewish Social and Economic History,* 1–70; Kosak, *Cultures of Opposition;* Kuznets, "Immigration of Russian Jews"; Lestchinsky, *Dos yidishe folk in tsifern;* Lestchinsky, "Di antviklung fun yidishn folk."

31. Kahan, *Essays in Jewish Social and Economic History,* 1–70; Klier and Lambroza, eds., *Pogroms;* Nathans, *Beyond the Pale;* Rubinow, *Economic Conditions;* Stanislawski, "Russian Jewry"; Stein, *Making Jews Modern.*

32. Glenn, *Daughters of the Shtetl;* Green, *The Pletzl of Paris;* Green, *Ready-to-Wear and Ready-to-Work;* Kosak, *Cultures of Opposition.*

33. CPN, F/M Solomon Barron, Chaim Sholom Barron to Harry Barron, April 10, 1919. This letter hints at the discord that could attend trans-Atlantic commerce even within a single family. During a severe dip in the feather market, the New York–based Harry Barron accused his Cape-based brother (likely Chaim Sholom) of charging inflated sums for ostrich chicks and subsequently refused to extend him the credit he requested.

34. On the centrality of Livorno to Mediterranean and extra-regional trade in the sixteenth through eighteenth centuries: Filippini, *Il Porto di Livorno;* Israel, *European Jewry in the Age of Mercantilism;* Israel, *Diasporas Within a Diaspora;* Lehmann, "A Livornese 'Port Jew'"; Lévy, *La nation juive portugaise;* Trivellato, *The Familiarity of Strangers;* Yogev, *Diamonds and Coral.* On ties between Livorno and North Africa, including those of feather families, see De Felice, *Jews in an Arab Land;* Rozen, "The Leghorn Merchants in Tunis"; Schroeter, *Merchants of Essaouira;* Schroeter, *The Sultan's Jew;* Triulzi, "Italian-Speaking Communities."

35. Schroeter, *Merchants of Essaouira;* Schroeter, *The Sultan's Jew.*

36. Edward Schuman to author, November 8, 2004, November 10, 2004.

37. For example, CPN, Isaac Nurick Exhibit [hereafter INE], "1909–1914 Letter book," Nurick-Andrade correspondence, May 16, 1910. To another associate Nurick advised: "You can use the ABC Code 5th edition or Lieber's [Standard Code] until, as we get further on in business, we can have a Private Code between us." CPN, INE, "1909–1914 Letter book," Nurick to H. P. Spiers, April 4, 1910. A more detailed analysis of Nurick's correspondence with Isach Hassan appears in Chapter 3.

38. ULC RNS, 8171/27 "Boyhood and the Family Background," 11.

39. In a general way, this conclusion echoes scholarship on medieval and early modern trans-hemispheric trading networks that have emphasized the importance of trust and reputation. I depart from this scholarship in emphasizing how crucial were the bonds of sub-ethnicity among Jewish traders; and also in drawing attention to the

particularities of individual commodity chains. Among the many sources on the importance of kinship, trust, and reputation for traders of earlier periods: Greif, *Institutions
and the Path to the Modern Economy;* Hancock, *Citizens of the World;* Muldrew, *The Economy of
Obligation;* Trivellato, *The Familiarity of Strangers.*

40. Schroeter, *Merchants of Essaouira,* 115.

41. Van Waart, *Paleise van die pluime,* 119–20.

42. Slezkine, *The Jewish Century.*

43. Among the dizzying number of works on changing norms of consumption in
the period, the following have influenced this study: Auslander, *Taste and Power;* Modern
Girl Around the World Research Group, "The Modern Girl Around the World";
Benson, *Counter Cultures;* Breward, *The Culture of Fashion;* De Grazia, *Irresistible Empire;*
De Grazia and Furlough, *The Sex of Things;* Leach, *Land of Desire;* Norton, "Tasting Empire"; Peiss, *Cheap Amusements;* Richards, *Commodity Culture;* Steele, *Paris Fashion;* Walkowitz, *City of Dreadful Delight.* Useful in summarizing and evaluating the burgeoning body
of literature on consumption have been: Roberts, "Gender, Consumption, and Commodity Culture"; Tiersten, "Redefining Consumer Culture"; Trentmann, "Beyond
Consumerism." Histories that attend to questions of supply include: Berg, "In Pursuit
of Luxury"; Levy, "Contemplating Delivery"; Mintz, *Sweetness and Power;* Ramamurthy,
"Why Is Buying a 'Madras' Cotton Shirt a Political Act?"; Zimmerman, "A German
Alabama in Africa."

44. *Report of the Ostrich Feather Commission Appointed to Enquire into the Ostrich Industry,* 26.

45. Clarke, "Fashion Meets Modern Demands"; "Ostrich-Farming."

46. Epstein, *The Rise and Fall of Diamonds;* Kanfer, *The Last Empire;* Proctor, "Anti-Agate:
The Great Diamond Hoax and the Semiprecious Stone Scam."

47. In the wake of the feather crash, some ostrich farmers in the Western Cape embarked on an active campaign to resuscitate and protect the feather industry. These efforts were two-tiered. On one hand, the farmers formed a cooperative movement that
aimed to encourage the government to oversee and protect the feather industry. On the
other, they attempted, by means of a "Propaganda Commission," to promote feather
fashion to would-be consumers at home and overseas. (Among the founding members
of this commission was Russell Thornton.) Such promotional efforts resulted in,
among other things, an extensive display on the ostrich industry at the British Empire
Exhibit of 1924 and an elaborate window display in London's Selfridge's Department
Store. The London-based acting trade commissioner for the Union of South Africa
oversaw the creation of the window display personally. The push for an ostrich farmers'
cooperative had severely negative repercussions for Jews in the industry. On farmers'
experience of and response to the feather crash: *Report of the Ostrich Feather Commission
Appointed to Enquire into the Ostrich Industry;* Board of Trade and Industries (South Africa),
"Report No. 55: The Ostrich Feather Industry." On the attempts to promote South
African ostrich plumes to consumers in London in the wake of the feather crash:

"Ostrich Feather Display in London"; "The Queen at Wembley Ostrich Feather Clipping"; "What Ostrich Feathers Are Doing." On the Propaganda Commission: Wormser, "The Ostrich Industry," 8–9. My thanks to Lynn Thomas for drawing the images in *South African Pictorial* to my attention.

48. Hooper, "Our Paris Letter." Historians of fashion have nuanced Hooper's arguments about the influence of Paris on global fashion, but have not fundamentally challenged her point: Buckley and Hilary, *Fashioning the Feminine*; Crane, *Fashion and Its Social Agendas*, 132–70; De Grazia, *Irresistible Empire*, 157–58; Doughty, *Feather Fashions and Bird Preservation*; Roberts, *Disruptive Acts*; Steele, *Paris Fashion*. Paris also set the world standard for superior feather dyeing and finishing, prompting some New York merchants to send their imported raw plumes to Paris to be finished: Clarke, "Fashion Meets Modern Demands"; Lefèvre, *Le commerce et l'industrie de la plume*, 265–71; Van Kleeck, *Artificial Flower Makers*, 144–90.

49. "The Feather Rage"; Martineau, "Present the Season of Plumes." See also De Courtais, *Women's Headdress*; Delpierre, *Chapeaux, 1750–1960*; Doughty, *Feather Fashions and Bird Preservation*; Lefèvre, *Le commerce et l'industrie de la plume*; Swadling, Wagner, and Laba, *Plumes from Paradise*.

50. Rappaport, "Art, Commerce, or Empire?"; Rappaport, *Shopping for Pleasure*; Steele, *Paris Fashion*; Walkowitz, *City of Dreadful Delight*; Wilson, *Adorned in Dreams*. For a subtle discussion of the development of modern "tastes" among male and female consumers: Norton, "Tasting Empire."

51. Hooper, "The Use and Care of Feathers."

52. An undated Chicago Feather Company style bulletin from this period offered some evidence of the year-round appeal of the plumes. It counseled would-be buyers: "It is always good style to use a handsome ostrich plume to match or harmonize with your tailored suit, your afternoon or evening gown. . . . In summer or winter nothing is more beautiful than the sweeping curves of the ostrich plume." Baker Library Historical Collections, Chicago Ostrich Feather Company Style Bulletin 3, "How to Trim a Hat at Home." The inherent sartorial flexibility of ostrich feathers was also commented on by American and British fashion observers, among others. The quotation regarding the feathers' appropriateness for women of all ages and hues comes from Hooper, "The Use and Care of Feathers." On American working-class women and the politics of hat choice: Enstad, *Ladies of Labor, Girls of Adventure*, 136, 147.

53. Images of a beplumed Bernhardt, among others of Paris' fin-de-siécle fashion world, may be found in Juin, *La parisienne*. For a discussion of Bernhardt's complex and widespread influence: Roberts, *Disruptive Acts*, 165–220.

54. "My Life by Daddy Ostrich" (undated), HL COF, Box 1, Folder "Ostrich Misc., 3 pieces."

55. Hooper, "The Use and Care of Feathers."

56. Board of Trade and Industries (South Africa), "Report No. 55: The Ostrich

Feather Industry," 6. Examples of Americans' and Europeans' uneasy response to feather wearing by non-white men and women in southern Africa may be found in, among other sources: Jackson and Rosenthal, *Trader on the Veld*, 55; Martin, *Home Life on an Ostrich Farm*, 110.

57. A representative of the London-based feather manufacturing firm of George Wills and Company told members of Britain's Trade Board that by the mid-1920s the trade in feather products was largely oriented toward "export to the Colonies," where fashion trends were "always behind" those in Europe. TNA, LAB 11/697/TB134/2/1927 "Revision of Scope," in particular the interview conducted with Mr. Dennick in September 1925. Research by Lynn Thomas on the modern girl in South Africa notes that Flora Ndobe, winner of a highly publicized beauty pageant featured in the 1932–33 issues of the popular *Bantu World*, posed in an ostrich feather tippet; Thomas, "The Modern Girl and Racial Respectability."

58. "Ostrich Feathers," *Scientific American* 7/46, July 31, 1852; "Ornamental Feathers," *Saturday Evening Post*, October 2, 1875; "Ostrich Plumes and Tips: A Great Increase in the Demand for Feathers," *New York Times*, September 24, 1882; "Natural History: The Feather Industry," *Forest and Stream; A Journal of Outdoor Life, Travel, Nature Study, Shooting, Fishing, Yachting* 26/9, March 25, 1886, 162; "The Manufacture of Ostrich Feathers," *Scientific American* 84/11, March 16, 1901, 164; Connor, "A Chapter on Ostrich Feathers"; Gouy, "Ostrich-Feathers"; Hall, *Second Report of the Factory Investigating Commission*; Harper, "The Feather Business"; Manson, *Work for Women*. The particular experience of London's feather handlers is detailed in TNA, LAB 2/835/2; TNA, LAB 2/835/3; TNA, LAB/11/697/TB134/2/1927; TNA, LAB 21682/OTB/OF4487/1921.

59. Bailkin, "Making Faces"; Buckley and Hilary, *Fashioning the Feminine*, 16–49; Nava, "The Cosmopolitanism of Commerce"; Rappaport, *Shopping for Pleasure*; Roberts, *Disruptive Acts*; Walkowitz, "The 'Vision of Salome'"; Wollen, "Fashion/Orientalism/the Body." And, though relative to a later moment: Roberts, "Samson and Delilah Revisited."

60. Hooper, "The Use and Care of Feathers." See also "Fashion Chat," *Pictorial Review*, January 1903, September 1904.

61. Walkowitz, "The 'Vision of Salome.'"

62. "The Queen at Wembley Ostrich Feather Clipping." Reference to the feathers of the Cawston Ostrich Farm of Pasadena, California, being purchased by the Smithsonian Museum may be found in HL COF, Box 3, Folder 1914. See also Amero, "The Southwest on Display"; Cawston Ostrich Farm, *Twenty-Fifth Anniversary Souvenir Catalogue*.

63. "A Loss on Ostrich Feathers," *The Times* (London), April 16, 1912, 21.

64. CPN, ASC 22/1–6 Aschman, George, "History of Oudtshoorn." The 1948 document is titled "Centenary of South Africa's Oldest Boom Town, Pocket Metropolis Which Came to Life in the Little Karoo, Fell from Grace But Is Now Blessed with Prosperity Again," 5.

65. "No Cruelty to Ostriches," *New York Times*, May 11, 1913. The oft-cited analogy with the cutting of human hair may be found in "Is Ostrich Farming Cruel?" *The Times* (London), August 17, 1886, 6. The second statement is attributed to the Jewish ostrich farmer and feather merchant Max Rose.

66. This change may be tracked through monthly auction reports reported by London's brokerage firms and published in *The Agricultural Journal of the Union of South Africa*. It was also described succinctly in *The Times* of London, where one report on the industry stated tersely: "The United States' law [of 1913] has had a marked effect on the London market. At the December sales there was a great drop in prices, while a vast quantity of plumage remained unsold." "The London Feather Sales," *The Times* (London), December 17, 1913, 23.

67. On the evolution of hat fashions in this period: De Courtais, *Women's Headdress*; McDowell, *Hats*.

68. Roberts, "Samson and Delilah Revisited"; Steele, *Paris Fashion*. On the thorny problem of feathers and motorized transport: Board of Trade and Industries (South Africa), "Report No. 55: The Ostrich Feather Industry," 5.

69. This was not an idiosyncratic feature of the feather market. The turn-of-the-century global grain market, too, was increasingly shaped by futures trading and speculation: Levy, "Contemplating Delivery."

70. In Morocco, the decline of the feather trade also closely paralleled the gradual disassimilation of Jews from Moroccan society. For more on how Jewish traders—and Jews more generally—were viewed by Muslims in Morocco after the feather industry's decline: Boum, "Muslims Remember Jews in Southern Morocco."

71. For example, James Buckland, one of Britain's leading anti-plumage lobbyists, wrote that the "clamour" of opposition to anti-plumage legislations "is being raised by a handful of dealers, who care for nothing but their own profits." These claims may well have been accurate. However, given the ethnic constitution of the feather trade, they were also weighted by historical stereotypes about the greed of the Anglo-Jewish merchant. Buckland, *Pros and Cons of the Plumage Bill*, 19. Similar accusations were aired in the *Pall Mall Gazette*, cited in "The Slaughter of Our Songsters," *Littell's Living Age*, February 23, 1889.

CHAPTER 1. THE CAPE OF SOUTHERN AFRICA

1. CPN, INE, "Feather Book [1912]," 19. This business ledger along with other of Nurick's records are displayed in an uncatalogued exhibit at the C. P. Nel Museum in Oudtshoorn.

2. Warnings to this effect were also voiced in *AJUSA* 3/1, January 1912, 146. On the depressed demand for feathers: CPN, INE, "Correspondence with Isach Hassan and associates," November 1 and 10, 1911.

3. "South African Produce Markets: Cape Town, Ostrich Feathers," *AJUSA* 4/1, July 4, 1912, 151.

4. Board of Trade and Industries (South Africa), "Report No. 55: The Ostrich Feather Industry."

5. The majority of these feathers were purchased from the Potgieter Brothers, the largest ostrich holders in the district. CPN, INE, "Feather Book [1912]," 24. On the Potgieter Brothers: Van Waart, *Paleise van die pluime.*

6. On the particular communities whence they came: *Krakenowo, Our Town in Lithuania;* Bakalczuk-Felin, *Yizkur-Bukh.*

7. On ostrich hunting by white travelers: Ballantyne, *Six Months at the Cape,* 53–87; Jackson and Rosenthal, *Trader on the Veld.*

8. Douglass, "Ostrich Farming"; Mosenthal and Harting, *Ostriches and Ostrich Farming;* Thornton, "The Ostrich Feather Industry in South Africa."

9. In 1865, census returns recorded only 80 domesticated birds in Cape Colony; in 1875, 32,247 were noted. Mosenthal and Harting, *Ostriches and Ostrich Farming;* Smit, *Ostrich Farming,* 7.

10. Board of Trade and Industries (South Africa), "Report No. 55: The Ostrich Feather Industry."

11. Van Waart, *Paleise van die pluime.*

12. On the social and economic developments in Oudtshoorn in this period: Appel, *Die distrik Oudtshoorn;* Smit, *Ostrich Farming;* Wormser, "The Ostrich Industry."

13. "The Home of the Ostrich," 366.

14. Ibid; Evans and Evans, "Lucerne Growing as a Fodder for Stock." For the most detailed study of the environmental factors that shaped the Oudtshoorn District: Appel, *Die distrik Oudtshoorn.*

15. Buirski, "Aspects of Material Life," 23–24.

16. *The Times* (London), November 29, 1864, 12.

17. *The Times* (London), October 2, 1876, 12. Arthur Douglass wrote a study of ostrich farming in South Africa with the express purpose of advising young British men on how to penetrate and succeed in the industry. Douglass, *Ostrich Farming in South Africa,* 26.

18. Christopher, "The Growth of Landed Wealth."

19. Buirski, "Aspects of Material Life," 52–53.

20. The number of wells can be measured by comparing the censuses of the Cape of Good Hope of 1891 and the Union of South Africa of 1911. *Results of a Census of the Colony of the Cape of Good Hope; Census of the Union of South Africa, 1911.*

21. Christopher, "The Growth of Landed Wealth."

22. Aschman, "Oudtshoorn," 133. For further discussion of Oudtshoorn's extravagance: Van Waart, *Paleise van die pluime.*

23. Buirski, "Aspects of Material Life," chapter 2.

24. Between these years, the population of Oudtshoorn grew from 5,377 to 10,930. *Results of a Census of the Colony of the Cape of Good Hope; Census of the Union of South Africa, 1911.*

25. The wider story of the loss of land, capital, and opportunities by colored people in the Cape is told in Keegan, *Rural Transformations.*

26. Albasu, *The Lebanese in Kano;* Dotson and Dotson, "The Economic Role of Non-Indigenous Ethnic Minorities"; Falola, "The Lebanese in Colonial West Africa"; Freund, *Insiders and Outsiders;* Hourani, *The Lebanese in the World;* Seidenberg, *Mercantile Adventurers;* Swanson, "The Asiatic Menace"; Winder, "The Lebanese in West Africa."

27. On Sephardi traders in southern Africa: Benatar, "El Kal Sefaradi de Lubum-bash"; Benatar and Pimienta-Benatar, *De Rhodes à Elisabethville;* Breun, "Rhodes, It's a Long Way"; Franco-Hasson, *Il etait une fois, l'ile des roses;* Kerem, "The Migration of Rhodian Jews to Africa and the Americas from 1900–1914"; Minerbi, *From Rhodes to Africa;* Rahmani, *Shalom Bwana.* My insight into these communities has been greatly advanced by a collection of oral histories conducted by Sergio Itzhak Minerbi with Jews (including Ben Atar, Léon Hasson, J. Israel, and Simon Israel) who resided or worked in the region. Transcripts of these interviews are held by the Hebrew University Institute for Contemporary Jewish History Oral History Department, Jerusalem. I am also enormously thankful to Moise Rahmani for sharing his voluminous personal archive of oral histories he conducted with Jewish residents of the former Belgian Congo. Most of these interviews took place in the 1990s in Brussels: they form the archival foundation for Rahmani's 2002 study cited above.

28. Foster, Tennant, and Jackson, *Statutes of the Cape of Good Hope, 1652–1886,* 2197.

29. Ibid., 2196–98.

30. Simon, "Historical Notes," 167.

31. According to Cape censuses, 251 Jews lived in the district in 1891 and nearly 800 in 1904 and 1913. However, as the feather industry was fueled by itinerant feather buyers, these figures likely vastly underestimated how many Jews actually operated in Oudtshoorn District. *Results of a Census of the Colony of the Cape of Good Hope; Census of the Union of South Africa, 1911.* I borrow the figure of 1,000–1,500 from Coetzee, "The Oudtshoorn Jewry Interviews"; Coetzee, "Immigrants to Citizens"; Coetzee, "Fires and Feathers."

32. M. P. V., "Jottings from South Africa: Oudtshoorn," *Jewish Chronicle,* November 15, 1901. A *Jewish Chronicle* article from 1887 stated that Oudtshoorn, the center of the feather buying trade, "is entirely in the hands of Jews." "Appeals from South Africa," *Jewish Chronicle,* March 3, 1887, no. 937, 13.

33. "Natural History: The Feather Industry."

34. Lists of newly licensed ostrich feather buyers were regularly published in the *Oudtshoorn Courant,* for example on December 1, 1888, March 25, 1890, February 2, 1893, and March 8, 1894.

35. A ruthlessly anti-Semitic depiction of an illegal ostrich feather buyer was created

by W. C. Scully, novelist and magistrate for the Oudtshoorn region. Scully, *Between Sun and Sand*, 29. The figure of 277 feather buyers licensed in 1913 is drawn from a Standard Bank Inspector's Report and cited in Coetzee, "Immigrants to Citizens," 7.

36. Much of the literature on South African Jewry emphasizes that Russian Jews left their homes out of a fear of pogrom violence or tsarist oppression. Scholars of the Russian (and to some extent American émigré) context, however, emphasize ambition as serving as a central "push" for would-be Jewish émigrés. On the forces that constrained Jews in Russia, see, among other sources: Kahan and Weiss, *Essays in Jewish Social and Economic History*; Klier and Lambroza, eds., *Pogroms*; Rogger, *Jewish Policies*.

37. Letters by South African "correspondents" to Yiddish and Hebrew newspapers published in the Russian Empire (notably *Ha-melits, Ha-tsefira, Ha-magid* and *Der fraynd*) reached Jewish readers with impressive regularity. Some of these letters have been catalogued: Grossman, "A Study in the Trends and Tendencies." Others have been translated: Hoffman, *Book of Memoirs*. A thorough study of these texts, however, remains to be written. On the negative images of Jews that emerged in this and other periods of South African history: Shain, *The Roots of Antisemitism*. For further exploration of the topic: Krut, "Building a Home"; Krut, "The Making of a South African Jewish Community"; Shain, *Jewry and Cape Society*; Shimoni, *Jews and Zionism*; Van Onselen, *Studies in the Social and Economic History*.

38. On Jews' role in the prostitution, liquor, diamond, and gold industries of South Africa: Bristow, *Prostitution and Prejudice*; Rosenthal, "On the Diamond Fields"; Van Onselen, *Studies in the Social and Economic History*; Van Onselen, "Jewish Marginality." Firsthand accounts of Jews' presence in gold and diamonds include: Cohen, *Reminiscences of Kimberly*; Feldman, *Motsudi*.

39. On the particular communities whence they came: *Krakenowo, Our Town in Lithuania*; Bakalczuk-Felin, *Yizkur-bukh*.

40. Salo Baron and Arcadius Kahn have described tanning and the leather trade as "an outstanding Jewish occupation" of Poland, Lithuania, and Russia. In interwar Poland, Jews represented over 40 percent of tanners and leather workers. Literature on Jews' involvement in textiles and tailoring—and on their creation of unions in both industries—is extensive. For a useful, if dated, bibliography on this topic: Baron, Kahan, and Gross, *Economic History of the Jews*, 171, 288–90. See also Mahler, *Yidn in amolikn poyln*; Mahler, *Yehude polin ben shete milhamot 'olam*. On Jews and the fur trade: Fisher, *The Russian Fur Trade*, 196–97.

41. The history of the Jewish *smous*, and popular views of him, has begun to be studied, but a comprehensive history remains to be written: Jowell and Folb, *Joe Jowell of Namaqualand*; Shain, "'Vant to Puy a Vaatch.'" Firsthand accounts include: Jackson and Rosenthal, *Trader on the Veld*; Locher, "The South African Trader"; Rybko, *Oyf di pleynen fun afrike*. A number of oral histories of *smous* and their families have been preserved by the UCT Archives.

42. CPN, F/M Solomon Barron.

43. "Licenses, Oudtshoorn, Ostrich Feather Buyers, £5," *Oudtshoorn Courant*, December 1, 1888, 1.

44. This information is assembled in "Residents' List of Oudtshoorn Jewry." This list mistakenly identifies 1889 as the year in which Nurick acquired his first feather buyer's permit. Isaac Nurick's granddaughter, Ann Harris, has described her grandfather's close relationship to Hotz: Ann Harris to author and extended Nurick family, November 23, 2004.

45. Thanks to Derrick Lewis for sharing his copy of this document with me. Standard Bank Archives, "Nurick and Son request for loan from Standard Bank, 1899."

46. The Queen's Street shul, built in 1888, was attended by the more established, wealthy, and Anglicized Jews in town. The orthodox St. John Street shul, built in 1896, was attended by more recent immigrants, who were likely to be less well off financially. Aschman, "Oudtshoorn," 123; Coetzee, "Immigrants to Citizens," 28.

47. Anne (Chana) Biderman to author and extended Nurick family, November 20, 2004.

48. Lewis, *The Sanders Story, a Family Saga.*

49. Derrick Lewis to author, November 3, 2004; Lewis, *The Sanders Story, a Family Saga.*

50. "A Jewish Wedding," *Oudtshoorn Courant*, March 9, 1893.

51. The most prominent Jewish feather buyers were included in commercial directories compiled in the early decades of the twentieth century. One directory from 1912 included more than a hundred Jewish business people, most of whom were feather buyers. *Donaldson's South African Directory; Braby's Cape Province Directory.* On the Nurick's motor car: Judith Landau to author and extended Nurick family, November 20, 2004; Derrick Lewis to Judith Landau, author, and extended Nurick family, November 20, 2004.

52. CPN, INE, "Feather Book [1914]."

53. Simon, "Historical Notes," 167. An incomplete sampling of 1,000 Jews (of approximately 1,253) who were naturalized in the Cape Colony between 1904 and 1907 includes 31 who called themselves "feather buyers." Many more self-identified as "speculators" or "hawkers," categories that no doubt encompassed feather buyers. Rabinowitz, *Cape Colony Jewish Naturalization Registers, 1903–1907,* available from http://www.jewishgen .org/SAfrica/natrec.htm.

54. Many of the small-scale feather buyers of Oudtshoorn resided on the road to Calitzdorp, a street known then as "Jewish Street." Hotels and boarding houses were also home to a great number. Feldman, *Oudtshoorn*, 99.

55. UCT BC, 949, 0117, Lily Jacobs, 15–23. On tensions between Boer farmers and Jewish feather buyers, see also Shain, *The Roots of Antisemitism*, 23–24.

56. UCT BC, 949, 0175, Alex Miller, 8.

57. Feldman, *Oudtshoorn*, 96.

58. Wallace and Caldecott, *Farming Industries of Cape Colony*, 21. Anxiety about Jews'

dominance of the feather trade was also expressed in the Afrikaans-language *Volksbode*, in which an editorial from 1893 lambasted Jewish participation in the feather trade. This editorial was rebutted in a letter to the *Oudtshoorn Courant* by Meyer Wolfsen, minister of the Hebrew Congregation of Oudtshoorn. "If the Jews were to give up feather buying," Wolfsen raged, "both trade and commerce in this town would collapse." M. Wolfsen, Letter to the editor, *Oudtshoorn Courant*, March 16, 1893. The original article from *Volksbode*, and the translation offered here, are analyzed in Shain, *The Roots of Antisemitism*, 23–24.

59. Anne Berman to author and extended Nurick family, November 20, 2004.

60. Nurick's business records include thirty-two such transactions brokered by "Abelkop and Rosenberg" during the course of three trips conducted in 1913 and 1914; the total Nurick was owed by contract farmers was £4,482. CPN, INE, "1909–1914 Letter book," "Trip 1 percent Abelkof and Rosenberg," undated.

61. The official history of the Standard Bank more or less absolves the institution of responsibility for encouraging speculation and the abuse of promissory notes. Instead, it lays blame on "speculative fever, which spread like a disease from which even some officials at the Standard Bank were not immune." Henry, *The First Hundred Years of the Standard Bank*, 79. For references to the bank's role in encouraging speculation, see Feldman, *Oudtshoorn*, 97; UCT BC, 949, 0175, Alex Miller. On bank inspectors' distrustful view of Jewish feather buyers: Shain, "'Vant to Puy a Vaatch,'" 117–19.

62. For American and European observers, the conflation of "Jew" and "speculator" was fueled, at least in part, by anxiety about Jews' prominence in the trade of commodity futures. This theme has not been explored at any length in secondary sources—for a fascinating recent parallel discussion, and further relevant citations: Levy, "Contemplating Delivery."

63. UCT BC, 949, 0175, Alex Miller, 16.

64. UCT BC, 949, 0130, Reggie Kahn, 18.

65. Feldman, *Oudtshoorn*, 99.

66. For this purpose, the wealthy maintained two homes, one on the farm and another, more lavish home in town. Others stayed in hotels like the Imperial, a favored (and notoriously rowdy) gathering place for the wealthier participants in the trade. Van Waart, *Paleise van die pluime*, 98–99.

67. While narrating his visit to an ostrich farm, Arthur Douglass noted that "all the labor on the farm is done by natives, who make excellent servants for managing stock." See also Mosenthal, *Ostriches and Ostrich Farming*, 207–15.

68. UCT BC, 949, 0130 Reggie Kahn, 2.

69. UCT BC, 949, 0117 Lily Jacobs, 14, 17.

70. Censuses conducted by the Cape of Good Hope in 1891 and 1911 suggest that during the feather boom, roughly 50 percent of male and female farm workers were non-white (a category that, in this region of the Cape at this time, tended to refer to colored people). According to these censuses, in 1891, a total of 4,076 men and 1,016

women were employed on farms in the Oudtshoorn District. "European or White workers" included 2,158 men and 467 women, while "Other than European or White" workers numbered 1,918 men and 549 women. In 1911, a total of 5,776 persons were estimated to work on farms, including 2,451 "European or White" males, 484 "European or White" females, 591 "South African Native" men and 117 "South African Native" women, and 1,623 male "Other Coloured" males and 410 "Other Coloured" females. *Results of a Census of the Colony of the Cape of Good Hope; Census of the Union of South Africa, 1911.*

71. In the early 1880s, ostrich farmers had discovered that plucking plumes, which was used as a method of harvesting the first farmed feathers, caused deterioration in the quality of a bird's plumes over time. Thereafter, ostrich farmers began clipping feathers close to their base, which caused no harm to the bird or to future feather growth. The remaining stub was removed some time later, after it had desiccated. Accounts of this transition were common in the popular press, as they provided implicit defense of the ostrich industry as being less cruel than was the collection of plumes from wild birds. See, among other sources, "Is Ostrich Farming Cruel?" *The Times* (London), August 17, 1896, 12; "Ostrich Farming in Cape Colony," *The Times* (London), November 5, 1910, 55; "No Cruelty to Ostriches," *New York Times*, May 11, 1913; Douglass, *Ostrich Farming in South Africa*, 74–79.

72. *The Times* (London), September 9, 1870, 11.

73. Mosenthal and Harting, *Ostriches and Ostrich Farming*, 230. Colored workers, especially women, were also employed as domestic workers in the homes of white families in Oudtshoorn District (here, as elsewhere in the Cape, Boer men and women resisted moving into the sphere of domestic work). This is evidenced in oral histories conducted with Jews who grew up in the region, as well as in secondary scholarship. For example: UCT BC, 949, 0107 Sybil Honikman, 57–58; 0027 Charles Brenner, 12; 0159 Arthur Lewin, 4. On Boer resistance to domestic work: Buirski, "Aspects of Material Life"; Van Onselen, *Studies in the Social and Economic History.*

74. Buirski, "Aspects of Material Life," 66.

75. According to a study published in the *Oudtshoorn Courant*, morbidity rates for tuberculosis were 13.3 per 1,000 feather sorters, 8.72 per 1,000 colored people, and 1.36 per 1,000 Europeans living in Oudtshoorn. *Oudtshoorn Courant*, 12 March 1914. The descriptions of feather sorting, borrowed from the Tuberculosis Commission's report, are cited in Buirski, "Aspects of Material Life," 68.

76. This is evident, too, in the fact that Jewish feather families who lived in town appear to have employed colored domestic workers as soon as they were financially able, no doubt for the status they afforded as much for the labors they performed. Sybil Honikman, daughter of a Jewish feather exporter based in Oudtshoorn, has remembered two colored employees working for her family: a live-in domestic worker named Rosie, and a driver by the name of Steven. Charles Brener has recalled that his family

employed a domestic worker even though his father was a small-scale and itinerant feather buyer. Arthur Lewin mentions his family employing several colored domestic workers, among them a maid, a cook, and a man who minded the horses, all of whom lived on the grounds of the Lewin house. From a rather badly damaged photograph, we learn that Isaac and Annie Nurick also relied on colored domestic workers. The photograph shows the couple seated in a horse-drawn cart with their first baby, Sarah (Cissie), in Annie's lap. Standing next to the carriage are two colored women and one colored man, all of whom are finely dressed and appear quite young. UCT BC, 949, 0107, Sybil Honikman, 57–58; 0027 Charles Brenner, 12; 0159 Arthur Lewin, 4. Thanks to Derrick Lewis for sharing with me his own copy of the photograph of Isaac and Annie Nurick, their child, and domestic workers. Lewis dates the photograph to 1894.

77. Before 1904, when the railway connecting Oudtshoorn and Port Elizabeth was completed, goods leaving Oudtshoorn were conveyed by horseback or ox wagon fifty-seven miles over the Swartberg mountains to Mossel Bay (where they could be loaded on ships and transported to Cape Town or overseas) or seventy miles over the mountains to Prince Albert Road, where the rail line commenced. On the state financing of mountain passes: Keegan, *Colonial South Africa*, 211.

78. Noble, ed., *Official Handbook*, 262, 326; Wormser, "The Ostrich Industry," 25–27. For an example of the kind of legislation the British government levied against ostrich imports: "An Act for the Better Preservation of Wild Ostriches (No. 12)."

79. Simon, "Historical Notes," 167.

80. Aschman, "Oudtshoorn"; Aschman, "A Childhood"; Feldman, *Oudtshoorn.*

81. On the development of scientific racism in South Africa: Dubow, *Scientific Racism.*

82. Berger, *Jewish Trails*; Feldman, *Shvarts un vays*; Leibowitz, "Vayse kafers"; Sherman, "Serving the Natives"; Titelstad, "Eating-Houses on the Witwatersrand"; Turrell, *Capital and Labour on the Kimberley Diamond Field*; Van Onselen, *Studies in the Social and Economic History.*

83. On perceptions of Jews by colonial administrators, missionaries, and other European settlers: *The South African Jewish Year Book*; Burke, *Lifebuoy Men, Lux Women*; Gray, "The Jew in the Economic Life in South Africa"; Saron and Hertz, eds., *The Jews in South Africa*; Shain, *The Roots of Antisemitism*; Shimoni, *Jews and Zionism.*

84. The most thorough study of anti-Semitic (or "anti-Peruvian," as it was locally known) sentiment in South Africa is Shain, *The Roots of Antisemitism*, 26–34. Additional relevant studies have already been cited.

85. Feldman, *Yidn in dorem-afrike*, 43–45.

86. On "whiteness" of Oudtshoorn Jewry: Coetzee, "Immigrants to Citizens"; Coetzee, "Fires and Feathers." Other sources that have explored the racial configuration of South African Jews have focused on the apartheid era and have been literary or memoiristic.

87. Duerden, "The Future of the Ostrich Industry."

88. In 1913 there were 776,000 ostriches in the Union of South Africa, and over 1 million cubic pounds of feathers valued at just under £3 million were exported; ibid., 2.

89. In Oudtshoorn, there was little investment in irrigation reform during the feather boom, particularly relative to other regions of the Cape. In 1914, farmers were still relying on relatively primitive irrigation techniques that inhibited rotation to other agricultural products. Buirski, "Aspects of Material Life," 24, 30; Godlonton, *Oudtshoorn and Its Farms.*

90. Reference to the storage of feathers in New York may be found in "South African Produce Markets," *AJUSA* 3/1, June 1912, 146.

91. CPN, INE, "Feather Book [1914]," 25 and 26. Some of these purchases Nurick undertook in partnership with one or more associates.

92. "South African Produce Markets," *AJUSA* 2/1, January–June 1914, 118.

93. Anne Biderman to author, November 17, 2004; Judith Landau to extended Nurick family and author, November 17, 2004.

94. Judith Landau to extended Nurick family and author, November 17, 2004; Ann Harris (neé Schech) to author and extended Nurick family, November 23, 2004. These memories appear to be confirmed by archival records: on July 26, 1918, after the death of his wife, Annie, Nurick oversaw the auction of the family's furniture, including even the oven door, for a total of £174.17. NASA CTA, vol. 13/1/144, "Nurick, Annie. Liquidation and Distribution Account," "Copy of vendor roll of sale held at Oudtshoorn on the 26th July, 1918 by I. Nurick." My thanks to Lynn Thomas for obtaining copies of this and other archival documents from NASA.

95. During the ostrich feather boom, feather buyers had routinely extended promissory notes in lieu of cash. In this, feather buyers were financially and conceptually supported by banks, foremost among them the Standard Bank, which had a branch in Oudtshoorn: Henry, *The First Hundred Years of the Standard Bank.*

96. CPN, INE, "Letter Book [1914]," "In the Court of the Resident Magistrate for the District of Steynsburg, In the matter between Arthur Bentley N.O. Plaintiff and Petrus Erasmus Smit and Daniel P. Smit, Defendants."

97. CPN, INE, "Letter Book [1914]," "From Joint Liquidator to Frank Rousseau [Notary Public in Steynburg] Esq. Re: D. P. and E. Smit, 17 October 1914."

98. CPN, INE, "Letter Book [1914]," "Notary Public to Messrs. I. Nurick and Co., 29 July, 1914."

99. CPN, INE, "Letter Book [1914]," "Notary Public to Messrs. I. Nurick and Co., 4 September, 1914."

100. The records of other legal battles Nurick was engaged in at this time are held by the National Archives of South Africa's Cape Town Archive Repository. See, for example, NASA CTA, vol. 2/1/1/757, "Illiquid case. Gideon Hendrik Van Zyl versus Pieter Jacob de Villiers and Isaac Nurick. Claim for the recover of money" and "Illiquid case. Isaak Nurick versus Philiop Cornelis Badenhorst, Action against breach of contract."

101. CPN, INE, "Letter Book [1914]," "In Bankruptcy. In the Matter of Isach Hassan."

102. NASA CTA, vol. 13/1/144, "Nurick, Annie. Liquidation and Distribution Account"; Isaac Nurick to Grand Magistrate of Cape Town, January 10, 1924; Oudtshoorn Magistrate to Cape Town Magistrate, October 13, 1924.

103. Anne Biderman to author and extended Nurick family, November 23, 2004. Reference to Isaac Nurick's departure is also made in Lewis, *The Sanders Story, a Family Saga.*

104. Nurick's descendants recalled that he died of nephritis and was buried in Jewish Carterhatch Lane cemetery, Enfield. A gravestone that may or may not be his documents a death on January 18, 1933. One of the children he saw before his death was his son Lyle, who had moved to London to attend dentistry school. Lyle even offered occasional financial support to his father, although it was not revealed to his Anglican children until after Lyle's own death. The other child with whom he had contact was his daughter Fanny, who visited London in the 1920s or '30s. According to Fanny's son, Isaac spoke of returning to Russia, which seems, given the era, a rather desperate fantasy. This information was conveyed by Fanny's son, Jonathan Blumberg, to Anne Biderman and then to me and the extended Nurick family: Anne Biderman to author and extended Nurick family, February 18, 2005. On Nurick becoming a hawker: Judith Landau to author, November 17 and 24, 2004; Anne Biderman to author and extended Nurick family, February 18, 2005; Anne Biderman to Derrick Lewis, June 27, 2003, sent to author by Derrick Lewis, November 4, 2004. On Lyle's secret: Richard Nurick to author, November 16, 2004. My sense of the tragedies that surrounded the Nurick family at this time owes much to a conversation with Richard Nurick, Rose Marie Nurick, Catherine James, and Pat Baldachin on June 25, 2006.

105. Smit, *Ostrich Farming,* 45. On the Calitzdorp side of the Oudtshoorn District, 1,130 farmers were rendered destitute by 1916. Buirski, "Aspects of Material Life," 72.

106. Van Waart, *Paleise van die pluime,* 125, 35.

107. Buirski, "Aspects of Material Life," especially chapter 4, and 78–85.

108. Lückhoff, "The Little Karroo," 254.

109. The dispersion and disintegration of Oudtshoorn's Jewish community in the second half of the twentieth century is ably described in Coetzee, "Immigrants to Citizens"; Coetzee, "Fires and Feathers."

110. Hirschbein, *Felker un lender,* 196.

111. Feldman, *Oudtshoorn,* 127.

112. Isidore Barron to author, March 24, 2004.

113. For example, "The Slump in Ostrich Feathers," *Oudtshoorn Courant,* March 17, 1914; "The Ostrich Feather Trade," *Oudtshoorn Courant,* April 14, 1914. The mood and public discourse of this period is analyzed in Coetzee, "Immigrants to Citizens," 55–58.

114. *Report of the Ostrich Feather Commission Appointed to Enquire into the Ostrich Industry;* Board of Trade and Industries (South Africa), "Report No. 55: The Ostrich Feather Industry."

115. Such disdain surfaced in conversation with Isidore and Carol Barron (March 26, 2004), and was aired in oral histories by Isidore Barron and Markus Monty conducted with Daniel Coetzee in 1999.

CHAPTER 2. LONDON

1. I. Salaman and Company Ostrich Feather Merchants first published contact information in the "Trades Directory" of the Post Office London Directory in 1870.

2. ULC RNS, 8171/27 "Boyhood and the Family Background," 11.

3. Edward Schuman recalls that his father, Philip R. Schuman, who founded P. R. Schuman Duster Company in New York in 1907, either attended London's auctions in person or relied on one of many assistants overseas. In such cases Schuman would receive, read, and mark his auction catalogue at home, thereby providing a bidding guide in absentia. Edward Schuman to author, November 9, 2004.

4. GLMS, Ms. 20508. Myer's name and address are handwritten on the cover.

5. A Lewis and Peat circular that reported on the auction of February 1879 describes the motivation behind this procedure: "A discussion arose on this occasion upon the insufficient time provided for the due examination of the Feathers; and a resolution was come to, that in the future, the sales take place at Eleven o'clock precisely; That no Feathers received at the warehouse after the Tuesday preceding the sale week shall be included in the ensuing auction; and that the Catalogues shall be issued, and the Feathers on shew on the Tuesday morning preceding the sales." GLMS, Ms. "Ostrich Feathers February Sales," Lewis and Peat Circular, February 19, 1879.

6. Douglass, *Ostrich Farming in South Africa*, 88.

7. Gouy, "Ostrich-Feathers," 376.

8. "Ostrich Plume Rivals. New York Favors South African Rather Than California Feathers—Reasons for the Preference," *New York Times*, October 26, 1903.

9. Although individual firms could be found in Manchester, Leeds, and Liverpool, London was the center of the Britain's feather trade throughout and after the feather boom. TNA, LAB 2/835/2.

10. Cain and Hopkins, *British Imperialism*; Cannadine, *Ornamentalism*; Hall, *The Industries of London*; Jones, *Outcast London*; McCusker, "The Demise of Distance"; Michie, *The City of London*; Nava, "The Cosmopolitanism of Commerce"; Schneer, *London 1900*; Walkowitz, "The 'Vision of Salome.'"

11. Jacobs, *Studies in Jewish Statistics*, 37–38. These figures are usefully summarized in Lipman, *Social History*, 79–82.

12. The figure of 90 percent is offered by the Ostrich Feather, Fancy Feather, and Artificial Flower Trade Board in a study of the industry conducted in roughly 1921. TNA, LAB 2/723/15. See also "Chief Inspector of Factories and Workshops Report, October 1886–87."

13. TNA, LAB 2/835/3, undated memorandum, likely early winter, 1919. A second version of this document, dated March 1921, is filed in TNA, LAB 11/697/TB134/2/1927.

14. The term "sweating" had its origins in the first half of the nineteenth century, when it was coined to refer to the reconfiguration of London's garment industry. "Sweating meant long and tedious hours of labor, abominably low wages, and degrading and unhealthy surroundings. . . . Above all, sweating meant the movement of work into unregulated premises, often the worker's home, but just as often any backroom, basement or garret shop—any place beyond the policing eye of the respectable artisan, manufacturer, or government inspector." Schmiechen, *Sweated Industries and Sweated Labor*, 3. See also "Select Committee of House of Lords on Sweating System Second Report"; Hall, *The Industries of London*; Jones, *Outcast London*. On the demographic transformation of Anglo-Jewry in general, and the East End, in particular, at this time: Feldman, *Immigrants and Workers*; Gartner, *The Jewish Immigrant in England*; Hourwich, "The Jewish Laborer in London"; Lipman, *Social History*; Newman, ed., *The Jewish East End*; Pollins, *Economic History of the Jews in England*; Williams, *The Making of Manchester Jewry*.

15. "de Pass, Alfred Aaron" and "Mosenthal, Alfred," *Encyclopaedia Judaica*. Further information on de Pass may be found in short biographies published in *The Jewish Chronicle*, April 12 and June 21, 1895.

16. Kelly's Post Office London Directories lists very few ostrich feather merchants prior to the 1860s.

17. Notes in the margin of this policy attest that one year later, in July 1825, the value of this man's household goods and book plates had dropped nearly by half, that he had lost his jewels and china, and that the worth of his wearing apparel had also eroded, rendering his net worth a mere £500. GLMS, Ms. 11936/500.

18. For Judah Imschwartz, GLMS, Ms. 11936/472, 11936/481; for Jacob Davies, GLMS, Ms. 11936/484, 11936/497, 11936/503 (June 24, 1824, November 20, 1824, July 5, 1825), 503.

19. Other factors relevant to the rise of the Cape ostrich industry included the invention of the ostrich incubator and the discovery of the superior quality of lucurne as ostrich feed. Keegan, *Colonial South Africa*, 211; Noble, ed., *Official Handbook*, 262, 326; Wormser, "The Ostrich Industry," 25–27. For an example of the kind of legislation levied against ostrich imports: "An Act for the Better Preservation of Wild Ostriches (No. 12)."

20. According to British House of Commons Parliamentary Papers, in 1858 the Cape of Good Hope was exporting 1,852 cubic pounds of ostrich feathers annually, a quantity valued at just over £12,000. "Chief Inspector of Factories and Workshops Report, October 1882–83," 64. Statistics about the relative quantity of ostrich feathers exported to London from North and South Africa are from Lefèvre, *Le commerce et l'industrie de la plume*, 344–46.

21. London's monopoly extended to the sale of feathers from the marabout and bird of paradise, both of which were imported from Calcutta, and the vulture and heron, which were imported from Brazil. Lefèvre, *Le commerce et l'industrie de la plume.* See also Méry, "Reseignements Commerciaux"; Mosenthal, *Ostriches and Ostrich Farming;* Oudot, *Le fermage des autruches en Algérie.*

22. "Trade in Ostrich Feathers," *Hunt's Mercantile Magazine* 38 (1858): 652.

23. "Protecting African Birds"; Baier, *An Economic History of Central Niger,* 88; Johnson, "Calico Caravans," 106.

24. Popular and scholarly accounts echoed this position. A 1907 article in the popular outdoor journal *Forest and Stream,* for example, explained to readers: "To-day the steamboat and the railroad tap this region [the upper Niger and center of the plumage trade], though they do not penetrate it. They have killed the desert caravan trade, and the ostrich feathers and heron plumes now take the steam route to the Atlantic." "Protecting African Birds." See also "Trade in Ostrich Feathers."

25. Walvin, *Fruits of Empire,* 31. British tea imports in the late nineteenth century increasingly favored Indian over Chinese leaves.

26. These statistics are from Lefèvre, *Le commerce et l'industrie de la plume,* 333–53. Lefèvre accumulated these figures from annual "Statistical Abstracts for Colonial and Other Possessions of United Kingdom," generated by the British House of Commons.

27. TNA, LAB 11/697/TB134/2/1927.

28. TNA, LAB 11/697/TB134/2/1927, "Revision of Scope," in particular, the interviews conducted in 1925 by Trade Board representatives with representatives of the firms of J. Davis Ltd, Greener Wiggell Ltd., A. Botibol, Messrs. Saillad and Cubbitt, G. Rose, Douglas Fergusson, and Messrs. J. Ferguson and Company. Other such surveys of the industry are documented in TNA, LAB 2/835/4; TNA, LAB 2/723/15.

29. "Chief Inspector of Factories and Workshops Report, October 1882–83," 32.

30. TNA, LAB 2/835/2.

31. This is based on my study of businesses that advertised in Kelly's London Post Office Directory under the categories "Ostrich Feather Manufacturer" and "Ostrich Feather Merchant" from 1860 to 1920. Additional ostrich feather specialists advertised themselves as "Feather Manufacturers" or "Feather Merchants." These four categories combined tally over one thousand entries.

32. The Ostrich and Fancy Feather and Artificial Flower Trade Board's mandate was derived from the Trade Boards Act of 1909, which was enforced by the (South African) Board of Trade until it was transferred to the Ministry of Labour in 1917. Originally the board's membership included three appointed members, twenty-two members who would represent the interests of employers, and eleven who would represent the interest of workers. However, the size of the committee shrank as the industry tapered: TNA, LAB 2/835/3; TNA, LAB 2/1682/OTB/OF4487. On the history of the board more

NOTES TO PAGES 63–66

generally: Foreman, *Shoes and Ships and Sealing-Wax*; Schmiechen, *Sweated Industries and Sweated Labor.*

33. "Possibilities of South Africa," *Wall Street Journal*, December 25, 1908, 6.

34. The names of the steamers that carried the feathers were printed in auction catalogues to facilitate buyers' identification of particular lots. For a fascinating reflection on how the overseas transport of Russian Jews and commercial interests collided: Krut, "Building a Home."

35. On docks as the nexus of London's imperial metropolis: Jones, *Outcast London*, chapter 5; Schneer, *London 1900*, chapter 3.

36. Lefèvre, *Le commerce et l'industrie de la plume*, 114; "Ostrich Plume Rivals. New York Favors South African Rather than California Feathers—Reasons for the Preference," *New York Times*, October 26, 1903.

37. London and Kano Trading also appears to have sent ostrich plumes to Lewis and Peat by rail from Liverpool to London, apparently after importing the feathers to Liverpool across the Atlantic. On paper, London and Kano Trading did maintain an office in London, at 16 St. Helen's Place, in the City, but its principal base was likely 3 New Quay, Liverpool. For the request to Lewis and Peat: LRO, 380 LON 1/2/252–430, letter from Lewis and Peat to London and Kano Trading Co. Ltd., May 27, 1914. For reference to the company shipping plumes from Liverpool to London: LRO, 380 LON 1/2/53, letter from London and Kano Trading Co. Ltd to Lewis and Peat, May 21, 1914.

38. UCT BC, 949, 0107 Sybil Honikman, 6–7.

39. UCT BC, 949, 0107 Sybil Honikman, 7.

40. Pollins, *Economic History of the Jews in England*, 42–60, 107–14. The name Figgis, which closely resembles such Anglo-Jewish names as Figes and Figg, suggests that this firm may have been owned by Jews, but no further evidence exists for this theory. Thanks to Todd Endelman for his suggestion in this vein.

41. Michie, *The City of London*, 42.

42. Ellis and Hale was, at this time, located on London's Lime Street. I am most grateful to Patricia Horton Webb of St. Albert, Canada, a distant relative of Thomas Hale by marriage, for sharing her research on the Hale family, including her genealogical findings detailing the occupations of Thomas Hale and Thomas Hale Jr. Patricia Horton Webb to author, March 2 and 7, 2006.

43. Henriques, *Marcus Samuel*, 31.

44. The Hales were not Jewish, and there is no evidence that other principal ostrich feather brokers were either, although Jews' movement into the feather trade corresponded with their occupying a greater (but still relatively small) percentage of London's brokerage firms than before. The shifting expertise of Ellis and Hale and Hale and Son may be tracked in Kelly's Post Office London Directory. On Jews' movement

into brokerage: Lipman, *Social History,* 79; Pollins, *Economic History of the Jews in England,* 46–47, 56–57.

45. What is more, the very popularization of feather wearing made unmediated feather sales inefficient. Milliners and millinery suppliers were unlikely to desire all of the forty-two types of feathers that could be identified by the expert. As Arthur Douglass suggested, feather sellers suffered from "a want of knowledge in making up the cases to suit the retail dealer." To explain this point, Douglass presented a list of actual feathers shipped from Port Elizabeth to London, pointing out that "the first, fourth, fifth, and tenth lines might suit a west-end retailer; whilst he could do nothing with the other lines; whilst a retailer from a manufacturing town might do with the cheaper lines, but could do nothing with the best lines." Douglass, *Ostrich Farming in South Africa,* 81–85, 91–92.

46. GLMS, Ms. 20509 "Ostrich Feathers, August Sale," Lewis and Peat, August 18, 1876; "Prices Current of Ostrich Feathers," Hale and Son, September 20, 1888; "Prices Current of Ostrich Feathers," Hale and Son, December 15, 1881.

47. Douglass, *Ostrich Farming in South Africa,* 87–88. One did not need to be suspicious of Jews per se to be wary of the insularity of London's feather industry; Douglass was not the only critic of the sway that British wholesalers and the London Produce Brokers' Association maintained over the feather industry. Some North and South African feather merchants (Jews among them) were also infuriated by the impenetrability of London's market, for it ensured that they were dependent on brokers, auctioneers, and London-based representatives, all of whose services cut into the exporters' profits.

48. Jones, *Outcast London,* 239.

49. Max Rose's brother Barney oversaw the London-based office of the family company. Two other brothers, Albert and Wulf, also appear to have resided in London and worked on Max's behalf. Aschman, "Oudtshoorn," 132. More details on Rose's personal and business history are preserved in drafts of Aschman's article, which may be found in UCT BC, 830 "Oudtshoorn Hebrew Congregation Archive." Other relevant sources include CPN, F/M "Max Rose" and J/C 5/1 "Joodse Artikles" and "Residents' List of Oudtshoorn Jewry."

50. On the longer history of business circulars and newspapers that emanated from London: McCusker, "The Demise of Distance."

51. GLMS, Ms. 20509 "Ostrich Feathers," Lewis and Peat, January 22, 1880. Merchants of other colonial goods were similarly invested in the character and reliability of their brokerage firms. Thus, for example, the circulars of Samuel Weiss and Company were marked with detailed character studies of the colonial brokers' on whom the firm relied, S. Figgis and Company among them. Cited in Kynaston, *The City of London,* 264–65.

52. GLMS, Ms. 20509, "Ostrich Feathers," Hale and Son, November 18, 1875.

53. "Chief Inspector of Factories and Workshops Report, October 1886–87." For a

popular press account that emphasizes the Jewish nature of London's ostrich feather manufactories: "The Slaughter of Our Songsters," *Littell's Living Age*, February 23, 1889.

54. TNA, LAB 2/835/4; TNA, LAB 2/723/15.

55. TNA, LAB 2/835/4.

56. In New York, by contrast, stringing was thought to require great physical strength, and was thus assigned to skilled male workers.

57. TNA, LAB 2/835/2; TNA, LAB 2/835/3; TNA, LAB/11/697/TB134/2/1927; TNA, LAB 21682/OTB/OF4487/1921. The papers on the quotidian work of Julia Davis Ltd's feather dyers, gathered by the board as it evaluated an appeal for retroactive insurance in 1932, is particularly rich: TNA, PIN 13/406.

58. The relative impact of seasonality on the ostrich feather and related industries is addressed in the last chapter. On the fancy feather trade relative to that of artificial flowers: Van Kleeck, *Artificial Flower Makers*; Van Kleeck, *A Seasonal Industry*.

59. "Chief Inspector of Factories and Workshops Report, October 1886–87," 83; "Select Committee of House of Lords on Sweating System Fourth Report," 271.

60. "Select Committee of House of Lords on Sweating System Second Report," 478.

61. "Chief Inspector of Factories and Workshops Report, October 1882–83," 32.

62. Ibid., 66; "Select Committee of House of Lords on Sweating System Fourth Report," 270. On the forty-eight-hour week: TNA, LAB 2/835/3.

63. "Annual Report of the Chief Inspector of Factories and Workshops, for 1903, Part I." For more on homework in the industry: TNA, LAB 2/213/TBM 111/37/1922; TNA, LAB 2/835/4; TNA, LAB 2/835/3.

64. Booth, *Life and Labour of the People in London.* On the low wages endemic to the industry: TNA, LAB/11/697/TB134/2/1927 "Revision of scope."

65. The remaining workers appear to have affiliated with the Amalgamated Tailors' and Garment Workers' Union, which claimed 310 feather workers in 1919, and the National Federation of Women Workers, with 100 members from the feather and flower trades combined. TNA, LAB 2/835/3.

66. The first minimum-wage pay scale was decided on by the Ostrich and Fancy Feather and Artificial Flower Trade Board in October 1919 and came into force the following month. Thereafter, the pay scale and formal definition of the industry was reevaluated almost annually. Notes on the original scale may be found in TNA, LAB 2/835/3; TNA, LAB/11/697/TB134/2/1927. Subsequent versions of wage scales determined by the board may be found elsewhere in the papers of the Trade Board, including TNA, LAB 2/213/TBM111/37/1922; TNA, LAB 2/213/TBM111/31/1922; TNA, LAB 2/695/24; TNA, LAB 83/1483/1919–1954.

67. TNA, LAB 214 Part I, "Minutes of Interview with Worker's Mother," September 28, 1922.

68. TNA, LAB2/1682/OTB/OCY395/1923; TNA, LAB 2/213/TBM111/31/1922; TNA, LAB 35/212; LAB 214 Part I and Part II.

69. "Yesterday's Police," *The Times* (London), January 31, 1882.

70. "Yesterday's Police," *The Times* (London), October 3, 1886.

71. The only other ostrich feather manufacturer to be exposed to such extensive scrutiny was A. Wiseburg, whose business practices were investigated by the board in 1924: TNA, LAB 2/1628/TBI/A/4250. A case against Julia Davis Ltd., a firm actively involved in the board's affairs, was also lodged in 1924, after the business had closed: TNA, PIN 13/406.

72. TNA, LAB 2/1630/TBI/A/13794/PtsI-III 6716295, "Ostrich and Fancy Feather and Artificial Flower Trade Board, A. Botibol and Co.," "Minute Sheet by Mr. Ezard, 25 November 1927."

73. The case against Botibol contains about as much verbiage as that produced by the entire run of the Trade Board's minutes, collected over the length of its roughly seventy-year operation. The reference to visiting a worker at home is dated September 26, 1927, and may be found in the opening notes of TNA, LAB 2/1630/TBI/A/1379/Pts I-III 6716295, "Ostrich and Fancy Feather and Artificial Flower Trade Board, A. Botibol and Co."

74. Handwritten note, January 12, 1927, found in ibid.

75. Ibid., Undated "Report of Proceedings under the Trade Boards Act." In the year Botibol's case was tried, he was the only feather manufacturer to be found guilty of keeping inadequate wage records and one of a dozen who failed to post notice of the board's minimum-wage rates. Only four employees in the industry besides his own were found to be owed arrears. TNA, LAB 35/213, "Report on Inspection and enforcement for the period from 1st January to 31 December, 1928." Reports of this kind for previous and subsequent years may be found in this folder and in TNA, LAB 35/212; TNA, LAB 35/214; and TNA, LAB 35/215.

76. TNA, LAB 2/1630/TBI/A/1379/Pts I-III 6716295, "Ostrich and Fancy Feather and Artificial Flower Trade Board, A. Botibol and Co.," "Report of Proceedings Under the Trade Boards Act."

77. Endelman, *The Jews of Britain*; Jones, *Outcast London*. On Jews' accused and actual links to sexual violence, the sex trade, and crime in London: Bristow, *Prostitution and Prejudice*; Feldman, *Englishmen and Jews*, chapter 2; Walkowitz, *City of Dreadful Delight*, chapter 7. On the blurring of boundaries between economic, sexual, and social crimes by members of the social reform movement: Koven, *Slumming*.

78. TNA, LAB 2/1630/TBI/A/1379/Pts I-III 6716295, "Ostrich and Fancy Feather and Artificial Flower Trade Board, A. Botibol and Co.," "Report of Proceedings Under the Trade Boards Act."

79. On the economic logic of "sweating," see, among other sources cited in this chapter: Hall, *The Industries of London*.

80. Walkowitz's original text reads: "To a considerable degree, before and after the war, the story of dance in London is the story of domestication, of the incorporation of transnational cultural forms into a national culture. This incorporation helped transform the metropolitan consumer economy." Walkowitz, "The 'Vision of Salome,'" paragraph 76, electronic edition.

81. The Salamans had deep roots in Britain: according to Myer's son Redcliffe Nathan Salaman, the family had migrated to Britain from either Holland or the Rhineland in the early eighteenth century, with, or so their descendant felt compelled to claim, "no infusion of Jewish blood from Eastern Europe in the families either of my father or my mother." ULC RNS, 8171/27 "Boyhood and the Family Background," 11.

82. The first theory, that the Solomon family name was changed to Salaman by mistake, was shared with me by Colin Cohen, great-nephew of Redcliffe Nathan Salaman. By Cohen's account, the change in spelling followed the error of a sign maker. Colin Cohen to author, May 11, 2006.

83. *Encyclopaedia Judaica*, "South Africa," see especially section titled "The Solomons"; Rabinowitz, "Saul Solomon and the Family of Saul Solomon."

84. "The Salamans," *Jewish Chronicle*, March 22, 1925, 25–26. The second account that links Isaac to St. Helena is found in the autobiographical writings of Redcliffe Nathan Salaman, who describes the story as "family tradition . . . which at least is possible." ULC RNS, 8171/27 "Boyhood and the Family Background," 10.

85. "Residents' List of Oudtshoorn Jewry."

86. GLMS, Ms. 14744, "April 2, 1863, Messrs. Isaac Salaman & Co. Deed of Copartnership."

87. ULC RNS, 8171/27 "Boyhood and the Family Background," 13.

88. Ibid., 12.

89. This deed from 1864 also documents that Myer and Nathan bought their married sisters Rachel and Betsy out of I. Salaman for the sum of £300 each, and that each of Isaac's seven children (including Rachel and Betsy) were henceforth entitled to equal shares of the dividends, income, and interest generated by I. Salaman and Company. Guildhall Salaman papers: GLMS, Ms. 14747, "Deed of settlement of proceeds of sale and stock, by Isaac Salaman."

90. ULC RNS, 8171/27 "Boyhood and the Family Background," 23, 24.

91. GLMS, Ms. 14740, "Myer Salaman and Sarah Solomon marriage settlement 1863."

92. GLMS, Ms. 8171/8, "Family Details."

93. The company's move to Monkwell House and out of retailing occurred sometime before 1863. ULC RNS, 8171/27 "Boyhood and the Family Background," 13.

94. GLMS, Ms. 19329, [Minutes from I. Salaman and Co. Board of Directors], "Meeting of 20 April 1918."

95. In the last two decades of the twentieth century, Myer and Nathan legally held

joint control over I. Salaman and Company, though in fact Nathan proved "devoid of any initiative" and "developed into a silent but most faithful partner" of Myer, who, "ably supported by his sisters" emerged as "the driving force" of the company. After a failed stint on the gold mines of California, Myer's brother Abraham took over the manufacturing side of things in London. Myer's daughter Betty and her husband, Charles Feist, meanwhile, oversaw the running of a Parisian office on rue St. Appoline. (This office was started by Myer in 1894 with the financial support of his brother Abraham.) Finally, Myer's son-in-law Alfred Aaron de Pass, who married his daughter Ethel Phoebe in 1888, became an active trustee of the company, a position he held well into the 1930s. Not coincidentally, de Pass was a merchant long experienced with overseas trade: his firm, de Pass, Spence and Company, helped develop the whaling, sealing, guano, fishing, angora, and sugar industries of the Cape Colony. ULC RNS, 8171/27 "Boyhood and the Family Background," 19–20; GLMS, Ms. 14745, Abraham Salaman to Myer Salaman, September 26, 1895. See also "Biography," *Jewish Chronicle*, April 12 and June 21, 1895.

96. GLMS, Ms. 20509, "Lewis and Peat January Ostrich Sales Auction Receipt," 1876.

97. When Myer died in his sixty-first year, in 1889, he distributed among twenty-five beneficiaries an estate valued at £288,674. This figure excluded the land in his possession. Although the capital value of this land at the time of Myer's death is unknown, by 1939 it had risen to £158,552. What is more, the Myer Salaman estate generated significant residuary capital: between 1912 and 1953, this component of his estate alone was calculated to exceed £675,000. Myer's brother and associate Nathan, though by some accounts the less motivated businessman, generated an even more imposing legacy. When Nathan died in 1905, nearly £375,000 was distributed among his beneficiaries, not including properties whose capital value would exceed £215,000 in thirty years' time. Over the course of the five decades since his death, Nathan's estate, which was initially divided among forty-six beneficiaries, yielded nearly half a million British pounds sterling worth of residuary capital. GLMS, Ms. 19321, Myer Salaman's will; GLMS, Ms. 19335, Nathan Salaman's will. A description of Nathan's legacy is offered in a correspondence from representatives of M. and N. Salaman Estates to Redcliffe Nathan Salaman, October 16, 1953: ULC RNS, 8171/8, "Family details." On Myer's inclination to "speculate like a bear": ULC RNS, 8171/27, "Boyhood and the Family Background," 28. On the real estate profits of I. Salaman and Company: Endelman, "Anglo-Jewish Scientists."

98. Van Kleeck, *Artificial Flower Makers*, especially chapter 7.

99. GLMS, Ms. 19329 vol. 2, [Minutes from I. Salaman and Company Board of Directors], "Meeting of 17 January 1917," 140.

100. Ibid., "Meeting of 16 July 1914," 41.

101. Ibid., "Meeting of 24 and 25 June 1919," 233.

102. Ibid., "Meeting of 31 January 1917," 143.

103. Ibid., "Meetings of 24 and 25 June 1919," 180.

104. Ibid., "Meeting of 30 April 1923," 3.

105. Ibid., "Meeting of 20 April 1918," 179.

106. Ibid., "Meeting of 17 January 1917," 140.

107. Ibid., "Meeting of 20 April 1918," 180.

108. Ibid.

109. *London Gazette*, August 21, 1914.

110. More detailed documentation about businesses that closed at this time were filed with the Board of Trade, including those that appear in the TNA, BT 31 series.

111. For example, the firm of Greener Wiggell Ltd. had by 1925 reduced its workforce from 250 to 156, and employed these workers only two-thirds of the normal work week. In the same year, the firm of Messrs. Saillad and Cubbit, which once employed 300 workers, admitted to employing only 57. TNA, LAB 11/697/TB134/2/1927, "Revision of Scope."

112. Undated letters to the board written sometime in 1927 by Florence Thomasson and Edith Button: TNA, LAB 2/1630/TBI/A/13794/PtsI-III 6716295, "Ostrich and Fancy Feather and Artificial Flower Trade Board, A. Botibol and Co." The young women's ages may be determined from an undated board list of A. Botibol and Company's employees, found in the same file.

113. TNA, LAB 11/697/TB134/2/1927, "Revision of Scope." Some of the firms the board spoke of dramatically reduced the scale of their operations, simultaneously diversifying by manufacturing fancy feathers, artificial flowers, or other related goods.

114. Ibid.

115. GLMS, Ms. 8171/45e, "Press Cuttings 1906–1955," "Will Fashion Kill the Ostrich? London Stocks of Feathers That Nobody Wants," unspecified journal, November 7, 1929.

116. Ibid.

117. GLMS, Ms. 19329 vol. 3, [Minutes from I. Salaman and Company Board of Directors], "Meeting of 2 June 1924," 65.

118. GLMS, Ms. 8171/45e, "Press Cuttings 1906–1955," "Will Fashion Kill the Ostrich? London Stocks of Feathers That Nobody Wants," unspecified journal, November 7, 1929.

119. GLMS, Ms. 19329 3, [Minutes from I. Salaman and Company Board of Directors], "Meeting of 9 June 1943," 182.

120. GLMS, Ms. 8171/8 "Family Details." On Redcliffe's scholarly career: Endelman, "The Decline of the Anglo-Jewish Notable"; Endelman, "'Practices of a Low Anthropologic Level'"; Endelman, "Anglo-Jewish Scientists." For a rather more personal reminiscence of Salaman and his work: Miller, *Relations*, 26–58.

121. "Select Committee of House of Lords on Sweating System Second Report"; "Select Committee of House of Lords on Sweating System Fourth Report"; Endel-

man, *The Jews of Britain;* Feldman, *Englishmen and Jews;* Feldman, *Immigrants and Workers;* Schmiechen, *Sweated Industries and Sweated Labor.*

CHAPTER 3. THE TRANS-SAHARAN TRADE

1. CPN, INE, "Letter Book [1914]," "In Bankruptcy. In the Matter of Isach Hassan." When interviewed in the 1970s by Rosemary Eshel, head of research and special projects at the Israel Museum, Hassan's grandson Cyril Raphael Rex Hassan (and, more recently, his daughter) detailed that the family's trade in esparto grass rooted them in Sfax, Sousse, and Tunis (in Tunisia), Oran (Algeria), as well as in Manchester, London, and Paris. I am grateful to Rosemary Eshel for sharing the fruits of her research with me.

2. References to the Hassans' prominence may be found in Baier, *An Economic History of Central Niger,* 72–73; Fituri, "Tripolitania, Cyrenaica, and Bilad as-Sudan Trade Relations," 128.

3. This study draws on a rich literature on the feather trade written by scholars of North Africa and West Africa, much of which is cognizant of Jews' role as feather financiers and plume exporters. Significantly, this scholarship does not follow the path of feathers or feather merchants overseas, severing the ostrich feather commodity chain on the southern shore of the Mediterranean and failing to situate the work of its merchants within the larger frames of global (or modern Jewish) history. By contrast, I aim to situate the regional feather trade and the Mediterranean Jewish feather merchants, financiers, and sorters who contributed to it in a larger, extra-continental story. See, for example: Austen, "The Trans-Saharan Slave Trade"; Austen, "Marginalization, Stagnation, and Growth"; Baier, "Trans-Saharan Trade and the Sahel"; Baier, *An Economic History of Central Niger;* Boahen, "The Caravan Trade"; Boahen, *Britain, the Sahara, and the Western Sudan;* Cordell, "Eastern Libya, Wadai and the Sanusiya"; Curtin, *The Atlantic Slave Trade;* Curtin, *Economic Change in Precolonial Africa;* Dunn, "The Trade of Tafilal"; Dyer, "Export Production in Western Libya"; Fituri, "Tripolitania, Cyrenaica, and Bilad as-Sudan Trade Relations"; Johnson, "Calico Caravans"; Lovejoy, "Commercial Sectors in the Economy of the Nineteenth-Century Central Sudan"; Miège, "Le commerce trans-saharien"; Miège, "Les juifs et le commerce transsaharien"; Newbury, "North African and Western Sudan Trade"; Pascon, *La maison d'Iligh;* Schroeter, *Merchants of Essaouira;* Walz, *Trade Between Egypt and Bilad as-Sudan.*

4. The remaining feather lots were exported directly to Europe from Aden, or sold by Jewish feather merchants to Europeans passing through the port city. English-language travel narratives make frequent mention of these merchants' on-board visitations; one account from 1860 advised that "it is quite necessary in some cases to use a stick to drive off these feather merchants"; another urged visitors that it was better simply not to disembark in Aden, amusing oneself, instead, in "buy[ing] an imitation

ostrich feather from a cheating Jew" who came on board for this purpose. Chadwick et al., *Ocean Steamships*, 270; Allen, *A Visit to Queensland*, 30. On Yemeni Jews' monopoly over Aden's feather trade: Hunter, *An Account of the British Settlement of Aden*, 109–10; *Encyclopedia Americana* (1919), 139; Semach, *Une mission de l'alliance au Yemen*; Ahroni, *The Jews of the British Crown Colony of Aden*, 46.

5. On the early history of Jews' involvement in trans-Saharan trade: Abitbol, "Juifs maghrébins"; Hirschberg, *A History of the Jews in North Africa*, 254–61. On the more general subject of Jewish trade in the medieval Islamic and Mediterranean world: Braudel, *The Mediterranean*; Goitein, *A Mediterranean Society*, especially vol. 1; Goitein, *Letters of Medieval Jewish Traders*.

6. Mark Dyer writes that in western Libya, "virtually all groups, both nomads and settled," hunted ostriches on occasion. Dyer, "Export Production in Western Libya," 126. Other sources refer to ostrich hunting in Damergu and Sennar. It was claimed by some European observers that "from religious scruple, the Mussulman is averse to the mode of plucking the feathers out of the live bird," a suggestion rendered spurious by the small-scale farming of ostriches in some parts of the Sahara and Sahel. This claim is found in an 1875 letter from M. Eugene Gros, "a merchant at Cairo and Paris, for many years connected with feather trade of Egypt," to Julius de Mosenthal: Mosenthal, *Ostriches and Ostrich Farming*, 233–34. Hunter, *An Account of the British Settlement of Aden*, 110.

7. Green, "Ostrich Eggs and Peacock Feathers." For a partial accounting of the export of ostrich feathers from Aden just prior to the modern feather boom (in 1874 and 1875): Hunter, *An Account of the British Settlement of Aden*, 109–10.

8. On ostrich cultivation in Niger: Baier, "Trans-Saharan Trade and the Sahel," 50. The letter cited above in n. 6 refers to ostrich breeding in Sudan. Reference to the farming of ostrich by "some tribes of Soudan, of the Upper Senegal, and of the Algerian frontiers" was also made in a letter by United States consul Alex Jourdan, based in Algiers, to the authors of a state-sponsored study on the feasibility of introducing ostrich farming to this country. *Ostrich Farming in the United States: Reports from the Consuls of the United States*, 582.

9. Perinbaum, "Social Relations," 424.

10. For more on the Ghadamasi diaspora and the commercial activity of Ghadamasi merchants, see Baier, "Trans-Saharan Trade and the Sahel"; Baier, *An Economic History of Central Niger*; Fituri, "Tripolitania, Cyrenaica, and Bilad as-Sudan Trade Relations"; Haarmann, "The Dead Ostrich"; Johnson, "Calico Caravans"; Miège, "Le commerce trans-saharien"; Mircher, *Mission de Ghadamès*; Newbury, "North African and Western Sudan Trade"; Schroeter, *Merchants of Essaouira*. On the Sanusiya in particular: Cordell, "Eastern Libya, Wadai and the Sanusiya"; Fituri, "Tripolitania, Cyrenaica, and Bilad as-Sudan Trade Relations." On the Swiri: Schroeter, "The Jews of Essaouira"; Schroeter, *Merchants of Essaouira*.

11. Boahen, *Britain, the Sahara, and the Western Sudan*, 107–8. On the Tuareg refreshment

stands, and the "landlady brokers" who ran them: Lovejoy and Baier, "The Desert-Side Economy of the Central Sudan." On the commercial relationships between Swiri merchants and Ait Baha transporters: Schroeter, "The Jews of Essaouira"; Schroeter, *Merchants of Essaouira*.

12. Slouschz, *Travels in North Africa*, 106–7.

13. Data on ostrich feather exports from Tripoli and elsewhere in North Africa has been refined and elaborated in a series of scholarly works. These studies, which rely on French and British consular and archival reports, include Baier, "Trans-Saharan Trade and the Sahel"; Baier, *An Economic History of Central Niger*; Fituri, "Tripolitania, Cyrenaica, and Bilad as-Sudan Trade Relations"; Johnson, "Calico Caravans"; Lovejoy, "Commercial Sectors in the Economy of the Nineteenth-Century Central Sudan"; Lovejoy and Baier, "The Desert-Side Economy of the Central Sudan"; Newbury, "North African and Western Sudan Trade." A brief but thorough discussion of the evolution of this historiography is offered in Lovejoy, "Commercial Sectors in the Economy of the Nineteenth-Century Central Sudan." The most thorough calculations have been provided in Baier, *An Economic History of Central Niger*, 234.

14. These figures, based on American and British consular reports, have been discussed by a number of sources. The precise statistics cited above are drawn from Baier, *An Economic History of Central Niger*, 74, tables 1 and 2; Fituri, "Tripolitania, Cyrenaica, and Bilad as-Sudan Trade Relations," 78, 126. See also Johnson, "Calico Caravans." Together, these authors counter an argument made by Newbury that the volume of trade on the three westernmost trade routes were in decline after 1875: Newbury, "North African and Western Sudan Trade."

15. Fituri, "Tripolitania, Cyrenaica, and Bilad as-Sudan Trade Relations," 71–76, 96–98.

16. Rozen, "The Leghorn Merchants in Tunis"; Simon, "The Socio-Economic Role of the Tripolitanian Jews." Still other Jewish merchants were subjects of France, Holland, Austria, and Spain: indeed, in Tripoli, Jews constituted all or the majority of these "foreign" groups. De Felice, *Jews in an Arab Land*, 11.

17. A list of 161 "unnationalized foreigners protected by consuls in Tripoli" was assembled in 1876 by American consul Michael Vital, who was stationed in Tripoli. This list includes both Muslims and Jews, but is dominated by the names of Jewish merchants and their families. Vital, "Correspondences of Michael Vital, Consulate of the United States of America, Tripoli of Barbary, to Department of State." I am thankful to Matthew Olson, archivist of Civilian Records at the United States National Archives and Records Administration for helping me locate Vital's correspondence.

18. "Ostrich Feathers," *El Telegrafo* 2, 26 Sivan 5652 (June 21, 1892), cited in Birmizrahi, *From Our Fathers' Newspapers*, 124–25. My thanks to Julia Phillips Cohen for alerting me to this source.

19. Miège, *Le Maroc et l'Europe*, vol. 3; Schroeter, *Merchants of Essaouira*; Schroeter, *The Sultan's Jew*.

20. Schroeter, *Merchants of Essaouira*, chapter 10; Schroeter, *The Sultan's Jew*.

21. The results of subsequent experiments in Algeria, Marseilles, and Grenoble were avidly covered in the *Bulletin de la société d'acclimatation*.

22. Early proponents of developing the ostrich feather industry in the central or eastern Sahara included two Frenchmen, the civil engineer Jules Oudot and H. Mircher, who was an officer. Both published extensive reports on the matter. Mircher, *Mission de Ghadamès*; Oudot, *Le fermage des autruches en Algérie*. These men's efforts were renewed in the early years of the twentieth century by Dr. J. Decorse, who was sent to French Sudan by the colonial government to investigate the viability of ostrich cultivation in the region. "Protecting African Birds." On this topic, see also Newbury, "North African and Western Sudan Trade."

23. "Protecting African Birds."

24. Fituri, "Tripolitania, Cyrenaica, and Bilad as-Sudan Trade Relations," 71–73; Johnson, "Calico Caravans," 97–100.

25. On European attitudes, policies, and ambitions regarding trans-Saharan trade, see Austen, "Marginalization, Stagnation, and Growth"; Johnson, "Calico Caravans." The rumination on the "apathy" of French colonials was offered by American consul Jourdan. Cited in *Ostrich Farming in the United States: Reports from the Consuls of the United States*, 577.

26. Israel, *Diasporas Within a Diaspora*, 173.

27. The original article, published in the *Annales du commerce extérieur*, is cited in "Trade in Ostrich Feathers."

28. For the most thorough exploration of the role of Sephardi merchants in establishing the centrality of Livorno and the Livornese Jewish diaspora as crucial mercantile hubs in the sixteenth through eighteenth centuries: Trivellato, *The Familiarity of Strangers*. See also Filippini, *Il porto di Livorno*; Israel, *European Jewry in the Age of Mercantilism*; Israel, *Diasporas Within a Diaspora*; Lehmann, "A Livornese 'Port Jew'"; Lévy, *La nation juive portugaise*; Yogev, *Diamonds and Coral*. On ties between Livorno and North Africa, including those of feather families: De Felice, *Jews in an Arab Land*; Rozen, "The Leghorn Merchants in Tunis"; Schroeter, *Merchants of Essaouira*; Schroeter, *The Sultan's Jew*; Triulzi, "Italian-Speaking Communities." On the history of ostrich products as objects of cultural and material exchange of an earlier period: Green, "Ostrich Eggs and Peacock Feathers."

29. The original article, published in *Annales du commerce extérieur*, is cited in "Trade in Ostrich Feathers."

30. As Daniel Schroeter has demonstrated, during the nineteenth century the "Berberisco" population of London was growing in number and visibility. Schroeter, *The Sultan's Jew*, especially 55–76. On the presence of Mediterranean Jewish firms in Paris: Vadala, "Une Colonie Tripolitaine."

31. This is referenced in Schroeter, "The Jews of Essaouira," 379. Jews' capacity as merchants in Morocco more generally is explored in detail in Schroeter, *Merchants of Essaouira*; Schroeter, *The Sultan's Jew.* The geographic dispersal of Moroccan Jewish merchants was also remarked upon by the Franco-Jewish Orientalist scholar Nahum Slouschz. Slouschz, *Travels in North Africa*, 104–11, 72. For a fascinating account of how Jewish merchants are remembered by Muslims in southern Morocco: Boum, "Muslims Remember Jews in Southern Morocco."

32. As there was not a market of feather consumers in North Africa, itinerant merchants were unlikely to deal in feathers. Fituri, "Tripolitania, Cyrenaica, and Bilad as-Sudan Trade Relations," 127; Goldberg, *Jewish Life in Muslim Libya*, 68–81; Simon, "Jewish Itinerant Peddlers in Ottoman Libya."

33. Hirschberg, *A History of the Jews in North Africa*, 168.

34. Hajjaj-Liluf, "Ha-kalkalah ve-hatmorot."

35. The numerous stops feathers made along the Nile and en route to and from the Red Sea were outlined in an 1875 letter by M. Goy, "one of principal ostrich feather merchants in Paris, and for more than 30 years well acquainted with details of NA feather trade," and Juilus de Mosenthal cited in Mosenthal, *Ostriches and Ostrich Farming*, 234–35. This is also described in Miège, "Le commerce trans-saharien," 100.

36. Haim Nahum, chief Sephardic rabbi of the Ottoman Empire, detailed how Yemeni Jews from Aden bought and sold feathers in the trading entrepôt of Dire Dawa, Ethiopia. This, he wrote, "is their specialty." Benbassa, *Haim Nahum*, 108. Most feathers exported from Aden in the late nineteenth century appear to have been imported in a raw state from Berbera and other Somali ports. After local manufacture by Yemeni Jews, these would be exported directly to London: Hunter, *An Account of the British Settlement of Aden*, 109–10.

37. Cited in Schroeter, "The Jews of Essaouira," 380.

38. This relationship of credit and commission is described in, among other sources, Pascon, *La maison d'Iligh*; Schroeter, *Merchants of Essaouira*, 109–10.

39. Baier, *An Economic History of Central Niger*, 57–78; Johnson, "Calico Caravans," 110.

40. When the return on feathers was high, this strategy paid off, with merchants increasing their gain by as much as 160 percent, but when the bottom fell out of the ostrich feather market, as it did several times during the late nineteenth century, many merchants, especially small-scale ones, were severely affected. Baier, *An Economic History of Central Niger*, 75–76; Johnson, "Calico Caravans," 110; Schroeter, "The Jews of Essaouira," 378.

41. Dyer, "Export Production in Western Libya," 126; Miège, "Le commerce trans-saharien," 100; Mosenthal and Harting, *Ostriches and Ostrich Farming*; Oudot, *Le fermage des autruches en Algérie*; Walz, *Trade Between Egypt and Bilad as-Sudan*, 38; Hunter, *An Account of the British Settlement of Aden*, 109.

42. Bird protectionists concerned about the destruction of the Saharan ostrich

warned that the wild birds in French possessions were "sure to be exterminated" if they continued to be killed for their plumage. These protectionists believed the solution to the pending crisis was to domesticate the ostrich. "Protecting African Birds."

43. Cited in Newbury, "North African and Western Sudan Trade," 240. On the importation and handling of feathers in Tripoli: Méry, "Reseignements commerciaux."

44. Cited in Fituri, "Tripolitania, Cyrenaica, and Bilad as-Sudan Trade Relations," 127. Fituri does not document the claim that feather sorting was undertaken in the Jewish district, but this point is echoed in other sources, for example Baier, *An Economic History of Central Niger*, 71. A comparison may be drawn with the early modern Moroccan sugar industry, which was more or less controlled by the sultan and farmed out to local Jewish merchants. Jews were also involved in Morocco's sixteenth-century sugar processing industry. Gottreich, *The Mellah of Marrakesh: Jewish and Muslim Space in Morocco's Red City*, 37. For a similar dismissive account of the techniques employed by Aden's Jewish feather handlers, who, it was claimed, "make a great mystery" of the manufacturing process: Hunter, *An Account of the British Settlement of Aden*, 109.

45. "Protecting African Birds"; Baier, *An Economic History of Central Niger*, 88; Johnson, "Calico Caravans," 106.

46. In South Africa, as we have seen, colored sorters were found to double their risk of contracting tuberculosis: in New York, feather handlers were disproportionately affected by ailments of the nose, throat, and ears: *Oudtshoorn Courant*, March 12, 1914; Hall, *Second Report of the Factory Investigating Commission*, 534–39.

47. With ostrich feathers, hides represented one of the principal agricultural goods exported from North Africa: like ostrich feathers, they were destined for Venice, Livorno, and Marseilles, port cities in which Jewish merchants were overrepresented. According to Mark Dyer, the purchase, processing, and export of animal skins from Tripoli was a monopoly of the local pasha, who employed Jewish merchants to conduct the work on his behalf. These merchants oversaw the trade within the country as a whole and oversaw the export of skins to Venice, Malta, and Livorno. Dyer, "Export Production in Western Libya," 125. Similarly, the trade of goatskins in Morocco was "entirely in the hands" of Jews from Essaouira and their co-religionists from the south. Schroeter, "The Jews of Essaouira," 377; Schroeter, *Merchants of Essaouira*, 83. Hides also constituted an essential commodity in the trade between Tunis and Livorno. Triulzi, "Italian-Speaking Communities."

48. Coffin, "Ostrich Feathers of Tripoli," 55.

49. Mathuisieulx, "Une mission en Tripolitaine," 32.

50. Cited in Goldberg et al., "Social and Demographic Aspects," 80, table 6.

51. Cited in De Felice, *Jews in an Arab Land*, 11.

52. The first feather firm established in Paris by Jewish merchants from Tripoli was that of Cesar Labi and Ange Arbib, which was established in 1860. Other Arbibs, including Abraham Arbib, already operated as ostrich feather merchants in the city: per-

haps they were members of the Venetian branch of the family and registered as Italians. Baier, *An Economic History of Central Niger*, 72, 90; Mathuisieulx, "Une mission en Tripolitaine." I am indebted to Rosemary Eshel for sharing her insights on the extended Arbib family: Rosemary Eshel to author, September 9–12, 2007.

53. Members of the Nahum family were important philanthropists in and beyond Tripoli, funding, for example, the building of a Talmud Torah in Tripoli, and a synagogue and Talmud Torah in the town of Homs (whence they exported alfalfa). Slouschz, *Travels in North Africa*, 9, 10, 45. The importance of the Hassans as ostrich magnates is also referenced in Mathuisieulx, "Une mission en Tripolitaine," 32. The Arbib family registered their line of ships in the British Mercantile Navy List and Maritime Directory.

54. On the Nahums' shipping capabilities: Slouschz, *Travels in North Africa*, 7. Evidence of a London-based member of the Hassan family evincing an interest in creating a shipping company is preserved in correspondence between Isach Hassan and a South African ostrich feather exporter, Isaac Nurick.

55. Rosemary Eshel to author, September 9–11, 2007.

56. Schroeter, *Merchants of Essaouira*, 34–42, 166. Further details of the holdings of the house of Corcos is presented in Miège, "Bourgeoisie juive du Maroc," 33.

57. Slouschz, *Travels in North Africa*, 105–6.

58. The Sephardim who settled in North Africa after the expulsion from Spain and Portugal were unique in adopting the language of the preexisting regional Jewish population rather than maintaining a Judeo-Spanish language (Ladino) or the language of the majority or state culture (Dutch, French, English, and so on). In other respects the Sephardic population of North Africa remained culturally and communally distinct from extant Jewish populations.

59. Schroeter, *Merchants of Essaouira*, 115.

60. Hajjaj-Liluf, "Ha-kalkalah ve-hatmorot."

61. Matthews, "Northwest Africa and Timbuctoo," 208.

62. Baier, *An Economic History of Central Niger*, 72.

63. Oudot, *Le fermage des autruches en Algérie*, 153.

64. Ibid., 145.

65. Mosenthal, *Ostriches and Ostrich Farming*, 233–34.

66. The original article, published in the *Annales du commerce extérieur*, is cited in "Trade in Ostrich Feathers."

67. This tale was conveyed by French consul Fléraud to the Ministry of Foreign Affairs in 1879. Cited in Newbury, "North African and Western Sudan Trade," 239–40.

68. Baier, *An Economic History of Central Niger*, 72. The latter quotation is Baier's own synopsis of the merchants' letter, with the original bracketed therein. Complaints by Cuthbert Jones were published in the February 1880 issue of *American Exporter* under the title "Warning to American Exporters."

69. Baier, *An Economic History of Central Niger*, 79–95. See also Austen, *African Economic History*; Baier, "Trans-Saharan Trade and the Sahel"; Boahen, "The Caravan Trade"; Cordell, "Eastern Libya, Wadai and the Sanusiya"; Fituri, "Tripolitania, Cyrenaica, and Bilad as-Sudan Trade Relations"; Johnson, "Calico Caravans"; Newbury, "North African and Western Sudan Trade."

70. On the uneven implementation of the *Tanzimat* reforms across the empire and to various ethnic and mercantile groups: Ahmad, *The Making of Modern Turkey*; Doumani, *Rediscovering Palestine*; Eldem, Goffman, and Masters, eds., *The Ottoman City*; Kayali, *Arabs and Young Turks*; Makdisi, *Culture of Sectarianism*; Masters, *Christians and Jews*.

71. Scholarly studies of the decline of the Livornese Jewish mercantile class of North Africa have tended to focus on Tunis. See, for example, Lévy, *La nation juive portugaise*; Rozen, "The Livornese Jewish Merchants"; Triulzi, "Italian-Speaking Communities." Jean-Louis Miège has also meditated on Jews' experience of the decline of trans-Saharan trade, though recent scholarship has questioned his chronology as faulty: Miège, "Le commerce trans-saharien"; Miège, "Les juifs et le commerce transsaharien."

72. These dynamics are explored in the following sources, as well as those aforementioned: Miège, "Bourgeoisie Juive du Maroc"; Miège, *Le Maroc et l'Europe*; Pascon, *La maison d'Iligh*; Schroeter, "The Jews of Essaouira"; Schroeter, *Merchants of Essaouira*; Schroeter, *The Sultan's Jew*.

73. The most comprehensive statistics on the feather trade have been assembled by Stephen Baier, who draws on earlier work by Charles Newbury and Marion Johnson, among others. Information on the feather trade in the first decade of the twentieth century is scarcer, but includes Fituri, "Tripolitania, Cyrenaica, and Bilad as-Sudan Trade Relations," 181.

74. Baier, *An Economic History of Central Niger*, 90; Slouschz, *Travels in North Africa*; Vadala, "Une colonie Tripolitaine."

75. Vadala, "Une colonie Tripolitaine."

76. The Arbib, Nahum, and Hassan families all moved into the esparto trade after the popularity of ostrich feathers waned. De Felice, *Jews in an Arab Land*, 316n.9. CPN, INE, "Letter Book [1914]," "In Bankruptcy. In the Matter of Isach Hassan."

77. Sargeant's findings indicate that these Parisian industrial populations overlapped far more than did their peer industries in New York and London; Van Kleeck, *Artificial Flower Makers*, 144–90.

78. Ibid., 180–81.

79. Sargeant found that the majority of Parisian feather and flower workers earned between $5.40 and $14.00 a week, depending on their experience and skill. This, by Sargent's account, rendered flower making among the better paid trades for Parisian women of the period. By contrast, ostrich feather workers in the city earned between $3.60 and $6.00 a week. Calculating their annual expenses, Sargeant concluded that these workers "will be unable to make the two ends meet at the end of the year." Ibid., 163. These find-

ings are echoed in Bonneff, "L'art de la fleur et de la plume." Workers in this industry benefited from the efforts of the Societé pour l'assistance paternelle aux enfants employes dans les industries des fleurs et des plumes, founded in 1866. The society offered courses, contests, awards, and even private boardinghouses for young girls moving into the industry. A union for women in the industry also operated in the 1890s. For more on the experiences of Parisian flower workers: Coffin, *The Politics of Women's Work*, 151–54.

80. Trivellato, *The Familiarity of Strangers*, chapter 1, section 1.4.

81. Notably, Raccah's operations also greatly outpaced those of Lebanese Catholic and Greek merchants in the industry. Hancock, *Survey of British Commonwealth Affairs*, 214–18.

82. Ibid., 217.

83. My sense of this company's operation is based on scrutiny of the firm's business records and correspondences, held by the Liverpool Record Office: LRO, 380 LON/1 and 380 LON/2. Limited additional information on the company may be found in Hancock, *Survey of British Commonwealth Affairs*, 215–16.

84. LRO, LON 1/2/52, J. R. Cousins, the London and Kano Trading Company, Liverpool, to London and Kano Trading Company, London, May 20, 1914.

85. This nugget of information may be derived from a letter between the two brokerage firms that handled the London and Kano Trading Company's feathers in Liverpool and London (respectively): LRO, LON 1/3/359-/381, Culverwell Brooks and Company [Brokers] to Lewis and Peat Brokers, June 19, 1914.

86. In the 1883 edition of Kelly's Directory, Hassan's business address was listed as 101 Leadenhall Street, in London's East End. Kelly's Directories Ltd., *The Post Office London Directory*.

87. CPN, INE, Hassan-Nurick correspondence, November 1, 1911.

88. CPN, INE, Hassan-Nurick correspondence, December 15, 1911.

89. Ibid. Hassan also tried to win over Nurick's support for his "new company" in correspondence, December 11, 1911.

90. CPN, INE, Hassan-Nurick correspondence, December 7, 1911.

91. Douglass, *Ostrich Farming in South Africa*, 90.

92. CPN, INE, Hassan-Nurick correspondence, December 15, 1911.

93. Ibid.

94. CPN, INE, Hassan-Nurick correspondence, November 6, 1912; CPN, INE, Hassan-Nurick correspondence, November 7, 1912.

95. CPN, INE, Hassan-Nurick correspondence, July 1, 1913.

96. Nixon, *Dreambirds*, 80.

CHAPTER 4. THE AMERICAN FEATHER WORLD

1. "Feather Workers Strike Again," *New York Times*, October 31, 1888. For further reference to the Working Women's Union: Henry, *Women and the Labor Movement*, 56.

2. On the number of women in the ostrich feather industry at this time: "The Duty of Women of Leisure to Women Who Work," *New York Evangelist*, November 1, 1888. This figure is likely an underestimation, for it excludes those home workers whose labors undergirded the ostrich feather trade.

3. Sometime in the summer of 1888, the Working Women's Union had represented another group of ostrich feather workers who faced a similarly drastic pay cut. Thanks to the financial outpouring of "other women of the same trade, who realized how much was at stake for themselves," and to the efficiency of the Working Women's Union, this work stoppage lasted but a week, after which, it seemed, "the girls were all at work again at their former wages, and under vastly improved conditions." "The Duty of Women of Leisure to Women Who Work," *New York Evangelist*, November 1, 1888.

4. "Isidore Cohnfeld Tricked," *New York Times*, December 8, 1888.

5. "Feather Workers' Strike," *New York Times*, December 7, 1888.

6. "Isidore Cohnfeld Tricked," *New York Times*, December 8, 1888.

7. *Compilation of Customs Laws and Digest of Decisions Thereunder Rendered by the Courts and the Board of United States General Appraisers.*

8. "Ostrich Feather Importers Protest Against High Duty," *New York Times*, September 23, 1904.

9. Hayden, "Speech: The Ostrich Industry."

10. "Feather Workers Return to Work," *New York Times*, March 21, 1889.

11. Glenn, *Daughters of the Shtetl*, 8–50; Kosak, *Cultures of Opposition*.

12. Crucially, this focus allows us to write Jews into the history of the American West, Southwest, and South without focusing on the centrality of small-town or urban Jewish communities—as has so much literature in the field—but, instead, by eroding what Hasia Diner has called "a regionally bifurcated story" of American Jewry. Diner, "Jewish Life in the American West," 51. Literature emphasizing the importance of Jewish communities of the West includes: Angel, "History of Seattle's Sephardic Community"; Cone, Droker, and Williams, *Family of Strangers*; Lowenstein, *The Jews of Oregon, 1850–1950*; Rischin, *The Jews of the West*; Rischin and Livingston, *Jews of the American West*; Tobias, *A History of the Jews in New Mexico*; Toll, *The Making of an Ethnic Middle Class*; Vorspan and Gartner, *History of the Jews of Los Angeles*.

13. In its global focus, this study departs from most scholarship on Jews and American industries, including the diamond, textile, ready-to-wear, fur, and motion picture industries, which has tended to pivot around the complex dynamics that fueled, agitated, and constantly transformed culture, class, and politics in single metropolitan centers. Cohen, *From Hester Street to Hollywood*; Gabler, *An Empire of Their Own*; Glenn, *Daughters of the*

Shtetl; Rogin, *Blackface, White Noise;* Shield, *Diamond Stories.* An exception to this trend is Green, *Ready-to-Wear and Ready-to-Work.*

14. Gouy, "Ostrich-Feathers."

15. "Ostrich Plumes and Tips: A Great Increase in the Demand for Feathers," *New York Times,* September 24, 1882; "Ostrich Plume Rivals. New York Favors South African Rather Than California Feathers—Reasons for the Preference," *New York Times,* October 26, 1903. The precise number of these workshops evades historical record, but their increase over the period of time in question has been documented. In 1870, when the United States Census first collected data on the feather industry, there were 73 factories employing 2,034 wage earners (the majority of them women) in the feather and flower industries combined; ten years later this figure had more than doubled, with 174 feather and flower factories employing a total of 3,577 women workers. By 1891 the number of combined factories had risen to 251 and the number of women workers to 5,319. How many of these factories and workers specialized in the handling of ostrich plumes has not been documented. New York State, "Homework in the Artificial Flower and Feather Industry in New York State (Special Bulletin No. 199)," 7–8.

16. Watson, "Homework in the Tenements," 778.

17. One journalistic account from 1894 suggested that "the majority of skilled [ostrich feather workers] are American girls," but offered no evidence to support its claim: J. Torrey Connor, "A Chapter on Ostrich Feathers," *Arthur's Home Magazine* 64/2, November 1894.

18. Edward Schuman to author, November 8, 2004.

19. New York State, "Homework in the Artificial Flower and Feather Industry in New York State"; Van Kleeck, *Artificial Flower Makers,* 29–34; Watson, "Homework in the Tenements," 772–81.

20. Many accounts from the period, and some secondary sources, emphasize first-generation Italian women's resistance to organizing, and how this affected relations between Jewish and Italian women in the garment industry. However, it is clear that Italian women did take part in socialist political movements, as in acts of organized resistance. On Italian women's movement into the feather trade and related industries: Odencrantz, *Italian Women in Industry;* Van Kleeck, *Artificial Flower Makers,* 34–37. On their relationship to labor politics in the period: Carnevale, "A Coat of Many Colors"; Enstad, *Ladies of Labor, Girls of Adventure,* 120; Gabaccia, *Militants and Migrants;* Glenn, *Daughters of the Shtetl,* 191–94; McCreesh, *Women in the Campaign to Organize Garment Workers,* 104.

21. In the ostrich feather, fancy feather, and artificial flower trades, Italian girls and women tended to engage in homework in greater numbers than their Jewish peers. For children, this resulted in high rates of non-attendance at school, poor eyesight, respiratory and contagious disease, and mortality. *Child Employing Industries: Proceedings of the Sixth Annual Conference, Boston, Massachusetts, January 13–16, 1910;* Kosak, "A Coat of Many Colors"; New York State, "Homework in the Artificial Flower and Feather Industry in

New York State"; Van Kleeck, *Artificial Flower Makers*, especially chapters 4 and 5; Van Kleeck, *A Seasonal Industry*. For a vivid picture of the homework conducted by Italian ostrich feather willowers, and reference to the dangers that arose for young Italians in the industry: Watson, "Homework in the Tenements," 772–81.

22. A summary of typical wages earned by women at this time may be found in Tentler, *Wage-Earning Women*, 18–19. On typical wages paid fancy feather and artificial flower workers: Manson, *Work for Women*, 29–36; New York State, "Homework in the Artificial Flower and Feather Industry in New York State"; Van Kleeck, *Artificial Flower Makers*, especially chapters 4 and 5.

23. On the average age of American women workers of the period: Tentler, *Wage-Earning Women*, 59. On the age of ostrich feather workers specifically: Van Kleeck, *Artificial Flower Makers*, 25.

24. Glenn, *Daughters of the Shtetl*, 79–89. See also Tentler, *Wage-Earning Women*, 85–114.

25. "Isidore Cohnfeld Tricked," *New York Times*, December 8, 1888.

26. "Feather Workers' Strike," *New York Times*, December 7, 1888.

27. "Isidore Cohnfeld Tricked," *New York Times*, December 8, 1888.

28. New York State, *Preliminary Report*, 275. On the ubiquity of small, unhygienic, Jewish-run workshops in New York's clothing industry at the time: Soyer, *A Coat of Many Colors*.

29. Watson, "Homework in the Tenements," 778. Watson refers here to New York's Upper East Side, where she identified eighteen factories or shops specializing in the willowing of ostrich plumes on one block between Second and Third Avenues.

30. Hall, *Second Report of the Factory Investigating Commission*, 534–39.

31. Van Kleeck, *Artificial Flower Makers*, 54.

32. New York State, *Preliminary Report*, 275.

33. Hall, *Second Report of the Factory Investigating Commission*, 339.

34. Occupational segregation by sex was typical of the garment industry as a whole: Dye, *As Equals and as Sisters*, 19.

35. The description of feather processing is drawn from: "Ostrich Feathers," *Scientific American* 7/46, July 31, 1852; "Ornamental Feathers," *Saturday Evening Post*, October 2, 1875; "Ostrich Plumes and Tips: A Great Increase in the Demand for Feathers," *New York Times*, September 24, 1882; "Natural History: The Feather Industry," *Forest and Stream: A Journal of Outdoor Life, Travel, Nature Study, Shooting, Fishing, Yachting* 26/9, March 25, 1886, 162; "Flower and Feather Manufacturing," *Scientific American* 70/25, June 23, 1894; "The Manufacture of Ostrich Feathers," *Scientific American* 84/11, March 16, 1901: 164; "The Ostrich Plume Craze," *Washington Post*, September 27, 1908, 9; "Making 'Willow' Plumes," *Los Angeles Times*, August 20, 1910; Clarke, "Fashion Meets Modern Demands"; Connor, "A Chapter on Ostrich Feathers"; Gouy, "Ostrich-Feathers"; Hall, *Second Report of the Factory Investigating Commission*; Harper, "The Feather Business"; Manson, *Work for Women*.

36. Gouy, "Ostrich-Feathers."

37. Ibid.

38. Watson, "Homework in the Tenements," 778.

39. The figure of fifty dollars is derived from "The Ostrich Plume Craze." The maximum salary for a willower is given as forty-five dollars in "Making 'Willow' Plumes"; "The Manufacture of Ostrich Feathers"; Manson, *Work for Women*, 31.

40. Gouy, "Ostrich-Feathers."

41. "Feather Workers Return to Work," *New York Times*, March 21, 1889.

42. On the experience of the earliest female strikers in New York and elsewhere: McCreesh, *Women in the Campaign to Organize Garment Workers*, 24–92; Orleck, *Common Sense and a Little Fire*, 31–41.

43. Antonovsky, ed., *The Early Jewish Labor Movement*; Epstein, *Jewish Labor in U.S.A.*, 108–32; Michels, *A Fire in Their Hearts*, 56–61.

44. Van Kleeck, *Artificial Flower Makers*, 11.

45. "Fashion Says Feathers—The Wonderful Effect of a Trifling Change," *Chicago Daily Tribune*, October 28, 1883. See also *Report on the Wages of Women in the Millinery Industry in Massachusetts*; Frankfurter and Dewson, *District of Columbia Minimum Wage Cases*; New York State, "Homework in the Artificial Flower and Feather Industry in New York State"; Van Kleeck, *Artificial Flower Makers*, especially chapter 3.

46. The Flower Makers' Union, founded in 1907 under the American Federation of Labor, was formed by Jewish women and girls from Russia, and members relied on Yiddish as their language of communication and agitation. In 1909 or 1910 the union initiated a failed attempt to unite with milliners, wire makers, and flower makers; roughly nine years later, it initiated its first organized strike. Van Kleeck, *Artificial Flower Makers*, 29, 36–37. On the affairs of this union and its successor, the Artificial Flower and Feather branch of Local 142 of the Ladies Neckwear Workers' Union: "Annual Report of the Woman's Trade Union League of New York"; New York State, "Homework in the Artificial Flower and Feather Industry in New York State." On Italians in the industry: Odencrantz, *Italian Women in Industry*. Seasonality was also an acute concern for garment and millinery workers: Van Kleeck, *A Seasonal Industry*; Waldinger, "International Ladies Garment Workers Union."

47. *Report on the Wages of Women in the Millinery Industry in Massachusetts*; Frankfurter and Dewson, *District of Columbia Minimum Wage Cases*; Hall, *Second Report of the Factory Investigating Commission*; New York State, "Report and Testimony Taken Before the Special Committee of the Assembly Appointed to Investigate the Conditions of Female Labor in the City of New York," 1027–30; New York State, *Preliminary Report*; New York State, "Homework in the Artificial Flower and Feather Industry in New York State"; Van Kleeck, *Artificial Flower Makers*; Van Kleeck, *A Seasonal Industry*.

48. See the reports published by New York State, cited above, and Van Kleeck, *Artificial Flower Makers*, 213.

49. The feather workers' strike does not appear to have been covered prominently by

New York's leading Yiddish socialist weekly of the time, *Di nyu-yorker yudishe folkstsaytung*, or by the daily *Yidishes tageblatt*. On these and other New York presses of the period: Epstein, *Jewish Labor in U.S.A.*, 253–71; Michels, *A Fire in Their Hearts*, 69–124. On the growing militancy of the Jewish labor movement, see also Kosak, "A Coat of Many Colors."

50. "The Duty of Women of Leisure to Women Who Work," *New York Evangelist*, November 1, 1888.

51. The impassioned bird protection advocate William Hornaday, who published extensively on the anti-plumage movement, for example, consistently wrote that "dealers in ostrich feathers are not concerned" with anti-plumage bills, "for ostrich feathers do not come from wild birds." Hornaday, "The Steam Roller of the Feather Importers in the United States Senate." This argument was echoed by protectionists on the other side of the Atlantic: Buckland, *Pros and Cons of the Plumage Bill*. On ostrich feather merchants' interest in disaggregating the industries: "No Cruelty to Ostriches," *New York Times*, May 11, 1913. The Audubon Society, for its part, approved of the use of ostrich feathers by the millinery trade, a fact that was cited in promotional literature by ostrich farmers and feather merchants. See, for example, Cawston Ostrich Farm, *Twenty-Fifth Anniversary Souvenir Catalogue*, 8.

52. See, for example, "Natural History: The Feather Industry." On the growth and popular response to the bird protection movement: Doughty, *Feather Fashions and Bird Preservation*.

53. *Report of the Ostrich Feather Commission Appointed to Enquire into the Ostrich Industry*; Board of Trade and Industries (South Africa), "Report No. 55: The Ostrich Feather Industry."

54. Hayden, "Speech: The Ostrich Industry," 60.

55. *Ostrich Farming in the United States: Reports from the Consuls of the United States*; Hayden, "Speech: The Ostrich Industry."

56. "Ostrich Raising."

57. Pisani, *From the Family Farm to Agribusiness*, 186–289; Stoll, *The Fruits of Natural Advantage*, 25–29. The American grain and feather markets were further linked by their reliance on speculation and futures trading: Levy, "Contemplating Delivery."

58. On the rise of California's fruit and citrus industry: Sackman, *Orange Empire*; Stoll, *The Fruits of Natural Advantage*. On struggles over irrigation: Hundley, *The Great Thirst*; Pisani, *From the Family Farm to Agribusiness*; Reisner, *Cadillac Desert*; Worster, *Rivers of Empire*.

59. For parallels in the fruit industry: Stoll, *The Fruits of Natural Advantage*, 63–93.

60. Another influential ostrich farming pioneer was Dr. Charles J. Sketchly, an Englishman who had raised ostriches in the Cape. Sketchly was the first to bring the birds to California, importing twenty to thirty of them from the Cape in 1883. (According to one source, twenty-two out of two hundred birds survived the journey.) They were sent via Buenos Aires and New York and settled in Anaheim on a farm established with Messrs. Stracey, Beauchamp, and Burkett. With the birds Sketchley brought four colored men and one colored woman who were, he claimed, "more familiar with the

ostrich than any native Africans." "Ostrich Farming in This Country." Another of these pioneers was E. J. Johnson, who brought twenty-three birds from the Cape to California's San Luis Rey valley in 1883 and formed branch farms in Coronado Beach and Riverside. Benjamin, "Ostrich Farming"; Cawston and Fox, *Ostriches and Ostrich Farming in California*; Holder, "An Ostrich Ranch"; Hovey, "American Ostrich Farming."

61. Felix J. Koch, "The Ostrich Feather Industry in the West vs. Africa," *Overland Monthly and Out West Magazine* 108/6, December 1891; Cawston and Fox, *Ostriches and Ostrich Farming in California*; Cawston Ostrich Farm, *Twenty-Fifth Anniversary Souvenir Catalogue.*

62. Hayden, "Speech: The Ostrich Industry," 58. Similar statistics are reported in Lee, "The Ostrich Industry in the United States."

63. Pickerell, "Ostrich Farming in Arizona," 399–400. Birds bred in Arizona from Cawston stock were in turn sold to ersatz ostrich farmers in other states. The correspondence of the Colorado Ostrich Farm, for example, documents one such farmer's inquiries into available stock from Arizona. Denver Public Library, "Colorado Ostrich Farm."

64. The ranch in San Jacinto had been rented by the Cawston Ostrich Farm in the early years of the twentieth century, but the organization's board of directors resolved to purchase it in May 1909. After this, all of Cawston's birds were brought to the ranch. HL COF, Box 1, Folder 2, "Deeds etc, Os. Farm November 24, 1909–July 28, 1928," Board of Directors' Minutes, May 19, 1909. For further particulars about the acquisition of this property: "New Home for Big Birds," *Los Angeles Times*, March 4, 1909. A number of occasionally conflicting early histories of the farm are found in publications by Cawston himself, including: Causton (Cawston), "Ostrich Farming in California"; Cawston, *Ostrich Farming in California*; Cawston and Fox, *Ostrich Farming in California*; Cawston and Fox, *Ostriches and Ostrich Farming in California*; Cawston Ostrich Farm, *Twenty-Fifth Anniversary Souvenir Catalogue.*

65. The lots in question were numbered 10–21. HL COF, Box 1, Folder 2, "Deeds etc, Os. Farm November 24, 1909–July 28, 1928," "Deed of Sale." The plot purchased was in Lincoln Park. A more detailed description of the property may be found in a letter by Herbert Vatcher Jr. to an unidentified potential buyer of the property, August 20, 1928. HL COF, Box 2, Folder "Debits, Credits, Assets (cnt.)."

66. Sackman, *Orange Empire*, 45. The quote is from tourist literature published in 1888. See also Stoll, *The Fruits of Natural Advantage*, 33–62.

67. Teisch, "'Home Is Not So Very Far Away.'"

68. Cawston and Fox, *Ostriches and Ostrich Farming in California.*

69. HL COF, Box 2, Folder "Contracts," "Cawston Ostrich Farm Prospectus," 3.

70. Cawston Ostrich Farm, *Twenty-Fifth Anniversary Souvenir Catalogue*, 10.

71. An image of these fantastic structures adorned a postcard sold to tourists at the Cawston Farm's shop. HL COF, Box 1, Folder "Ostrich misc., 3 pieces," "A Prize Flock, Cawston Ostrich Farm, South Pasadena, Calif."

72. HL COF, Box 1, Folder "Ostrich misc., 3 pieces"; The Seaver Center, Natural History Museum of Los Angeles County, George N. Wilkie Collection, P-123, Photos 1–29. Fortunately for the birds, other sources attest that their normal diet consisted heavily of alfalfa and grain. "Pluck Many Birds," *Los Angeles Times*, December 10, 1910.

73. Raibmon, *Authentic Indians;* Sackman, *Orange Empire.*

74. HL COF, Box 2, Folder "Contracts," "Cawston Ostrich Farm Prospectus," 2.

75. On the manufacture of Cawston feathers in New York: "Ostrich Raising"; Hovey, "American Ostrich Farming." Reference to the finest Cawston feathers being saved for California consumers appears in Hovey's article and also in Bicknell, "An American Ostrich Farm."

76. HL COF, Box 2, Folder "Contracts," "Cawston Ostrich Farm Prospectus," 4. In 1920 it was estimated that 50,000 to 100,000 visitors flocked to the farm each year, earning the business $8,300–$15,000. Herbert Vatcher Jr. to an unidentified potential buyer of the property, August 20, 1928. HL COF, Box 2, Folder "Debits, Credits, Assets (cnt.)."

77. "The Manufacture of Ostrich Feathers."

78. Ibid.

79. On the company's lease of space on South Broadway: "Change of Feathers," *Los Angeles Times*, January 31, 1909.

80. HL COF, Box 2, Folder "Debits, Credits, Assets (cnt.)," "Undated Lists of Employees."

81. M. Iwata appears on two undated "List of Employees," once as a "Janitor and Miscl. work[er]," and once as a porter. C. (or G.) Ching worked as one of the company's dyers. HL COF, Box 2, Folder "Debits, Credits, Assets, cnt."

82. Cawston Ostrich Farm, *Twenty-Fifth Anniversary Souvenir Catalogue*, 9.

83. HL COF, Box 2, Folder "Contracts," "Cawston Ostrich Farm Prospectus," 1.

84. The Chicago store was located at 108 Michigan Avenue, the New York store at 500 Fifth Avenue, the San Francisco store at 54 Geary Street, and the Los Angeles store at 723 South Broadway. HL COF, Box 1, Folder "Ostrich misc, 3 pieces," Cawston Ostrich Farm stationery.

85. On the relatively high price of Cawston plumes: Willey, "Raising Ostriches." On the farm's success at world fairs: Cawston Ostrich Farm, *Twenty-Fifth Anniversary Souvenir Catalogue.* On the display of other California produce in world fairs and garden shows: Sackman, *Orange Empire*, 34–39.

86. A newspaper article claimed that some New York feather merchants favored retail stores uptown rather than in the traditional center of feather sales, the Lower East Side, so that "women may see their wares displayed in big show windows." Sellers insisted that domestic ostrich feathers were "gaining every year on the imported article." "Ostrich Plume Rivals," *New York Times*, October 26, 1903. Other positive reviews of Cawston plumes include: "Behold the Wonders of the Window in the Los Angeles Fashion Festival," *Los Angeles Times*, September 25, 1913.

87. During the promotional campaign of 1913, advertisements for Cawston feathers appeared in *Butterick Trio, Ladies Home Journal, Women's Home Companion, Pictorial Review, McCalls,* and *Modern Priscilla.* HL COF, Box 2, Folder "Credits and Assets, 1909–1935," Miscellaneous Cawston Ostrich Farm accounting information.

88. "California Ostrich Trade," *Los Angeles Times,* January 1, 1914.

89. "Ostrich Plume Rivals," *New York Times,* October 26, 1903.

90. HL COF, Box 1, Folder "Ostrich misc. 3 pieces," "Souvenir of the Cawston Ostrich Farm in California" (c. 1903).

91. HL COF, Box 3, Folder "1910–1913," Ernest Vatcher to Bert Vatcher, August 16, 1912.

92. UAL WFS, Box 6, Folder 6, W. F. Staunton to State Tax Company of Arizona, December 10, 1914. The quotation is from Staunton, who served as a principal investor and director of the Western Land and Cattle Company, which was formed from the ashes of the Pan-American Ostrich Company in 1914; UAL WFS, Box 6, Folder 6, W. F. Staunton to A. Lincoln Rowland, July 18, 1922. More detail on the collapse of the first and creation of the second company may be found in Staunton's papers in this archive.

93. HL COF, Box 3, Folder "1910–1913," Ernest Vatcher to Bert Vatcher, August 16, 1912.

94. Ibid.

95. In an undated list of employees, the Cawston Farm recorded wages paid its factory workers. At $30–35 per week, dyers earned the most, followed by washers ($13.25 per week), preparers ($7–18 per week), and sewers ($6–12 per week). Out of step with New York wages was the sum paid to the company's curlers, which ranged from $3.50 to $8 per week. HL COF, Box 2, Folder "Debits, Credits, Assets, cnt.," "List of Employees."

96. "Local Syndicate Buys Cawston Ostrich Farm," *Los Angeles Times,* November 21, 1911.

97. Archival material in the British National Archives' Public Records office records that E. P. Cawston, solicitor, was a founding investor in the Graaff Reinet Ostrich and Lucerne Farms Ltd., which was created in 1912. Cawston remained involved in this operation until the early winter of 1913: the business itself folded the following year. TNA, BT 31/21086/125785, "No. of Company: 125785; Graaff Reinet Ostrich and Lucerne Farms Ltd." On Edwin Cawston Jr.: "George Cawston Is Pneumonia Victim," *Los Angeles Times,* November 16, 1918.

98. HL COF, Box 1, Folder "Deeds, etc. Ostrich Farm November 24, 1909–July 28, 1928," E. P. Cawton to Herbert Vatcher, October 24, 1910.

99. The local press that covered Cawston's departure appeared duped by—and, indeed, downright enthusiastic about—what was in fact financial gerrymandering on the part of the farm's management. "Local Syndicate Buys Cawston Ostrich Farm," *Los Angeles Times,* November 21, 1911.

100. NA, BT 31/13611/115860, "No. of Company: 115860; Cawston Ostrich Farm Ltd."

101. HL COF, Box 3 Folder "1914," Unsigned letter by "President" (Jonathan S. Dodge) to J. A. Stein, May 2, 1914.

102. Ernest Vatcher also aspired to open his own feather manufacturing company that would be utilized by the Cawston Farm. The Vallely and Vatcher Incorporated Feather Manufacturers did open shop in Los Angeles, but there is no evidence that the Cawston Farm relied on it. HL COF, Box 2, Folder "Printed Material from 1911–1912," Vallely and Vatcher business card. The challenge of finding laborers to pick, process, or prepare for sale agricultural products in California was ubiquitous in this period. See, for example, Stoll, *The Fruits of Natural Advantage*, chapter 5.

103. HL COF, Box 2, Folder "Debits, Credits, and Assets, Cawston Ostrich Farm," J. A. Stein to Cawston Ostrich Farm, December 1, 1912.

104. HL COF, Box 1, Folder "Deeds, etc. Ostrich Farm November 24, 1909–July 21, 1928," "List of Stockholders Cawston Ostrich Farm." Lists of stockholders in 1920, complete with the number of stocks in each party's possession, may be found in Box 2, Folder "Debits, Credits, Assets (cnt.)."

105. Reference to the average dividends may be found in HL COF, Box 1, Folder "Deeds, etc. Ostrich Farm November 24, 1909–July 28, 1928," E. P. Cawston to Herbert Vatcher, October 24, 1910.

106. HL COF, Box 2, Folder "Credits and Assets, 1909–1935," Fred H. Ralsten to Jonathan S. Dodge, September 16, 1914.

107. HL COF, Box 2, Folder "Credits and Assets, 1909–1935," Jonathan S. Dodge to Stockholders, June 16, 1914.

108. HL COF, Box 2, Folder "Debits, Credits, and Assets, Cawston Ostrich Farm," "J. A. Stein Account."

109. HL COF, Box 3, Folder "1914," Jonathan S. Dodge to J. A. Stein, May 2, 1914.

110. On the quantity of Western Land and Cattle Company feathers in Fish's possession: UAL WFS, Box 6, Folder 6, A. N. Gage to W. F. Staunton, May 27, 1921; Staunton to F. F. Klingerman, March 9, 1925. On the value of feathers sold by Fish on behalf of the company from 1919 to 1924: UAL WFS, Box 6, Folder 6, W. F. Staunton to F. F. Klingerman, March 9, 1925.

111. UAL WFS, Box 6, Folder 6, W. F. Staunton to O. B. Fish, June 23, 1924. For a similar tone: W. F. Staunton to O. B. Fish, August 20, 1922.

112. HL COF, Box 2, Folder "Debits, Credits, and Assets, Cawston Ostrich Farm," "J. A. Stein Account." On the repeated and unfair assessment of investors: HL COF, Box 3 Folder "1914," Unsigned letter (likely by R. D. Davis, director and vice president of the farm in 1914) to Fred Ralsten, July 23, 1914.

113. Ibid.

114. Ibid.

115. Ibid. On the sale of the San Jacinto property: "Ostrich Farm's a Dairy Ranch," *Los Angeles Times*, June 27, 1914.

116. HL COF, Box 1, Folder "Atlanta Ostrich Farm," Walter Solomon, landlord, to Cawston Ostrich Farm, April 20, 1915.

117. "Ostriches Get Wet," *Los Angeles Times*, January 4, 1916; "Ostriches Are Cheap," *Los Angeles Times*, May 9, 1919.

118. New York State, "Homework in the Artificial Flower and Feather Industry in New York State," 20.

119. The quip originally appeared in an unspecified issue of the satirical journal *Puck* and was reprinted in "Pebbles," *The Independent*, December 14, 1914.

120. "Locked Out!" *Life*, December 10, 1914, 64.

121. Amero, "The Southwest on Display."

122. HL COF, Box 1, Folder "Deeds, etc., Ostrich Farm November 24, 1909–July 28, 1928," "Indenture of Lease made by Sun Drug Company, lessor, and Cawston Ostrich Farm, lessee." On the farm's acquisition of this lease: "Change of Feathers," *Los Angeles Times*, January 31, 1909.

123. HL COF, Box 1, Folder "Deeds, etc., Ostrich Farm November 24, 1909–July 28, 1928," "Flint and Jutten to Cawston Ostrich Farm, 23 January, 1917."

124. HL COF, Box 1, Folder "Deeds, etc., Ostrich Farm November 24, 1909–July 28, 1928," "Assets and Liabilities, December 31st 1920." By manipulating the value of its illiquid assets, the farm managed to claim an even balance by the close of the calendar year of 1920, but this was a desperate and transparent sleight of hand. Among the assets mentioned in the firm's year-end recordkeeping were equipment and inventories with a paper value of over $25,000: in practice these goods were all but useless, as there was no demand for feathers or the manufacturing supplies required to prepare them.

125. HL COF, Box 3, Folder "1914," unsigned letter (likely by R. D. Davis, director and vice president of the farm in 1914) to Fred Ralsten, July 23, 1914.

126. "Ostrich Coming Back," *New York Times*, April 12, 1919. Articles in this vein ran throughout the month in the *New York Times* and frequently thereafter; for example, "Trimmings for Hats," *New York Times*, April 6, 1919; "For Summer Millinery," *New York Times*, April 27, 1919; "Ostrich Industry Revived," *Los Angeles Times*, September 2, 1920.

127. "C. Vanderbilt, Jr. Wed Before 3,000," *New York Times*, April 30, 1919.

128. "New Winter's Hats Pass Grand Review," *New York Times*, August 5, 1919.

129. "Ostrich Feather Sale," *New York Times*, July 11, 1919; "Ostrich Feather Prices Rising," *New York Times*, September 18, 1919.

130. HL COF, Box 3, Folder "1919," Bert Vatcher to Leon Shaw, May 29, 1919. Lillian Vatcher had been involved in the company since its early years, serving as secretary under her maiden name, Lillian Craig.

131. "Mosely, Alfred," *Encyclopaedia Judaica*.

132. Teisch, "'Home Is Not So Very Far Away,'" 140–41.

133. Ibid., 154.

134. Mosely, *Reports of the Delegates of the Mosely Industrial Commission*, 6.

135. HL COF, Box 3, Folder "1915–1918," "Synopsis of Imperial Trip, 14 April 1917."

136. HL COF, Box 3, Folder "1919," Bert Vatcher to Lillian Vatcher, April 3, 1919; Bert Vatcher to Leon Shaw, May 29, 1919.

137. HL COF, Box 3, Folder "1919," Bert Vatcher to Jonathan Dodge, May 4, 1919. George Mosely returned the affection, unfailingly concluding his professional correspondence to Vatcher with "love to Mrs. Vatcher and the kiddies."

138. HL COF, Box 3, Folder "1919," Bert Vatcher to Lillian Vatcher, April 3, 1919.

139. HL COF, Box 3, Folder "1929," Bert Vatcher to Jonathan Dodge, May 4, 1919.

140. Ibid. Reference to Stein being "not in funds" appears in HL COF, Box 3, Folder "1929," S. Shaw (cashier of the National Bank of Pasadena) to Bert Vatcher, November 1, 1918.

141. HL COF, Box 3, Folder "1929," Bert Vatcher to Jonathan Dodge, May 4, 1919. This letter also contains Vatcher's assessment that Mosely's "crowd not only has lots of money but are the squarest people."

142. HL COF, Box 3, Folder "1919," Bert Vatcher to Lillian Vatcher, April 3, 1919.

143. HL COF, Bert Vatcher to Leon Shaw, May 29, 1919, Box 3, Folder "1919."

144. HL COF, Box 3, Folder "1919," Telegram by Bert Vatcher to Miss Manning (secretary, Cawston Ostrich Farm), June 1, 1919.

145. "Ostrich Feather Sale Called Off," *New York Times*, November 12, 1919. See also "Ostrich Feather Prices Rising," *New York Times*, September 18, 1919; "Fewer Ostriches," *New York Times*, September 12, 1919, "Ostriches Killed Off as Price Falls," *Washington Post*, March 20, 1927.

146. UAL WFS, Box 6, Folder 6, Dr. John Dennett to Arthur Gage, June 6, 1920. Fish's feather business was located first at 33 East Tenth Street and subsequently at 64 East Eleventh Street. In a letter to his associates in Arizona, Fish mentioned being pushed out of the former location by a "profiteering" landlord who "speculated" in real estate, but one suspects, given the timing of the move, that it in fact represented a desperate downsizing of his operation. UAL WFS, Box 6, Folder 6, O. B. Fish to W. F. Staunton, August 8, 1922, August 25, 1922.

147. HL COF, Box 2, Folder "Credits and Assets 1909–1919," Lillian Vatcher to Bert Vatcher, July 12, 1919.

148. HL COF, Box 3, "1929," Jonathan Dodge to Bert Vatcher, May 6, 1919.

149. HL COF, Box 1, Folder 2, "Deeds etc., Ostrich Farm November 24, 1909–July 28, 1928," George [Mosely?] to Bert Vatcher, May 10, 1921.

150. HL COF, Box 1, Folder 2, "Deeds etc., Ostrich Farm November 24, 1909–July 28, 1928," George [Mosely?] to McDevitt, May 10, 1921.

151. HL COF, Box 1, Folder 2, "Deeds etc., Ostrich Farm November 24, 1909–July 28, 1928," Payment receipt signed by Miss C. Manning (secretary, Cawston Ostrich Farm), July 21, 1920.

152. UAL WFS, Box 6, Folder 6, O. B. Fish to W. F. Staunton, September 15, 1921.

153. UAL WFS, Box 6, Folder 6, O. B. Fish to W. F. Staunton, June 22, 1922, August 8, 1922, May 24, 1924.

154. HL COF, Box 1, Folder 2, "Deeds etc., Ostrich Farm November 24, 1909–July 28, 1928," agreement between William Ellis Lady and Cawston Ostrich Farm, September 12, 1923.

155. On the demands of stockholders: HL COF, Box 3, Folder "1927–1928," John A. Goodrich to Ernest Vatcher, March 31, 1928. On the liabilities of the Cawston farm and business: HL COF, Box 1, Folder "Credits and Assets, 1909–1935," Bert Vatcher to George M. Wiley, Chamber of Commerce, April 9, 1927.

156. HL COF, Box 2, Folder "Debits, Credits, and Assets, cnt.," Cawston Ostrich Farm to C (illegible), August 20, 1928. Documents promoting the sale of the Vatcher family house are in the same folder.

157. The California Zoological Society was formed in May 1935 and claimed among its animal stock the Cawston birds and animals from the former Selig Zoo. HL COF, Box 1, Folder "Zoological Society."

158. "Where the Dye Is Cast: Feather Merchant to the World," *Los Angeles Times*, August 11, 1977.

159. A subsidiary corrective is also provided to the scholarship on American agriculture, which neglects Jews and Jewishness as categories of analysis. A telling example of the former trend appears in Steven Stoll's marvelous study of the California fruit industry. Stoll devotes considerable time to discussing the professional ventures of Harris Weinstock, who "spent forty years of his life navigating and formalizing the relationship between California fruit growers and the markets for their produce," but, though mentioning Weinstock's Jewishness, teases out no relevance from this fact. Stoll, *The Fruits of Natural Advantage*, 64–74. An exception to this trend is the literature on Jewish cooperative farming ventures.

CONCLUSION

1. Penslar, *Shylock's Children*, 60.

Abitbol, Michel. "Juifs maghrébins et commerce transsaharien au moyen-age." In *Communautés juives des marges sahariennes du maghreb*, edited by Michel Abitbol, 229–52. Jerusalem: Institut Ben-Zvi, 1982.

———. "Juifs maghrébins et commerce transsaharien du VIIIe au XVe Siècles." In *Le sol, la parole et l'écrit: mélanges en hommage à Raymond Mauny*, 561–78. Paris: Société française d'histoire d'outre-mer, 1981.

"An Act for the Better Preservation of Wild Ostriches (No. 12)." In *Laws in Colonies as to Trespass and Preservation of Game:* House of Commons Parliamentary Papers, 1871.

Ahmad, Feroz. *The Making of Modern Turkey.* London: Routledge, 1993.

Ahroni, Reuben. *The Jews of the British Crown Colony of Aden: History, Culture, and Ethnic Relations.* Leiden: E. J. Brill, 1994.

Albasu, S. A. *The Lebanese in Kano: An Immigrant Community in a Hausa Society in the Colonial and Post-Colonial Periods.* Kano, Nigeria: Kabs Print Services, 1995.

Allen, Charles H. *A Visit to Queensland and Her Goldfields.* London: Chapman and Hall, 1900.

Amero, Richard W. "The Southwest on Display at the Panama-California Exposition, 1915." *The Journal of San Diego History* 36, no. 4 (1990).

Angel, Marc D. "History of Seattle's Sephardic Community." *Western States Jewish Historical Quarterly* (1974): 22–30.

"Annual Report of the Chief Inspector of Factories and Workshops, for 1903, Part I." In *Command Papers; Reports of Commissioners:* House of Commons Parliamentary Papers, 1904.

"Annual Report of the Woman's Trade Union League of New York." New York: The League, 1920–22.

Antonovsky, Aaron, ed. *The Early Jewish Labor Movement in the United States.* New York, 1961.

Appel, A. *Die distrik Oudtshoorn tot die tagtigerjare van die 19de Eeu: 'n sosio-ekonomiese studie.* Pretoria: Die Staatsdrukker, 1988.

Aschman, George. "A Childhood in Oudtshoorn." *Jewish Affairs*, May 1969: 26–29.

————. "Oudtshoorn in the Early Days." In *The Jews in South Africa, a History*, edited by Gustav Saron and Louis Hotz, 121–37. London: Oxford University Press, 1955.

Auslander, Leora. "'Jewish Taste'? Jews, and the Aesthetics of Everyday Life in Paris and Berlin, 1933–1942." In *Histories of Leisure*, edited by Rudy Koshar, 299–318. Oxford: Berg, 2002.

————. *Taste and Power: Furnishing Modern France.* Berkeley: University of California Press, 1996.

Austen, Ralph A. *African Economic History: Internal Development and External Dependency.* London: James Currey, 1987.

————. "Marginalization, Stagnation, and Growth: The Trans-Saharan Caravan Trade in the Era of European Expansion, 1500–1900." In *The Rise of Merchant Empires: Long-Distance Trade in the Early Modern World, 1350–1750*, edited by James Tracy, 311–50. Cambridge: Cambridge University Press, 1990.

————. "The Trans-Saharan Slave Trade: A Tentative Census." In *The Uncommon Market: Essays in the Economic History of the Atlantic Slave Trade*, edited by Henry A. Gemery and Jan S. Hogendorn, 23–76. New York: Academic, 1979.

Baier, Stephen. *An Economic History of Central Niger.* Oxford: Clarendon, 1980.

————. "Trans-Saharan Trade and the Sahel: Damergu, 1870–1930." *The Journal of African History* 18, no. 1 (1977): 37–60.

Bailkin, Jordanna. "Making Faces: Tattooed Women and Colonial Regimes." *History Workshop Journal*, no. 59 (2005): 33–56.

Bakalczuk-Felin, Meilech. *Yizkur-bukh fun rakishok un umgegnt.* Johannesburg: Aroysgegebn fun der rakisher landsmanshaft in Yohanesburg South Africa, 1952.

Ballantyne, R. M. *Six Months at the Cape; or, Letters to Periwinkle from South Africa.* London: J. Nisbet, 1878.

Barlow, Tani, et al. "The Modern Girl Around the World: A Research Agenda and Preliminary Findings." *Gender and History* (forthcoming).

Baron, Salo Wittmayer, Arcadius Kahan, and Nachum Gross. *Economic History of the Jews.* New York: Schocken, 1975.

Benatar, Gaby E. "El kal sefaradi de Lubumbashi (en el Zaire)." *Los Muestros*, no. 22 (1996).

Benatar, Jacqueline, and Myriam Pimienta-Benatar. *De Rhodes à Elisabethville, l'odyssée d'une communauté Sépharade.* Paris: Editions SIIAC, 2000.

Benbassa, Esther, ed. *Haim Nahum: A Sephardic Chief Rabbi in Politics, 1892–1923.* Tuscaloosa: University of Alabama Press, 1995.

Benson, Susan Porter. *Counter Cultures: Saleswomen, Managers, and Customers in American Department Stores, 1890–1940.* Urbana: University of Illinois Press, 1986.

Berg, Maxine. "In Pursuit of Luxury: Global History and British Consumer Goods in the Eighteenth Century." *Past and Present,* no. 182 (2004): 85–142.

Berger, Nathan. *Jewish Trails Through Southern Africa: A Documentary.* Johannesburg: Kayor, 1976.

Birmizrahi, Rifat. *Lo Ke Meldavan Nustros Padres / Babalarimizin Gazetlerindin (From Our Fathers' Newspapers).* Istanbul, 2006.

Boahen, A. Adu. *Britain, the Sahara, and the Western Sudan, 1788–1861.* Oxford: Clarendon, 1964.

———. "The Caravan Trade in the Nineteenth Century." *The Journal of African History* 3, no. 2 (1961): 349–59.

Board of Trade and Industries (South Africa). "Report No. 55: The Ostrich Feather Industry." 1925.

Bodian, Miriam. *Hebrews of the Portuguese Nation: Conversos and Community in Early Modern Amsterdam.* Bloomington: Indiana University Press, 1997.

Bonacich, Edna. "A Theory of Middleman Minorities." *American Sociological Review* 38, no. 5 (1973): 583–94.

Bonacich, Edna, and Richard P. Appelbaum. *Behind the Label: Inequality in the Los Angeles Apparel Industry.* Berkeley: University of California Press, 2000.

Bonneff, Léon Bonneff Maurice. "L'art de la fleur et de la plume." In *La vie tragique des travailleurs, enquêtes sur la condition économique et morale des ouvriers et ouvrières d'industrie,* 323–35. Paris: M. Rivière, 1914.

Booth, Charles. *Life and Labour of the People in London.* London: Macmillan, 1902.

Boum, Aomar. "Muslims Remember Jews in Southern Morocco: Social Memories, Dialogic Narratives, and the Collective Imagination of Jewishness." University of Arizona, 2006.

Braby's Cape Province Directory. Durban, 1900.

Braudel, Fernand. *The Mediterranean and the Mediterranean World in the Age of Philip II.* New York: Harper & Row, 1972.

Breun, Roger. "Rhodes, It's a Long Way." *Los Muestros,* no. 32 (1998).

Breward, Christopher. *The Culture of Fashion: A New History of Fashionable Dress.* Manchester: Manchester University Press, 1995.

Bristow, Edward J. *Prostitution and Prejudice: The Jewish Fight Against White Slavery, 1870–1939.* New York: Schocken, 1983.

Buckland, James. *Pros and Cons of the Plumage Bill.* London: Racquet Court Press, n.d. (ca. 1920).

Buckley, Cheryl, and Hilary Fawcett. *Fashioning the Feminine: Representation and Women's Fashion from the Fin-de-Siécle to the Present.* London: Tauris, 2002.

Buirski, Peter. "Aspects of Material Life in Oudtshoorn, 1860–1927, with Particular Reference to the Labouring Poor." B.A. Honours, University of Cape Town, 1983.

Burke, Timothy. *Lifebuoy Men, Lux Women: Commodification, Consumption, and Cleanliness in Modern Zimbabwe.* Durham: Duke University Press, 1996.

Cain, P. J., and A. G. Hopkins. *British Imperialism: Innovation and Expansion, 1688–1914.* London: Longman, 1993.

Cannadine, David. *Ornamentalism: How the British Saw Their Empire.* Oxford: Oxford University Press, 2001.

Carnevale, Nancy C. "Culture of Work: Italian Immigrant Women Homeworkers in the New York City Garment Industry, 1890–1914." In *A Coat of Many Colors: Immigration, Globalism, and Reform in the New York City Garment Industry,* edited by Daniel Soyer, 141–68. New York: Fordham University Press, 2005.

Causton (Cawston), Edwin. "Ostrich Farming in California." *Pearson's Magazine* (1896): 184–87.

Cawston, Edwin. *Ostrich Farming in California.* Norwalk, Los Angeles County, 1887.

Cawston, Edwin, and Charles E. Fox. *Ostriches and Ostrich Farming in California.* Los Angeles: Washington Garden Ostrich Farm, Bentley & Sutton Print, 1887.
———. *Ostrich Farming in California.* Los Angeles: Bentley & Sutton Print, 1887.

Cawston Ostrich Farm. *Twenty-Fifth Anniversary Souvenir Catalogue and Feather Price List.* South Pasadena, California, 1911.

Census of the Union of South Africa, 1911. Pretoria: Government Printing and Stationery Office, 1913.

Cesarani, David, ed. *Port Jews: Jewish Communities in Cosmopolitan Maritime Trading Centres, 1550–1950.* London: Frank Cass, 2002.

Chadwick, French Ensor, A. E. Seaton, William H. Rideing, John H. Gould, J. D. Jerrold Kelley, and Ridgely Hunt. *Ocean Steamships; a Popular Account of Their Construction, Development, Management and Appliances.* New York: C. Scribner's Sons, 1891.

Chaudhuri, Napur. "Shawls, Jewelry, Curry and Rice in Victorian Britain." In *Western Women and Imperialism: Complicity and Resistance,* edited by Napur Chaudhuri and Margaret Strobel, 231–46. Bloomington: Indiana University Press, 1992.

"Chief Inspector of Factories and Workshops Report, October 1882–83." In

Command Papers; Report of Commissioners: House of Commons Parliamentary Papers, 1884.

"Chief Inspector of Factories and Workshops Report, October 1886–87." In *Command Papers; Report of Commissioners:* House of Commons Parliamentary Papers, 1888.

Child Employing Industries. Proceedings of the Sixth Annual Conference, Boston, Massachusetts, January 13–16, 1910. Pamphlet; No. 124; Variation: National Child Labor Committee (U.S.). Pamphlet; No. 124. New York, 1910.

Chirot, Daniel, and Anthony Reid. *Essential Outsiders: Chinese and Jews in the Modern Transformation of Southeast Asia and Central Europe.* Seattle: University of Washington Press, 1997.

Christopher, A. J. "The Growth of Landed Wealth in the Cape Colony, 1860–1910." *Historia* 22, no. 1 (1977): 53–61.

Coetzee, Daniel. "Fires and Feathers: Acculturation, Arson, and the Jewish Community in Oudtshoorn, South Africa, 1914–1948." *Jewish History*, no. 19 (2005): 143–87.

———. "Immigrants to Citizens: Civil Integration and Acculturation of Jews into Oudtshoorn Society, 1874–1999." M.A. Thesis, University of Cape Town, 2000.

———. "The Oudtshoorn Jewry Interviews: Synopses." M.A. Thesis, University of Cape Town, 1999.

Coffin, Judith. *The Politics of Women's Work: The Paris Garment Trades, 1750–1915.* Princeton: Princeton University Press, 1996.

Coffin, William. "Ostrich Feathers of Tripoli." *Monthly Consular and Trade Reports* 347 (1909).

Cohen, Louis. *Reminiscences of Kimberley.* London: Bennett, 1911.

Cohen, Robert. *Jews in Another Environment: Surinam in the Second Half of the Eighteenth Century.* Leiden: Brill, 1991.

Cohen, Sarah Blacher. *From Hester Street to Hollywood: The Jewish-American Stage and Screen.* Bloomington: Indiana University Press, 1983.

Compilation of Customs Laws and Digest of Decisions Thereunder Rendered by the Courts and the Board of United States General Appraisers. Washington: Government Printing Office, 1908.

Cone, Molly, Howard Droker, and Jacqueline Williams. *Family of Strangers: Building a Jewish Community in Washington State.* Seattle: Washington State Jewish Historical Society, 2003.

Connor, J. Torrey. "A Chapter on Ostrich Feathers." *Arthur's Home Magazine* 64, no. 2 (1894).

Cordell, Dennis D. "Eastern Libya, Wadai and the Sanusiya: A Tariqa and a Trade Route." *The Journal of African History* 18, no. 1 (1977): 21–36.

Crane, Diana. *Fashion and Its Social Agendas: Class, Gender, and Identity in Clothing.* Chicago: University of Chicago Press, 2000.

Curtin, Philip D. *The Atlantic Slave Trade: A Census.* Madison: University of Wisconsin Press, 1969.

———. *Cross-Cultural Trade in World History.* Cambridge: Cambridge University Press, 1984.

———. *Economic Change in Precolonial Africa; Senegambia in the Era of the Slave Trade.* Madison: University of Wisconsin Press, 1975.

De Courtais, Georgine. *Women's Headdress and Hairstyles in England from AD 600 to the Present Day.* London: B. T. Batsford, 1973.

De Felice, Renzo. *Jews in an Arab Land: Libya, 1835–1970.* Austin: University of Texas Press, 1985.

De Grazia, Victoria. *Irresistible Empire: America's Advance Through Twentieth-Century Europe.* Cambridge: Harvard University Press, 2005.

De Grazia, Victoria, and Ellen Furlough. *The Sex of Things: Gender and Consumption in Historical Perspective.* Berkeley: University of California Press, 1996.

Delpierre, Madeleine. *Chapeaux, 1750–1960: Musée de la mode et du costume.* Paris: Le Musée, 1980.

Diner, Hasia R. "American West, New York Jewish." In *Jewish Life in the American West: Perspectives on Migration, Settlement, and Community,* edited by Ava Fran Kahn, 33–52. Los Angeles: Autry Museum of Western Heritage in association with University of Washington Press, Seattle, 2002.

Donaldson's South African Directory. Capetown: K. Donaldson.

Dotson, Floyd, and Lillian O. Dotson. "The Economic Role of Non-Indigenous Ethnic Minorities in Colonial Africa." In *Colonialism in Africa, 1870–1960,* edited by Peter Duignan and L. H. Gann, 565–631. Stanford: Hoover Institute, 1988.

Doughty, Robin W. *Feather Fashions and Bird Preservation: A Study in Nature Protection.* Berkeley: University of California Press, 1975.

Douglass, Arthur. "Ostrich Farming." In *Official Handbook: History, Productions and Resources of the Cape of Good Hope,* edited by John Noble, 256–62. Cape Town: S. Solomon, 1886.

———. *Ostrich Farming in South Africa.* London: Cassell, Petter, Galpin, 1881.

Doumani, Beshara. *Rediscovering Palestine.* Berkeley: University of California Press, 1995.

Dubow, Saul. *Scientific Racism in Modern South Africa.* Johannesburg: Witwatersrand University Press, 1995.

Duerden, J. E. "The Future of the Ostrich Industry." *Agricultural Journal of the Union of South Africa* 1, no. 3 (1911): 348–51.

——. *Ostrich Feather Investigations.* Port Elizabeth, 1907.

Dunn, Ross. "The Trade of Tafilalt: Commercial Change in Southeast Morocco on the Eve of the Protectorate." *African Historical Studies* 4, no. 2 (1971): 271–304.

Dye, Nancy Schrom. *As Equals and as Sisters: Feminism, the Labor Movement, and the Women's Trade Union League of New York.* Columbia: University of Missouri Press, 1980.

Dyer, Mark. "Export Production in Western Libya, 1750–1793." *African Economic History,* no. 13 (1984): 117–36.

Eisenberg, Ellen. *Jewish Agricultural Colonies in New Jersey, 1882–1920.* Syracuse: Syracuse University Press, 1995.

Eldem, Edhem, Daniel Goffman, and Bruce Masters, eds. *The Ottoman City Between East and West: Aleppo, Izmir, and Istanbul.* Cambridge: Cambridge University Press, 1999.

Encyclopaedia Judaica. 16 vols. Jerusalem: Encyclopaedia Judaica, 1971.

Endelman, Todd M. "Anglo-Jewish Scientists and the Science of Race." *Jewish Social Studies* 11, no. 1 (2004): 52–92.

——. "The Decline of the Anglo-Jewish Notable." *The European Legacy* 4, no. 6 (1999): 58–71.

——. *The Jews of Britain, 1656 to 2000.* Berkeley: University of California Press, 2002.

——. "'Practices of a Low Anthropologic Level': A *Shehitah* Controversy of the 1950s." In *Food in the Migrant Experience,* edited by Anne J. Kershen, 77–97. Aldershot: Ashgate, 2002.

Enstad, Nan. *Ladies of Labor, Girls of Adventure: Working Women, Popular Culture, and Labor Politics at the Turn of the Twentieth Century.* New York: Columbia University Press, 1999.

Epstein, Edward Jay. *The Rise and Fall of Diamonds: The Shattering of a Brilliant Illusion.* New York: Simon and Schuster, 1982.

Epstein, Melech. *Jewish Labor in U.S.A.: An Industrial, Political and Cultural History of the Jewish Labor Movement.* New York: Ktav, 1969.

Evans, E., and O. Evans. "Lucerne Growing as a Fodder for Stock." *Agricultural Journal of the Cape of Good Hope* 16–17 (1901–2): 812–21 and 16–25.

Falola, Toyin. "The Lebanese in Colonial West Africa." In *People and Empires in African History: Essays in Memory of Michael Crowder,* edited by J. F. Ade Ajayi, J. D. Y. Peel, and Michael Crowder. London: Longman, 1992.

Feldman, D. M. *Immigrants and Workers, Englishmen and Jews: Jewish Immigration to the East End of London, 1880–1906.* London: Cambridge University Press, 1985.

Feldman, David. *Englishmen and Jews: Social Relations and Political Culture, 1840–1914.* New Haven: Yale University Press, 1994.

Feldman, Leybl. *Motsudi; vi azoy ikh bin gevorn a diment-greber.* Johannesburg: L. Feldman, 1962.

———. *Oudtshoorn, Jerusalem of Africa.* Translated by Lilian Dubb and Sheila Barkusky; edited by Joseph Sherman. Johannesburg: Friends of the Library, University of Witwatersrand, 1989.

———. *Oudtshoorn, Yerushalayim d'Afrike.* Johannesburg: Sterling, 1940.

———. *Yidn in dorem-afrike.* Vilna, 1937.

Feldman, Rakhmiel. *Shvarts un vays: dertseylungen fun dorem-afrike.* Warsaw: R. Feldman, 1935.

Ferguson, Niall. *The House of Rothschild.* New York: Viking, 1998.

Filippini, Jean Pierre. *Il porto di Livorno e la Toscana (1676–1814).* Naples: Edizioni scientifiche italiane, 1998.

Fisher, Raymond Henry. *The Russian Fur Trade, 1550–1700.* Berkeley: University of California Press, 1943.

Fituri, Ahmed Said. "Tripolitania, Cyrenaica, and Bilad as-Sudan Trade Relations During the Second Half of the Nineteenth Century." Ph.D. diss., University of Michigan, 1982.

Foreman, Susan. *Shoes and Ships and Sealing-Wax: An Illustrated History of the Board of Trade, 1786–1986.* London: H.M.S.O., 1986.

Foster, Joseph, Hercules Tennant, and Edgar Michael Jackson. *Statutes of the Cape of Good Hope, 1652–1886.* Cape Town: W. A. Richards, 1887.

Franco-Hasson, Elisa. *Il etait une fois, l'île des roses.* Brussels: Clepsydre, 1995.

Frankfurter, Felix, and Molly Dewson. *District of Columbia Minimum Wage Cases.* New York: Steinberg, 1923.

Freund, Bill. *Insiders and Outsiders: The Indian Working Class of Durban, 1910–1990.* Portsmouth, N.H.: Heinemann, 1995.

Gabaccia, Donna R. *Militants and Migrants: Rural Sicilians Become American Workers.* New Brunswick, N.J.: Rutgers University Press, 1988.

Gabler, Neal. *An Empire of Their Own: How the Jews Invented Hollywood.* New York: Doubleday, 1989.

Gartner, Lloyd P. *The Jewish Immigrant in England, 1870–1914.* Detroit: Wayne State University Press, 1960.

Glenn, Susan A. *Daughters of the Shtetl: Life and Labor in the Immigrant Generation.* Ithaca: Cornell University Press, 1990.

Gmelch, Sharon Bohn. "Groups That Don't Want In: Gypsies and Other Artisan, Trader, and Entertainer Minorities." *Annual Review of Anthropology* 15 (1986): 307–30.

Godlonton, B. G. *Oudtshoorn and Its Farms.* Cape Town: Press Advertising, 1914.

Goitein, S. D. *Letters of Medieval Jewish Traders.* Princeton: Princeton University Press, 1974.

————. *A Mediterranean Society: The Jewish Communities of the Arab World as Portrayed in the Documents of the Cairo Geniza.* 6 vols. Berkeley: University of California Press, 1967.

Goldberg, Harvey. *Jewish Life in Muslim Libya: Rivals and Relatives.* Chicago: University of Chicago Press, 1990.

Goldberg, Harvey, Michelle Schenberger, Marcia Walerstein, and Orit Zvi. "Social and Demographic Aspects of the Jewish Community in Tripoli During the Colonial Period." In *Judaisme d'afrique du nord aux XIXe–XXe siècles: histoire, société et culture,* edited by Michel Abitbol, 67–86. Jerusalem: Institut Ben-Zvi, 1980.

Goldberg, Robert. "Zion in Utah: The Clarion Colony and Jewish Agrarianism." In *Jews of the American West,* edited by Moses Rischin and John Livingston. Detroit: Wayne State University Press, 1991.

Gottreich, Emily. *The Mellah of Marrakesh: Jewish and Muslim Space in Morocco's Red City.* Bloomington: Indiana University Press, 2007.

Gouy, Marius A. "Ostrich-Feathers: From the Bird to the Bonnet." *Frank Leslie's Popular Monthly* 29, no. 3 (1890): 376.

Graetz, Michael. *The Jews in Nineteenth-Century France: From the French Revolution to the Alliance Israélite Universelle.* Stanford: Stanford University Press, 1996.

Gray, J. L. "The Jew in the Economic Life in South Africa." Johannesburg: Society of Jews and Christians, 1920.

Green, Nancy L. *The Pletzl of Paris: Jewish Immigrant Workers in the Belle Epoque.* New York: Holmes and Meier, 1986.

————. *Ready-to-Wear and Ready-to-Work: A Century of Industry and Immigrants in Paris and New York.* Durham: Duke University Press, 1997.

Green, Nile. "Ostrich Eggs and Peacock Feathers: Sacred Objects as Cultural Exchange Between Christianity and Islam." *Al-Masaq* 18, no. 1 (2006): 27–66.

Greif, Avner. *Institutions and the Path to the Modern Economy: Lessons from Medieval Trade:* Cambridge: Cambridge University Press, 2006.

Grossman, Michael Pesah. "A Study in the Trends and Tendencies of Hebrew and Yiddish Writings in South Africa." Ph.D. diss., University of Witwatersrand, 1973.

Gsell, Stéphane, and Ad. H. A. Delamare. *Exploration scientifique de l'algérie pendant les années, 1840–1845.* Paris: E. Leroux, 1912.

Guershon, Isaac. "Kippur on the Amazon: Jewish Emigration from Northern Morocco in the Late Nineteenth Century." In *Sephardi and Middle Eastern Jewries, History and Culture in the Modern Era,* edited by Harvey Goldberg. Bloomington: Indiana University Press, 1996.

Gutwein, Daniel. "Economics, Politics, and Historiography." *Jewish Social Studies* 1, no. 1 (1994): 94–114.

Haarmann, Ulrich. "The Dead Ostrich: Life and Trade in Ghadames (Libya) in the Nineteenth Century." *Die Welt des Islams* 38, no. 1 (1998): 9–94.

Hajjaj-Liluf, Yaakov. "Ha-kalkalah ve-hatmorot be-ta'asuka be-meah ha-19." Edited by Haim Saadon. Jerusalem: Institute Ben-Zvi, forthcoming.

Hall, George A., et al. *Second Report of the Factory Investigating Commission.* Vol. 2, *Legislature; 1913. Senate Doc.; No. 36.* Albany: J. B. Lyon, 1913.

Hall, Peter Geoffrey. *The Industries of London Since 1861.* London: Hutchinson University Library, 1962.

Hancock, David. *Citizens of the World: London Merchants and the Integration of the British Atlantic Community, 1735–1785.* Cambridge: Cambridge University Press, 1995.

Hancock, W. K. *Survey of British Commonwealth Affairs.* Vol. 2. London: Oxford University Press, 1937.

Harper. "The Feather Business." *The Friend, a Religious and Literary Journal* 52, no. 12 (1878).

Hayden, Carl. "Speech: The Ostrich Industry." *Congressional Record: Proceedings and Debates of the 62nd Congress, Third Session* 49, no. 5 (1913): 57–61.

Heinze, Andrew R. *Adapting to Abundance: Jewish Immigrants, Mass Consumption, and the Search for American Identity.* New York: Columbia University Press, 1990.

Henriques, Robert David Quixano. *Marcus Samuel: First Viscount Bearsted and Founder of the 'Shell' Transport and Trading Company, 1853–1927.* London: Barrie and Rockliff, 1960.

Henry, Alice. *Women and the Labor Movement.* New York: George H. Doran, 1923.

Henry, J. A. *The First Hundred Years of the Standard Bank.* London: Oxford University Press, 1963.

Hirschbein, Peretz. *Felker un lender: rayze-ayndrukn fun nayzayland, avstralie, dorem-afrike 1920–1922.* Vol. 2, *Ale verk.* Vilna: Kletskin, 1929.

Hirschberg, H. Z. *A History of the Jews in North Africa.* Vol. 1. Leiden: Brill, 1974.

Hoffman, N. D. *Book of Memoirs.* Translated by Lilian Dubb and Sheila Barkusky. Cape Town: Kaplan Centre for Jewish Studies and Research, 1996.

"The Home of the Ostrich." *The Agricultural Journal of the Union of South Africa* 5 (1913): 359–68.

Hornaday, William T. "The Steam Roller of the Feather Importers in the United States Senate." 1913.

Hourani, Albert Habib. *The Lebanese in the World: A Century of Emigration.* London: Centre for Lebanese Studies, 1992.

Hourwich, Isaac. "The Jewish Laborer in London." *The Journal of Political Economy* 13, no. 1 (1912): 89–98.

Hundley, Norris. *The Great Thirst: Californians and Water, 1770s–1990s.* Berkeley: University of California Press, 1992.

Hunter, Frederick Mercer. *An Account of the British Settlement of Aden in Arabia.* London: Cass, 1968.

Hyman, Paula. *The Emancipation of the Jews of Alsace.* New Haven: Yale University Press, 1991.

Isaacman, Allen F., and Richard L. Roberts. *Cotton, Colonialism, and Social History in Sub-Saharan Africa.* Portsmouth, N.H.: Heinemann, 1995.

Israel, Jonathan I. *Diasporas Within a Diaspora: Jews, Crypto-Jews and the World Maritime Empires, 1540–1740.* Boston: Brill, 2002.

———. *Empires and Entrepôts: The Dutch, the Spanish Monarchy, and the Jews, 1585–1713.* London: Hambledon, 1990.

———. *European Jewry in the Age of Mercantilism, 1550–1750.* Oxford: Clarendon, 1985.

Jackson, Albert, and Eric Rosenthal. *Trader on the Veld.* Cape Town: A. A. Balkema, 1958.

Jacobs, Joseph. *Studies in Jewish Statistics, Social, Vital and Anthropometric.* London: D. Nutt, 1891.

Johnson, Marion. "Calico Caravans: The Tripoli–Kano Trade After 1880." *The Journal of African History* 17, no. 1 (1976): 95–117.

Jones, Gareth Stedman. *Outcast London: A Study in the Relationship Between Classes in Victorian Society.* Oxford: Clarendon, 1971.

Jowell, Phyllis, and Adrienne Folb. *Joe Jowell of Namaqualand: The Story of a Modern-Day Pioneer.* Vlaeberg: Fernwood, 1994.

Juin, Hubert. *La parisienne: les élégantes les célébritéis et les petites femmes, 1880–1914.* Paris: A. Barret, 1978.

Kahan, Arcadius. *Essays in Jewish Social and Economic History,* edited by Roger Weiss. Chicago: University of Chicago Press, 1986.

Kanfer, Stefan. *The Last Empire: De Beers, Diamonds, and the World.* New York: Farrar, Straus and Giroux, 1993.

Kaplan, Marion A. *The Making of the Jewish Middle Class: Women, Family, and Identity in Imperial Germany.* New York: Oxford University Press, 1991.

Karp, Jonathan. *The Politics of Jewish Commerce: Economic Thought and Emancipation in Europe, 1638–1848.* New York: Cambridge University Press, 2008.

Kayali, Hasan. *Arabs and Young Turks: Ottomanism, Arabism and Islamism in the Ottoman Empire, 1908–1918.* Berkeley: University of California Press, 1997.

Keegan, Timothy J. *Colonial South Africa and the Origins of the Racial Order.* Charlottesville: University Press of Virginia, 1996.

———. *Rural Transformations in Industrializing South Africa: The Southern Highveld to 1914.* Basingstoke: Macmillan, 1987.

Kelly's Directories Ltd. *The Post Office London Directory.* London.

Kerem, Yitzchak. "The Migration of Rhodian Jews to Africa and the Americas from 1900–1914." *Los Muestros,* no. 47 (2002): 24–30.

Klier, John D., and Shlomo Lambroza, eds. *Pogroms: Anti-Jewish Violence in Modern Russian History.* Cambridge: Cambridge University Press, 1992.

Kosak, Hadassa. *Cultures of Opposition: Jewish Immigrant Workers, New York City, 1881–1905.* Albany: State University of New York Press, 2000.

———. "Tailors and Troublemakers: Jewish Militancy in the New York Garment Industry, 1889–1910." In *A Coat of Many Colors: Immigration, Globalism, and Reform in the New York City Garment Industry,* edited by Daniel Soyer, 115–40. New York: Fordham University Press, 2005.

Koven, Seth. *Slumming: Sexual and Social Politics in Victorian London.* Princeton: Princeton University Press, 2004.

Krakenowo, Our Town in Lithuania: The Story of a World That Has Passed: Reminiscences Collected to Celebrate the Diamond Jubilee of the Krakenowo Sick Benefit and Benevolent Society. Edited by Krakenowo Sick Benefit and Benevolent Society. Johannesburg: The Society, 1961.

Krut, Riva M. "Building a Home and a Community: Jews in Johannesburg, 1886–1913." D.Phil. thesis, University of London, 1985.

———. "The Making of a South African Jewish Community in Johannesburg, 1886–1914." In *Class, Community and Conflict: South African Perspectives*, edited by Belinda Bozzoli, 135–59. Johannesburg: Raven, 1987.

Kurlansky, Mark. *Cod: A Biography of the Fish That Changed the World*. New York: Walker, 1997.

———. *Salt: A World History*. New York: Walker, 2002.

Kuznets, Simon. "Immigration of Russian Jews to the United States: Nature and Background and Structure." *Perspectives in American History* 9 (1975): 35–126.

Kynaston, David. *The City of London: Golden Years, 1890–1914*. Vol. 2. London: Chatto and Windus, 1994.

Leach, William. *Land of Desire: Merchants, Power, and the Rise of a New American Culture*. New York: Pantheon, 1993.

Lee, A. R. "The Ostrich Industry in the United States." *Annual Report of the Bureau of Animal Industry for the Year 1909* (1911): 233–38.

Lefèvre, Edmond. *Le commerce et l'industrie de la plume pour parure*. Paris: L'auteur, 1914.

Lehmann, Matthias. "A Livornese 'Port Jew' and the Sephardim of the Ottoman Empire." *Jewish Social Studies* 11, no. 2 (2005): 51–76.

Leibowitz, Shmeul. "Vayse kafers." *Foroys* (1937): 18–19.

Lemire, Beverly. *Fashion's Favourite: The Cotton Trade and the Consumer in Britain, 1660–1800*. Oxford: Oxford University Press, 1991.

Lestschinsky, Jacob. "Di antviklung fun yidishn folk far di letste 100 yor." *Shriftn far ekonomik un statistik* 1 (1928): 1–64.

———. *Dos yidishe folk in tsifern*. Berlin: Klal-farlag, 1922.

Levy, Jonathan Ira. "Contemplating Delivery: Futures Trading and the Problem of Commodity Exchange in the United States, 1875–1905." *American Historical Review* 111, no. 2 (2006): 307–32.

Lévy, Lionel. *La nation juive portugaise: Livourne, Amsterdam, Tunis, 1591–1951*. Paris: Harmattan, 1999.

Lewis, Derrick. 2003. *The Sanders Story, a Family Saga*. Southern Africa Jewish Genealogy Web Site, www.jewishgen.org/SAfrica/family-histories/sanders/index-1.htm.

Lipman, V. D. *Social History of the Jews in England, 1850–1950*. London: Watts, 1954.

Lovejoy, Paul E. "Commercial Sectors in the Economy of the Nineteenth-Century Central Sudan: The Trans-Saharan Trade and the Desert-Side Salt Trade." *African Economic History*, no. 13 (1984): 85–116.

Lovejoy, Paul E., and Stephen Baier. "The Desert-Side Economy of the Central Sudan." *International Journal of African Historical Studies* 8 (1975): 551–81.

Lowenstein, Steven. *The Jews of Oregon, 1850–1950*. Portland: Jewish Historical Society of Oregon, 1987.

Lückhoff, H. "The Little Karroo." Thesis, University of Cape Town, 1946.

McCreesh, Carolyn D. *Women in the Campaign to Organize Garment Workers, 1880–1917*. New York: Garland, 1985.

McCusker, John J. "The Demise of Distance: The Business Press and the Origins of the Information Revolution in the Early Modern Atlantic World." *American Historical Review* 110, no. 2 (2005): 295–321.

McDowell, Colin. *Hats: Status, Style, and Glamour*. New York: Rizzoli, 1992.

Mahler, Raphael. *Yehude Polin ben shete milhamot 'olam; historyah kalkalit-sotsyalit le-or ha-statistikah*. Tel Aviv: Devir, 1968.

——. *Yidn in amolikn Poyln: in likht fun tsifern: di demografishe un sotsyal-ekonomishe struktur fun yidn: in kroyn-poyln in XVIII yorhundert*. Warsaw: Yidish bukh, 1958.

Makdisi, Ussama. *The Culture of Sectarianism: Community, History, and Violence in Nineteenth-Century Lebanon*. Berkeley: University of California Press, 2000.

Manson, George J. *Work for Women*. New York: G. P. Putnam's Sons, 1883.

Martin, Annie. *Home Life on an Ostrich Farm*. London: George Philip and Son, 1890.

Maskiell, Michelle. "Consuming Kashmir: Shawls and Empires, 1500–2000." *Journal of World History* 13, no. 1 (2002): 27–65.

Masters, Bruce. *Christians and Jews in the Ottoman Arab World: The Roots of Sectarianism*. Cambridge: Cambridge University Press, 2001.

Mathuisieulx, Mehier de. "Une Mission en Tripolitaine." In *Renseignements Coloniaux et Documents*, 20–33. Paris: Le Comité, 1903.

Matthews, Felix A. "Northwest Africa and Timbuctoo." *Journal of the American Geographical Society of New York* 13 (1881): 196–219.

Mendes-Flohr, Paul. "Werner Sombart's 'The Jews and Modern Capitalism.'" *Leo Baeck Institute Yearbook*, no. 21 (1979): 87–107.

Méry, G. "Reseignements commerciaux sur le mouvement des echanges entre la Tripolitaine et se soudan central." *Bulletin du comité de l'Afrique française* (1893): 2–4.

Meyer, Maisie J. *From the Rivers of Babylon to the Whangpoo: A Century of Sephardi Jewish Life in Shanghai*. Lanham, Md.: University Press of America, 2003.

Michels, Tony. *A Fire in Their Hearts: Yiddish Socialists in New York*. Cambridge: Harvard University Press, 2005.

Michie, R. C. *The City of London: Continuity and Change, 1850–1990*. Basingstoke, Hampshire: Macmillan Academic and Professional, 1992.

Miège, Jean-Louis. "Bourgeoisie juive du Maroc au 19e siècle." In *Judaisme d'Afrique*

du Nord aux XIXe–XXe siècles: histoire, société et culture, edited by Michel Abitbol,
25–36. Jerusalem: Institut Ben-Zvi, 1980.

———. "Le commerce trans-saharien au XIXe siècle: essai de quantification."
Revue de l'occident musulman et de la Méditerranée, no. 32 (1981–2): 93–111.

———. "Les juifs et le commerce transsaharien au dix-neuvième siècle." In
Communautés juives des marges sahariennes du Maghreb, edited by Michel Abitbol,
391–406. Jérusalem: Institut Ben-Zvi, 1982.

———. *Le Maroc et l'Europe, 1830–1894.* Paris: Presses Universitaires de France,
1961.

Miller, Jane. *Relations.* London: Jonathan Cape, 2003.

Minerbi, Sergio Itzhak. *From Rhodes to Africa: The Jews Who Built the Congo, Mr. Elie
Eliachar Annual Memorial Lecture.* Jerusalem: Misgav Yerushalayim, 1989.

Mintz, Sidney Wilfred. *Sweetness and Power: The Place of Sugar in Modern History.*
New York: Viking, 1985.

Mircher, H. *Mission de Ghadamès.* Alger: Typ. Duclaux, 1863.

Morawska, Ewa T. *Insecure Prosperity: Small-Town Jews in Industrial America, 1890–1940.*
Princeton: Princeton University Press, 1996.

Mosely, Alfred. *Reports of the Delegates of the Mosely Industrial Commission.* New York:
Arno, 1973.

Mosenthal, Julius de, and James Edmund Harting. *Ostriches and Ostrich Farming.*
London: Trübner, 1879.

Mosse, Werner Eugen. *Jews in the German Economy: The German-Jewish Economic Elite,
1820–1935.* Oxford: Clarendon, 1987.

Moxham, Roy. *Tea: Addiction, Exploitation, and Empire.* New York: Carroll and Graf,
2003.

Muldrew, Craig. *The Economy of Obligation: The Culture of Credit and Social Relations
in Early Modern England.* New York: St. Martin's, 1998.

Nathans, Benjamin. *Beyond the Pale, the Jewish Encounter with Late Imperial Russia.*
Berkeley: University of California Press, 2002.

Nava, Mica. "The Cosmopolitanism of Commerce and the Allure of Difference:
Selfridges, the Russian Ballet and the Tango, 1911–1914." *International Journal of
Cultural Studies* 1, no. 2 (1998): 163–96.

Newbury, C. W. "North African and Western Sudan Trade in the Nineteenth
Century: A Re-Evaluation." *The Journal of African History* 7, no. 2 (1966):
233–46.

Newman, Aubrey, ed. *The Jewish East End, 1840–1939.* London: Jewish Historical
Society of England, 1981.

New York State. "Homework in the Artificial Flower and Feather Industry in New York State (Special Bulletin No. 199)." Edited by Department of Labor. New York, 1938.

———. *Preliminary Report of the Factory Investigating Commission.* Vol. 2, *Legislature; 1913. Senate Doc.; No. 36.* Albany: J. B. Lyon, 1912.

———. "Report and Testimony Taken Before the Special Committee of the Assembly Appointed to Investigate the Conditions of Female Labor in the City of New York." New York, 1896.

Nixon, Rob. *Dreambirds: The Strange History of the Ostrich in Fashion, Food, and Fortune.* New York: Picador USA, 2000.

Noble, John, ed. *Official Handbook. History, Productions and Resources of the Cape of Good Hope.* Cape Town: S. Solomon, 1886.

Norton, Marcy. "Tasting Empire: Chocolate and the European Internalization of Mesoamerican Aesthetics." *American Historical Review* 111, no. 3 (2006): 660–91.

Odencrantz, Louise. *Italian Women in Industry: A Study of Conditions in New York City.* New York: Russell Sage Foundation, 1919.

Orleck, Annelise. *Common Sense and a Little Fire: Women and Working-Class Politics in the United States, 1900–1965.* Chapel Hill: University of North Carolina Press, 1995.

"Ostriches from the Soudan: Mr. R. W. Thornton's Story." *South African Agricultural Journal* (1912): 807–13.

Ostrich Farming in the United States: Reports from the Consuls of the United States at Algiers, Cape Town, and Buenos Ayres, on Ostrich Raising and Ostrich Farming in Africa, in the Argentine Republic, and in the United States. Washington, D.C.: Government Printing Office, 1882.

Oudot, Jules. *Le Fermage des autruches en Algérie: incubation artificielle.* Paris: Challamel Ainé, 1880.

Pascon, Paul. *La maison d'Iligh et l'histoire sociale du Tazerwalt.* Rabat: Smer, 1984.

Peiss, Kathy Lee. *Cheap Amusements: Working Women and Leisure in Turn-of-the-Century New York.* Philadelphia: Temple University Press, 1986.

Pendergrast, Mark. *Uncommon Grounds: The History of Coffee and How It Transformed Our World.* New York: Basic, 1999.

Penslar, Derek Jonathan. *Shylock's Children: Economics and Jewish Identity in Modern Europe.* Berkeley: University of California Press, 2001.

Perinbaum, B. Marie. "Social Relations in the Trans-Saharan and Western Sudanese Trade: An Overview." *Comparative Studies in Society and History* 15, no. 4 (1973): 416–36.

Phillips, Philip, and Alexander Clark. *Song Pilgrimage Around and Throughout the World*

Embracing a Life of Song Experiences, Impressions, Anecdotes, Incidents, Persons, Manners, Customs, Sketches, and Illustrations Throughout Twenty Different Countries. Chicago: Fairbanks, Palmer, 1880.

Pickerell, Watson. "Ostrich Farming in Arizona." In *Yearbook of the United States Department of Agriculture,* 399–406. Washington, D.C.: Government Printing Office, 1905.

Pisani, Donald J. *From the Family Farm to Agribusiness: The Irrigation Crusade in California and the West, 1850–1931.* Berkeley: University of California Press, 1984.

Pollan, Michael. *The Botany of Desire: A Plant's Eye View of the World.* New York: Random House, 2001.

Pollins, Harold. *Economic History of the Jews in England.* London: Rutherford, 1982.

Proctor, Robert. "Anti-Agate: The Great Diamond Hoax and the Semiprecious Stone Scam." *Configurations* 9, no. 3 (2001): 381.

"Protecting African Birds." *Forest and Stream: A Journal of Outdoor Life, Travel, Nature Study, and Shooting* 69, no. 16 (1907): 1.

Rabinowitz, Ann. 2003. Cape Colony Jewish Naturalization Registers, 1903–1907. Southern Africa Jewish Geneology Web Site, http://www.jewishgen.org/SAfrica/natrec.htm.

Rabinowitz, M. "Saul Solomon and the Family of Saul Solomon." In *The South African Jewish Year Book,* 231–35. Johannesburg: South African Jewish Historical Society, 1929.

Rahmani, Moise. *Shalom Bwana, la saga des Juifs du Congo.* Paris: Romillat, 2002.

Raibmon, Paige Sylvia. *Authentic Indians: Episodes of Encounter from the Late-Nineteenth-Century Northwest Coast.* Durham: Duke University Press, 2005.

Ramamurthy, Priti. "Why Is Buying a 'Madras' Cotton Shirt a Political Act? A Feminist Commodity Chain Analysis." *Feminist Studies* 30, no. 1 (2004): 734–70.

Rappaport, Erika Diane. "Art, Commerce, or Empire? The Rebuilding of Regent Street, 1880–1927." *History Workshop Journal,* no. 53 (2002): 95–117.

———. "Packaging China: Foreign Articles and Dangerous Tastes in the Mid-Victorian Tea Party." In *The Making of the Consumer: Knowledge, Power and Identity in the Modern World,* edited by Frank Trentmann. Oxford: Berg, 2006.

———. *Shopping for Pleasure: Women in the Making of London's West End.* Princeton: Princeton University Press, 2000.

Reisner, Marc. *Cadillac Desert: The American West and Its Disappearing Water.* New York: Viking, 1986.

Report of the Ostrich Feather Commission Appointed to Enquire into the Ostrich Industry,

Including Two Minority Reports. Presented to Both Houses of Parliament by Command of His Excellency the Governor-General. Cape Town: Cape Times, 1918.

Report on the Wages of Women in the Millinery Industry in Massachusetts. Bulletin; No. 20, May, 1919; Variation: History of Women; Reel 908, No. 7578. Boston: Wright and Potter, 1919.

"Residents' List of Oudtshoorn Jewry." South African Friends of Beth Hatefutsoth Country Communities Project.

Results of a Census of the Colony of the Cape of Good Hope, as on the Night of Sunday, the 5th April, 1891. Cape Town: W. A. Richards, 1892.

Results of a Census of the Colony of the Cape of Good Hope, as on the Night of Sunday, the 17th April, 1904. Cape Town: Government Printer, 1905.

Richards, Thomas. *The Commodity Culture of Victorian England: Advertising and Spectacle, 1851–1914.* Stanford: Stanford University Press, 1990.

Rischin, Moses. *The Jews of the West, the Metropolitan Years.* Waltham, Mass.: Published by the American Jewish Historical Society for the Western Jewish History Center of the Judah L. Magnes Memorial Museum, Berkeley, California, 1979.

Rischin, Moses, and John Livingston. *Jews of the American West.* Detroit: Wayne State University Press, 1991.

Roberts, Mary Louise. *Disruptive Acts: The New Woman in Fin-de-Siècle France:* Chicago: University of Chicago Press, 2002.

———. "Gender, Consumption, and Commodity Culture." *American Historical Review,* no. 103 (1993): 817–44.

———. "Samson and Delilah Revisited: The Politics of Women's Fashion in 1920s France." *American Historical Review* 98, no. 3 (1993): 657–84.

Roberts, Richard L. *Two Worlds of Cotton: Colonialism and the Regional Economy in the French Soudan, 1800–1946.* Stanford: Stanford University Press, 1996.

Robinson, Leonard George. *The Agricultural Activities of the Jews in America.* New York: American Jewish Committee, 1912.

Rogger, Hans. *Jewish Policies and Right-Wing Politics in Imperial Russia.* Berkeley: University of California Press, 1986.

Rogin, Michael Paul. *Blackface, White Noise: Jewish Immigrants in the Hollywood Melting Pot.* Berkeley: University of California Press, 1996.

Rosenthal, Eric. "On the Diamond Fields." In *The Jews in South Africa, a History,* edited by Gustav Saron and Louis Hotz, 105–20. London: Oxford University Press, 1955.

Rozen, Minna. "The Leghorn Merchants in Tunis and Their Trade with Marseilles at the End of the 17th Century." In *Les relations intercommunautaires juives en*

Méditerranée occidentale, XIIIe–XXe siècles, edited by Jean Louis Miège, 51–59. Paris: Editions du centre national de la recherche scientifique, 1984.

———. "The Livornese Jewish Merchants in Tunis and the Commerce with Marseilles at the End of the Seventeenth Century." *Michael,* no. 9 (1985): 87–129.

Rozenblit, Marsha L. *The Jews of Vienna, 1867–1914: Assimilation and Identity.* Albany: State University of New York Press, 1983.

Rubinow, I. M. *Economic Conditions of the Jews in Russia.* Vol. 15. New York: U.S. Bureau of Labor Bulletin, 1907 (reprinted, New York, 1976).

Rybko, Wolf. *Oyf di pleynen fun Afrike.* Johannesburg: Pacific, 1961.

Sackman, Douglas Cazaux. *Orange Empire: California and the Fruits of Eden.* Berkeley: University of California Press, 2005.

Semach, Yomtov. *Une mission de l'alliance au Yemen.* Paris: Siège de la Société, 1910.

Saron, Gustav, and Louis Hertz, eds. *The Jews in South Africa, a History.* London: Oxford University Press, 1955.

Schmiechen, James A. *Sweated Industries and Sweated Labor: The London Clothing Trades, 1860–1914.* Urbana: University of Illinois Press, 1984.

Schneer, Jonathan. *London 1900: The Imperial Metropolis.* New Haven: Yale University Press, 1999.

Schorsch, Jonathan. *Jews and Blacks in the Early Modern World.* Cambridge: Cambridge University Press, 2004.

Schroeter, Daniel J. "The Jews of Essaouira (Mogador) and the Trade of Southern Morocco." In *Communautés juives des marges sahariennes du Maghreb,* edited by Michel Abitbol, 365–90. Jerusalem: Institut Ben-Zvi, 1982.

———. *Merchants of Essaouira: Urban Society and Imperialism in Southwestern Morocco, 1844–1886.* Cambridge: Cambridge University Press, 1988.

———. *The Sultan's Jew: Morocco and the Sephardi World.* Stanford: Stanford University Press, 2002.

Scully, W. C. *Between Sun and Sand: A Tale of an African Desert.* Cape Town: J. C. Juta, 1898.

Seidenberg, Dana April. *Mercantile Adventurers: The World of East African Asians, 1750–1985.* New Delhi: New Age International, 1996.

"Select Committee of House of Lords on Sweating System Fourth Report." In *Command Papers; Report of Commissioners:* House of Commons Parliamentary Papers, 1889.

"Select Committee of House of Lords on Sweating System Second Report." In *Command Papers; Report of Commissioners:* House of Commons Parliamentary Papers, 1888.

Shain, Milton. *Jewry and Cape Society: The Origins and Activities of the Jewish Board of Deputies for the Cape Colony.* Cape Town: Historical Publication Society, 1983.

———. *The Roots of Antisemitism in South Africa.* Charlottesville: University Press of Virginia, 1994.

———. "'Vant to Puy a Vaatch': The Smous and Pioneer Trader in South African Jewish Historiography." *Jewish Affairs*, September (1987): 111–28.

Sherman, Joseph. "Serving the Natives: Whiteness as the Price of Hospitality in South African Yiddish Literature." *Journal of Southern African Studies* 26, no. 3 (2000): 505–21.

Shield, Renée Rose. *Diamond Stories: Enduring Change on 47th Street.* Ithaca: Cornell University Press, 2002.

Shimoni, Gideon. *Jews and Zionism: The South African Experience, 1910–1967.* Cape Town: Oxford University Press, 1980.

Simon, John. "Historical Notes and Commentary." In *Oudtshoorn: Jerusalem of Africa*, edited by Joseph Sherman, 129–98. Johannesburg: Friends of the Library, University of Witwatersrand, 1989.

Simon, Rachel. "Jewish Itinerant Peddlers in Ottoman Libya: Economic, Social, and Cultural Aspects." In *Decision Making and Change in the Ottoman Empire*, edited by Caesar E. Farah, 293–304. Kirksville, Mo.: Thomas Jefferson University Press, 1993.

———. "The Socio-Economic Role of the Tripolitanian Jews in the Late Ottoman Period." In *Communautés juives des marges sahariennes du maghreb*, edited by Michel Abitbol, 321–28. Jerusalem: Institut Ben-Zvi, 1982.

Slezkine, Yuri. *The Jewish Century.* Princeton: Princeton University Press, 2004.

Slouschz, Nahum. *Travels in North Africa.* Philadelphia: Jewish Publication Society of America, 1927.

Smit, D. J. v Z. *Ostrich Farming in the Little Karoo.* Pretoria: South African Department of Agricultural Technical Services, 1963.

The South African Jewish Year Book. Johannesburg: South African Jewish Historical Society, 1929.

Soyer, Daniel, ed. *A Coat of Many Colors: Immigration, Globalism, and Reform in the New York City Garment Industry.* New York: Fordham University Press, 2005.

Stanislawski, Michael. "Russian Jewry, the Russian State, and the Dynamics of Russian Jewish Emancipation." In *Paths of Emancipation: Jews, States, and Citizenship*, edited by Pierre Birnbaum and Ira Katznelson, 262–85. Princeton: Princeton University Press, 1995.

————. *Tsar Nicholas I and the Jews: The Transformation of Jewish Society in Russia, 1825–1855.* Philadelphia: Jewish Publication Society of America, 1983.

Stansky, Peter. *Sassoon: The Worlds of Philip and Sybil.* New Haven: Yale University Press, 2003.

Steele, Valerie. *Paris Fashion: A Cultural History.* New York: Oxford University Press, 1988.

Stein, Sarah Abrevaya. "Falling into Feathers: Jews and the Trans-Atlantic Ostrich Feather Trade." *Journal of Modern History* 79/4 (2007).

————. *Making Jews Modern: The Yiddish and Ladino Press in the Russian and Ottoman Empires.* Bloomington: Indiana University Press, 2003.

Stoll, Steven. *The Fruits of Natural Advantage: Making the Industrial Countryside in California.* Berkeley: University of California Press, 1998.

Swadling, Pamela, Roy Wagner, and Billai Laba. *Plumes from Paradise: Trade Cycles in Outer Southeast Asia and Their Impact on New Guinea and Nearby Islands Until 1920.* Coorparoo DC, Queensland, Australia: Papua New Guinea National Museum in association with Robert Brown and Associates, 1996.

Swanson, Maynard W. "The Asiatic Menace: Creating Segregation in Durban, 1870–1900." *International Journal of African Historical Studies* 16, no. 3 (1983): 401–21.

Teisch, Jessica. "'Home Is Not So Very Far Away': Californian Engineers in South Africa, 1868–1915." *Australian Economic History Review* 45, no. 2 (2005): 139–60.

Tentler, Leslie Woodcock. *Wage-Earning Women: Industrial Work and Family Life in the United States, 1900–1930.* New York: Oxford University Press, 1979.

Thomas, Lynn. "The Modern Girl and Racial Respectability in 1930s South Africa." *Journal of African History* 47, no. 3 (2006): 1–30.

Thornton, Russel William. "The Ostrich Feather Industry in South Africa." *South African Journal of Science* 12 (1915): 272–79.

Tiersten, Lisa. "Redefining Consumer Culture: Recent Literature on Consumption and the Bourgeoisie in Western Europe." *Radical History Review*, no. 57 (1993): 116–59.

Titelstad, B. M. "Eating-Houses on the Witwatersrand, 1902–1979." M.A. Thesis, University of Witwatersrand, 1991.

Tobias, Henry Jack. *A History of the Jews in New Mexico.* Albuquerque: University of New Mexico Press, 1990.

Toll, William. *The Making of an Ethnic Middle Class: Portland Jewry over Four Generations.* New York: State University of New York Press, 1982.

Trentmann, Frank. "Beyond Consumerism: New Historical Perspectives on Consumption." *Journal of Contemporary History* 39, no. 3 (2004): 373–401.

Triulzi, Allesandro. "Italian-Speaking Communities in Early Nineteenth Century Tunis." *Revue de l'occident musulman et de la Méditerranée* 9 (1971): 153–84.

Trivellato, Francesca. *The Familiarity of Strangers: The Sephardic Diaspora, Livorno, and Cross-Cultural Trade in the Early Modern Period.* New Haven: Yale University Press, 2008.

Turrell, Robert Vicat. *Capital and Labour on the Kimberley Diamond Fields, 1871–1890.* Cambridge: Cambridge University Press, 1987.

Vadala, R. "Une colonie tripolitaine à Paris dans le commerce des plumes d'autruche." *Renseignements coloniaux* (1924): 89.

Van Kleeck, Mary. *Artificial Flower Makers.* New York: Survey Associates, 1913.

———. *A Seasonal Industry: A Study of the Millinery Trade in New York.* New York: Russell Sage Foundation, 1917.

Van Onselen, Charles. "Jewish Marginality in the Atlantic World: Organised Crime in the Era of the Great Migrations, 1880–1914." *South African Historical Journal* 43 (2000): 96–137.

———. *Studies in the Social and Economic History of the Witwatersrand, 1886–1914.* 2 vols. Harlow, Essex, 1982.

Van Waart, Sue. *Paleise van die pluime: 'n vertelboek oor Oudtshoorn en die volstruisveersage.* Pretoria: J. P. van der Walt, 1990.

Vital, Michael. "Correspondences of Michael Vital, Consulate of the United States of America, Tripoli of Barbary, to Department of State." In *Despatches from United States Consuls in Tripoli, 1796–1885.* Washington, D.C.: National Archives and Records Service, General Services Administration.

Vorspan, Max, and Lloyd P. Gartner. *History of the Jews of Los Angeles.* Philadelphia: Jewish Publication Society of America, 1970.

Waldinger, Rodger. "International Ladies Garment Workers Union: Women, Industry Structure, and Collective Action." In *Women, Work, and Protest: A Century of U.S. Women's Labor History,* edited by Ruth Milkman, 86–105. London: Routledge and Kegal Paul, 1987.

Walkowitz, Judith R. *City of Dreadful Delight: Narratives of Sexual Danger in Late-Victorian London.* Chicago: University of Chicago Press, 1992.

———. "The 'Vision of Salome': Cosmopolitanism and Erotic Dancing in Central London, 1908–1918." *American Historical Review* 108, no. 2 (2003).

Wallace, Robert, and Harry Stratford Caldecott. *Farming Industries of Cape Colony.* London: P. S. King and Son, 1896.

Walvin, James. *Fruits of Empire: Exotic Produce and British Taste, 1660–1800.* New York: New York University Press, 1997.

Walz, Terence. *Trade Between Egypt and Bilad as-Sudan, 1700–1820.* Cairo: Institut français d'archéologie orientale du Caire, 1978.

Watson, Elizabeth C. *Homework in the Tenements.* New York: National Consumers' League, 1911.

Willey, Day Allen. "Raising Ostriches in the United States." *Scientific American* 90, no. 14 (1904): 275.

Williams, Bill. *The Making of Manchester Jewry, 1740–1875.* New York: Manchester University Press/Holmes and Meier, 1976.

Wilson, Elizabeth. *Adorned in Dreams: Fashion and Modernity.* Berkeley: University of California Press, 1987.

Winder, R. Bayley. "The Lebanese in West Africa." *Comparative Studies in Society and History* 4, no. 3 (1962): 296–333.

Wollen, Peter. "Fashion/Orientalism/the Body." *New Formations,* no. 1 (1987): 5–33.

Wormser, Margaretha Francina. "The Ostrich Industry in South Africa." M.A. thesis, University of South Africa, 1930.

Worster, Donald. *Rivers of Empire: Water, Aridity, and the Growth of the American West.* New York: Pantheon, 1985.

Yogev, Gedalia. *Diamonds and Coral: Anglo-Dutch Jews and Eighteenth-Century Trade.* New York: Leicester University Press, 1978.

Zimmerman, Andrew. "A German Alabama in Africa: The Tuskegee Expedition to German Togo and the Transnational Origins of West African Cotton Growers." *American Historical Review* 110, no. 5 (2005): 1337–61.

ACKNOWLEDGMENTS

This book could not have been written without the financial support of a National Endowment for the Humanities Fellowship and a Charles A. Rys-kamp Research Fellowship from the American Council of Learned Societies. Additional sponsorship came from the Hadassah-Brandeis Institute, Maurice Amado Foundation Research Fund in Sephardic Studies, Memorial Foundation for Jewish Research, and University of Washington's Department of History, Jackson School of International Studies, Graduate School Fund for Excellence and Innovation, and Jewish Studies Program.

Jordanna Bailkin and Lynn Thomas have provided community and collabo-ration of the rarest sort. Steven J. Zipperstein was the first scholar to read my manuscript in its entirety, offering invaluable commentary, guidance, and succor. Leora Auslander, David Biale, Michael Bonine, Aomar Boum, Daniel Coetzee, David Feldman, Susan Glenn, Richard Kirkendall, Matthias Lehmann, Tony Michels, David N. Myers, Derek Penslar, Daniel Schroeter, Milton Shain, and Francesca Trivellato were generous readers, critics, and interlocutors. I am particularly indebted to Todd Endelman for his many insights and for point-ing me toward crucial archival material. Aron Rodrigue has been an unflagging mentor and friend.

Perhaps my largest debt is to those with personal ties to the feather world who shared family histories, documents, and hospitality and who imbued my story—and my research experience—with a humanity that transcends the archive. Isidore and Carole Barron, third-generation South African ostrich farmers and feather exporters (on the Barron side), were unstintingly gener-ous during my time in Oudtshoorn. Members of the extended family of the South African Jewish feather merchant Isaac Nurick—among them Derrick

Lewis, Anne (Chana) Biderman, Harris and Ann Ralph, Judith Landau, and Jonathan Blumberg—included me as they shared and debated the history of their family over email. Time spent in the Garden Café in Regent's Park with other Nurick descendants, including Richard Nurick, Rose Marie Nurick, Catherine James, and Patricia Baldachin, represented one of the most delightful moments of my research. Edward Schuman, whose father founded the first American ostrich feather duster firm, patiently answered many questions about the P. R. Schuman Duster Company. Colin Cohen, grandson of Myer Salaman, was generous with his knowledge of the history of I. Salaman and Company Ostrich Feather Merchants. Rob Nixon provided insights gleaned from his own ostrich explorations; Patricia Horton Webb, Robyn Lichter, and Rosemary Eshel shared genealogical research on Hale and Son Colonial Produce Brokers, the Morris family, and the Arbib and Hassan families (respectively). Willie Zelowitz was kind enough to give me an insiders' account of the contemporary feather industry and an unforgettable tour of the Los Angeles warehouse and manufactory of Mother Plucker Feathers.

Portions of this work were fruitfully shared with participants in workshops and lecture series sponsored by the University of Washington's Department of History; the George L. Mosse Program in History at the University of Wisconsin, Madison; the Institute for Jewish Studies at University College, London; Stanford University's Mediterranean Studies Forum and Taube Center for Jewish Studies; the Maurice Amado lecture series at the University of California, Los Angeles; New York University's Goren-Goldstein Center for American Jewish History and Columbia University's Institute for Israel and Jewish Studies; the University of California, Davis' Department of History, and the Center for Jewish Studies at the University of California, Santa Cruz. I am thankful to my colleagues and hosts at these events.

Many archivists and librarians aided my research. Hilda Boshoff and the C. P. Nel Museum and Archive of Oudtshoorn allowed me unfettered access to their collection, going so far as to permit me to treat an exhibit of Isaac Nurick's business papers as an extended part of their archive. Janine Dunlop at the Manuscripts and Archives Division of the University of Cape Town Libraries was of great help in advance of and during my research at her institution, as was Bill Frist at the Huntington Library in Pasadena, California. As I explored their collections, the staffs of the Guildhall Library Manuscripts

Section, the National Archives of the United Kingdom, Cambridge University Libraries, Hoover Institute Library and Archives, the Kaplan Centre for Jewish Studies and Research at the University of Cape Town, Harvard University's Ernst Mayer Library, and the Baker Library of Harvard Business School have been accommodating beyond measure. Roger Hull helped me peruse the papers of the London and Kano Trading Company, held by the Liverpool Records Office, Ellen Zazzarino of the Denver Public Library shared her institution's holdings on the Colorado Ostrich Farm, and Roger Myers, Special Collections Librarian and Archivist at the University of Arizona Libraries, offered aid as I explored William F. Staunton's papers. Naomi Musiker generously shared archival sources from the South African Jewish Board of Deputies of Johannesburg, as did Anna Wright, Curator of Images at the Museum of London. Closer to home, the University of Washington Libraries' interlibrary loan staff has executed miracles.

Others obtained sources crucial to this project. Harvey Goldberg led me, via Yaacov Hajjaj-Liluf and Pedetzur Benatiyah, to treasured images of a Jewish-owned ostrich feather workshop in Tripoli owned by the Or-Shalom Center, Bat-Yam. Lynn Thomas obtained copies of precious documents from the South African National Archive that I overlooked during my own research in Cape Town: Alta LeRoux did the same at the C. P. Nel Museum in Oudtshoorn. Saul Issroff, editor of the Southern Africa Jewish Genealogy Special Interest Group (SASIG) Web site, has been generous with research leads and introductions. Jerome Manin allowed me to reproduce images from his extraordinary collection of ostrich miscellany, www.struthie.com. I am grateful to the following research assistants for their capable aid: Elizabeth Angell, Magdalena Góram Rachel Berry, Spencer Lamm, and Shantel Martinez.

At Yale University Press, Alex Larson oversaw publication logistics with skill and speed. And, crucially, Ileene Smith has helped imagine this book, shaping and editing it in ways that can only be described as artful. I thank her, especially, for encouraging me to free my prose.

I am blessed with incredible colleagues too numerous to mention, including (in addition to those already named) Cynthea Bogel, Olga Borovaya, Stephanie Camp, Jim Gregory, Ali Igmen, Selim Kuru, Katharyne Mitchell, Uta Poiger, Joshua Schreier, Matt Sparke, and Glennys Young. Sarah Friedman and Andrew Solomon have soothed me with the perfect combination of adventure and hospitality. Joan Abrevaya's munificence has made life sweeter, and Rebecca Stein and Andrew Janiak have offered the best in friendship, conversation, and humor. My father, Richard Stein, carefully read and commented on the manuscript. Far more important than his practical assistance is his scholarly and personal integrity, which provide a model toward which I aspire. It is from my mother, Carole Stein, that I learned that lively conversation, probing questions, and vivid histories are the stuff of life. If I am able to glean a fraction of the truth of my historical subjects that she can from strangers, I will have done my job well.

Ira and Julius have borne the fact that their mother is writing a book on ostriches with remarkable aplomb: surely few other children in Seattle can count the bird among their first representational art subjects or have traveled to Oudtshoorn in utero. Last but not least, an inestimable debt is owed to Fred: my first and best reader, loyal advocate, and muse. There is no research trip he has not encouraged me to undertake, no page of this book that does not bear his mark, and no moment that I am not thankful for his wisdom and companionship.

INDEX

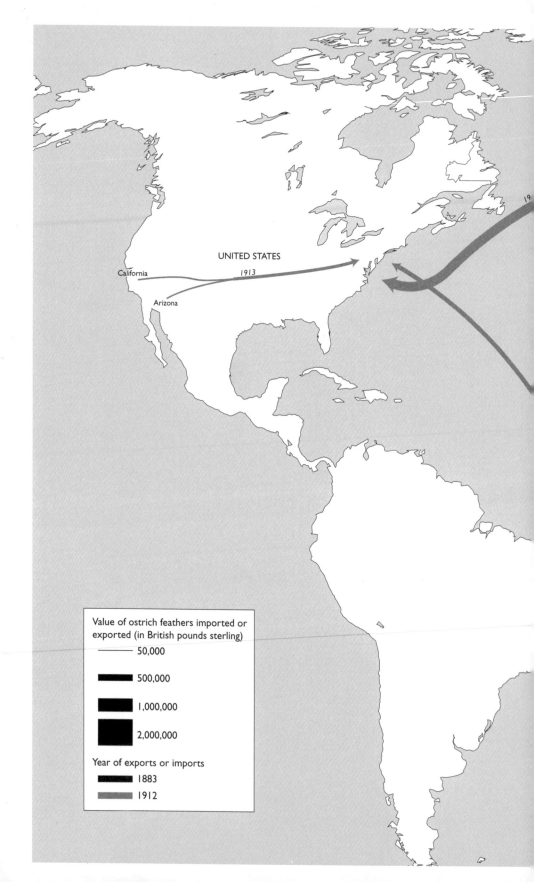

UNITED STATES

California

Arizona

1913

19

Value of ostrich feathers imported or
exported (in British pounds sterling)

—————— 50,000

▬▬▬▬ 500,000

██████ 1,000,000

██████ 2,000,000

Year of exports or imports

▬▬▬▬ 1883

▬▬▬▬ 1912